T

A COLOURGUIDE

Fourth Edition

Penina Coopersmith
Photography by Vincenzo Pietropaolo

FORMAC PUBLISHING COMPANY LIMITED

CONTENTS

Formac Publishing Company Limited acknowledges the support of the Cultural Affairs Section, Nova Scotia Department of Tourism and Culture. We acknowledge the support of the Government of Canada through the Book Publishing Industry Development Program (BPIDP) for our publishing activities.

For Cataloguing in Publication Data and photo credits, please see page **256**.

CONTENTS

Formac Publishing Company Limited
5502 Atlantic Street
Halifax, Nova Scotia, B3H 1G4
www.formac.ca

Distributed in the United States by:
Casemate
2114 Darby Road, 2nd Floor
Havertown, PA, USA, 19083

Distributed in the United Kingdom by:
Portfolio Books Limited
Unit 5, Perivale Industrial Park
Horseden Lane South
Greenford, UK
UB6 7RL

Printed and bound in Canada

See detailed maps of Toronto neighbourhoods and districts

🚍 401	Multi-lane highway
	Main arterial road
	GO transit line
	Subway/light rapid transit
🚌	Bus station
🚆	Train station
	Parkland
CN Tower ●	Selected site

Map legend applies to all walking tour maps

Greater Toronto Area

Lake Ontario

N

0   kilometres   5

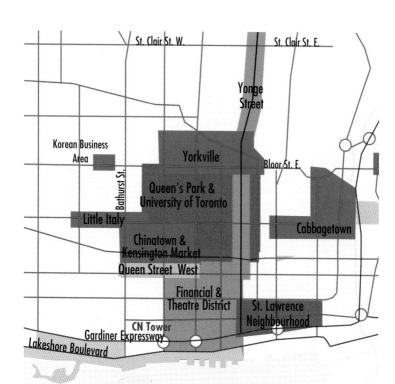

St. Clair St. W. St. Clair St. E.

Yonge Street

Korean Business Area

Bathurst St.

Yorkville

Bloor St. E.

Queen's Park & University of Toronto

Little Italy

Cabbagetown

Chinatown & Kensington Market

Queen Street West

Financial & Theatre District

St. Lawrence Neighbourhood

CN Tower

Gardiner Expressway

Lakeshore Boulevard

Toronto Islands

▲ CENTRAL TORONTO HOTELS MAP

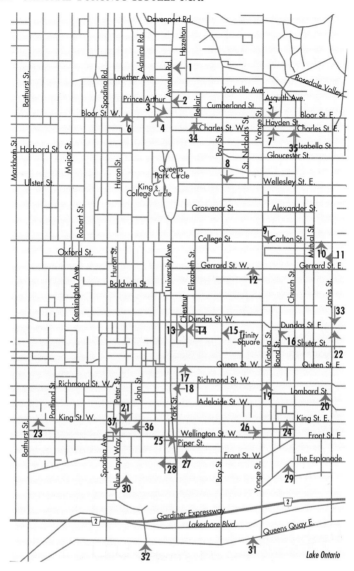

1. Howard Johnson Inn Yorkville
2. Four Seasons Hotel
3. Park Hyatt Hotel
4. Hotel Inter-Continental
5. Toronto Marriott Bloor Yorkville
6. Quality Hotel
7. Comfort Hotel
8. Sutton Place Hotel
9. Days Inn
10. Best Western Primrose Hotel
11. Ramada Hotel & Suites
12. Delta Chelsea Hotel
13. Metropolitan Hotel
14. Toronto Colony Hotel
15. Toronto Marriott Eaton Centre
16. Bond Place Hotel
17. Sheraton Centre
18. Toronto Hilton
19. Cambridge Suites Hotel
20. Quality Hotel Downtown
21. Holiday Inn
22. Grand Hotel & Suites
23. Executive Motor Hotel
24. King Edward Hotel
25. Strathcona Hotel
26. Hotel Victoria
27. Royal York Hotel
28. Crowne Plaza Toronto Centre
29. Novotel Toronto Centre
30. Renaissance Toronto Hotel at Skydome
31. Westin Harbour Castle
32. Radisson Plaza Hotel Admiral
33. Madison Manor
34. Windsor Arms
35. Town Inn
36. Le Germain
37. SoHo Metropolitan

CENTRAL TORONTO RESTAURANTS MAP ▲

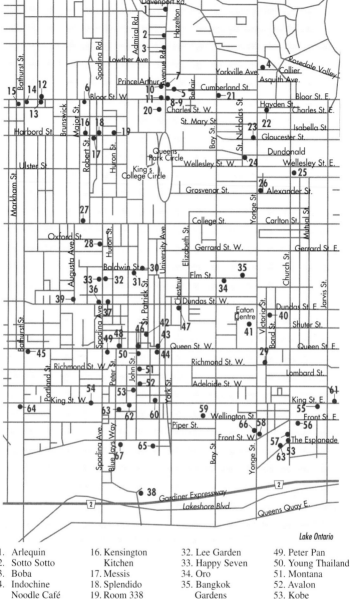

1. Arlequin
2. Sotto Sotto
3. Boba
4. Indochine Noodle Café
5. Jacques' Bistro
6. Goldfish
7. Truffles
8. Black and Blue
9. Prego della Piazza
10. Host
11. Pho Hung
12. Country Style Hungarian
13. Pauper's
14. Zizi Trattoria
15. Southern Accent
16. Kensington Kitchen
17. Messis
18. Splendido
19. Room 338
20. J.K. ROM
21. Pangaea
22. Focaccia
23. Ethiopian House
24. Segovia
25. Byzantium
26. Carman's
27. Free Times Café
28. Lucky Dragon
29. Terroni
30. Café la Gaffe
31. Wah Sing
32. Lee Garden
33. Happy Seven
34. Oro
35. Bangkok Gardens
36. Vien Dong
37. Champion House
38. Rain
39. Ban Vainpha
40. Torch Bistro
41. Cultures
42. Ematei
43. Queen Mother
44. Tiger Lily's
45. The Paddock
46. Express Café
47. Lai Wah Heen
48. Rivoli
49. Peter Pan
50. Young Thailand
51. Montana
52. Avalon
53. Kobe
54. Rodney's
55. Biagio
56. C'est What?
57. Le Papillon
58. Shopsy's
59. Canoe
60. Il Fornello
61. Hiro Sushi
62. La Fenice
63. Bier Markt
64. Wheat Sheaf
65. Accolade
66. Marché
67. 360

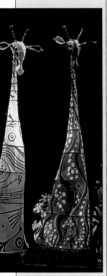

Welcome to this guide to Toronto!

The *Toronto Colourguide* will help you get the most out of your stay in the lively, appealing city of Toronto. The introductory chapters, Exploring Toronto and A Brief History, provide an overview of the city.

The maps in the introductory section give you a helpful general view of the city, and offer a guide to the organization of this book. The Overview Map shows routes into the city and main highways and streets. Its legend applies to all the maps in the book, so it is worth taking the time to orient yourself with its help. The Neighbourhoods Map shows the city's downtown neighbourhoods and districts, and contains an inset showing subway routes and stops. Each of these neighbourhoods is covered in its own chapter which you will find in the section entitled Neighbourhoods and Districts. The Hotels Map and Restaurants Map provide you with a quick and handy reference for recommended accommodation and dining downtown.

The book is divided into three main sections. The first, Toronto's Top Attractions, contains articles that will guide you to the famous as well as the less-familiar (but no less interesting) sites and attractions in the city.

The second section, Neighbourhoods and Districts, contains ten chapters that provide walking tours of ten of the city's most interesting communities.

Finally, section three contains select listings, with practical information on everything you'll want to do or find in Toronto: accommodations; dining; nightlife; attractions; festivals and events; theatres; shopping; galleries; sports; outdoor recreation — even special travel services and tips. Information on attractions and sites described in the first or second sections is also included in the listings.

This book is an independent guide. Its author and contributors have made their recommendations and suggestions based solely on what they believe to be the best, most interesting and most appealing sites and attractions. No payments or contributions of any kind are solicited or accepted by the creators or the publishers of this guide.

In a city as lively as Toronto, things change quickly. The safest thing to do about information you're relying on in this book is to confirm it with a brief phone call.

If your experience doesn't match what you read here — or if you think we've missed one of Toronto's best features — please let us know. Write us at the address on the contents page (page 3).This book is the work of author Penina Coopersmith and photographer Vincenzo Pietropaolo. Several chapters have been contributed by authors who are local experts in their fields:

KAREN BROWN (Dining) has been reviewing restaurants for *Toronto Life* for the past ten years.

SKY GILBERT (Gay Toronto) writer, director, and drag queen extraordinaire, is one of Canada's most controversial artistic forces. Mr. Gilbert is also an award-winning play-wright whose work has been performed in many major cities including New York, London and Toronto, where he is also the founder of Buddies in Bad Times Theatre. He is currently turning his protean energies to poetry and film-making.

JOYCE GUNHOUSE and JUDY CORNISH (Shopping) met at Ryerson Polytechnic University, where both were studying Fashion Design. With a sense of humour and style, they have been creating their collection, Comrags, since 1983. Many awards, international distribution and a flagship store have made Comrags one of Canada's best-known and loved designer labels.

CHRISTOPHER HUME (Art) has been the art and architecture critic at the *Toronto Star* since the early 1980s. He has written for major publications in Canada and the U.S. and appears regularly on radio and television. He lives in downtown Toronto.

ADAM STERNBERGH (Nightlife) is Senior Editor at *Saturday Night* magazine.

VINCENZO PIETROPAOLO has been photographing Toronto for over 25 years. His photojournalism and landscape, portrait and architecture photography has been widely published.

VIT WAGNER (Theatre and Dance) is a drama critic for the *Toronto Star*. During his more than a dozen years at the paper, he has covered the theatre scene in Toronto, from the big commercial musicals to the smaller avant-garde productions. He has also reported on the Stratford and Shaw festivals.

DEREK CHEZZI (Sports) has written for a variety of newspapers and magazines including the *Globe and Mail, Toronto Life, Maclean's* and *Elm Street.*

BETTY ZYVATKAUSKAS (Day Trips) writes a weekly travel column, "Day Tripper," for the *Globe and Mail.* She is the author of *Great Getaways: the Best Day Trips in Southern Ontario.*

JON KAPLAN (Symphony, Chamber Music and Opera) has been theatre editor at *NOW* magazine for nearly two decades, reviewing stage productions, opera and classical CDs. He has been theatre editor at CJRT-FM and is the Toronto correspondent for the London-based *Plays International* and the New York-based *Back Stage.*

JOHN MILLER (Glenn Gould) is the Toronto-based Executive Director of The Glenn Gould Foundation and a specialist in Canadian cultural affairs.

— The Publishers

EXPLORING TORONTO

Toronto's past and present make it a great place to visit: a clean, safe, modern city that is easy to get around and offers lots to see and do. Detailed information about climate, travel arrangements, currency, customs, accommodation, emergency care and other vital data can be found in the listings at the back of this guide. In-depth descriptions of Toronto's top attractions and activities, and walking tours of Toronto's many pleasant downtown and midtown neighbourhoods, follow. First, though, we offer a quick introduction to finding your way around.

Before you come, you might want to contact Ontario Travel, the Ontario government's tourist hotline (1-800-668-2746) or Tourism Toronto (1-800-499-2554 from outside the city, or 416 203-2500 from within), both of which will happily send you free pamphlets and answer questions about accommodation, special events and the like.

POLE ART ON SPADINA

The quickest way downtown for those arriving at Lester B. Pearson International Airport is by limousine or taxi. Only slightly less convenient are the big comfortable buses that run every half-hour or so to the subway stations closest to the airport and straight downtown to the major hotels. The price of the bus is about one-third that of a taxi. If you are coming in by train, you will arrive at Union Station, right downtown and opposite the Royal York Hotel. If you are flying in from Ottawa, Montreal or London (ON), try for a flight to the City Centre Airport. As its name implies, it takes you right downtown, to the old Toronto Island Airport, where you can take a free shuttle to (and from) Union Station. Those arriving by car, or planning to rent one at the airport, should ask about parking when booking

DOWNTOWN
TORONTO AT NIGHT

their accommodation.

In truth, however, most visitors will find they hardly need or want a car, except perhaps to visit the Toronto Zoo or other attractions located at the city's edges. Within town, you will quickly learn that while driving is no problem, parking is. Fortunately, Toronto's transit system is excellent. Its buses, subways and streetcars traverse 877 miles (1,412 km) of streets and will get you just about anywhere you want to go within the city. For fares, schedule and route information, call the Toronto Transit Commission (TTC), (416 393-4636) for 24-hour, automated information on major attraction routing, parking, fares and so on. Of course, you can always hail a cab. But one of the great joys of Toronto is that it is a delightful city to walk in, which is why part of this guide has been structured around neighbourhood tours to take on foot.

After you have yourself settled, but before plunging into attractions or neighbourhoods, there are a few activities that will help you get acquainted with Toronto. Several companies provide guided tours that will give you a sense of the city's scale and layout while introducing you to major attractions like City Hall, Harbourfront, SkyDome and the CN Tower. Each, of course, offers some special little twist. Greyhound Lines (416 594-3310) uses double-decker buses and permits you to hop on and off as you choose, Toronto Hippo Tours (416 703-4476) employs amphibious vehicles that plop into the lake after touring the downtown for an up-close view of the harbour, the Niagara Airbus tour (1-800-268-8111) includes a trip up the CN Tower, while Toronto Tours Ltd. (City Tour) (416 868-0400) picks you up at your hotel. Prices range from $30 to $50 per adult depending on the length of the tour.

PARAMOUNT AND
CHAPTERS AT
RICHMOND AND
JOHN

In the summer, free or low-cost walking tours are run by the City of Toronto's Parks Department (416 392-1111) and Heritage Toronto (416 338-0684), all of them led by knowledgeable guides, often local historians of note. Information about these and other city-organized tours — as well as special events — can also be obtained from Access Toronto (416

CN TOWER AT DUSK

338-0338). The Royal Ontario Museum's ROMwalks (416 586-3313) are also excellent.

Smaller operators also offer a variety of interesting tours, usually on foot. A Taste of the World (416 923-6813) has been introducing visitors and natives alike to Toronto's many cuisines for a decade. Now it has added ghost and literary walks to its foodie tours. Ghost walks are offered by Haunted Toronto (416 487-9017), too.

In the past, outfits that designed custom tours usually catered only to large groups. Now, however, a growing number of companies will work with family-sized units or even individuals. Among these are Toronto Footsteps (416 483-5483); Lost World Tours (416 947-0778, 1-888 567-9753), which promises to make you a "Torontonian for a day"; Civitas Cultural Resources (416 996-1550), which focuses on Toronto's history; and Art Insite (416 979-5704), which specializes in visits to the studios of artists and craftspeople as well as galleries. All these companies need some lead time — a day or two — to line things up, so if possible, they should be called before you arrive. Prices vary depending on the number of people in your group and the length of the tour, but $20 to $30 per person is about average.

For a view of the city from its harbour, nothing beats the ferry boat rides to Toronto's islands (see p. 94), but for a guided tour, you might prefer a one-hour trip on the ships of the Mariposa Cruise Line (416 203-0178) or Toronto Tours Ltd. (Harbour Tour) (416 868-0400) or Toronto Harbour Tours (416 260-5555). These cruises range from $12 to $25 for adults. As a special summer treat, you can go sailing on the Great Lakes Schooner Company's *Challenge* (416 260-6335).

For a bird's-eye view, it is hard to beat a trip up to the top of the CN Tower, unless of course you want to get really adventurous and go sky-high with The Helicopter Company (416 203-3280). To help you plan your days and evenings back on earth, pick up a free copy of *NOW* or *eye*, weekly newspapers published Thursdays, both of which have complete listings for theatre, music, dance, films, the club and restaurant scene and special events. *Toronto Life*, a monthly magazine, also provides listings, as well as the latest Toronto gossip.

TORONTO ISLANDS FERRY

A BRIEF HISTORY

When *Fortune* magazine ranked Toronto as the best city in the world for living, playing and working, it did so almost apologetically. "How can you fault the safest city in North America?" the authors began. And then, after warmly praising Toronto for its desirable downtown neighbourhoods, its ethnic diversity, its multitude of restaurants, galleries, parks and clubs, and its lively theatre scene, they looked for something to criticize. The winter weather, they pointed out, is cold and damp.

This attitude is quintessentially Torontonian: enthusiastically acknowledge being number one, then apologize with a slightly puzzled air and start discussing the weather. The puzzlement comes from the memory, fresh in the minds of many, of only recently having been a backwater. Admittedly, Paris and London once were backwaters — but that was in the days of Roman legions. By contrast, many Torontonians recall clearly when a night on the town meant a two-hour drive to Buffalo.

Today, the problem is glut: more than 2,000 restaurants, hundreds of them top-notch, represent almost every ethnic cuisine imaginable; dozens of live performances take place daily, enough to make Toronto the third-ranking theatre centre in the English-speaking world (after London and New York); galleries dot the city and family-oriented fun comes in a wide variety of forms. Toronto is a major centre not only of finance, but of publishing, broadcasting, emerging electronic technologies, fashion and the arts generally. Of late, the city has acquired a new sobriquet: Hollywood North. Not only has it hosted North America's — if not the world's — premier film festival for over a quarter of a century, but each year hundreds of films and TV shows are shot on its streets.

As a bonus, for residents and visitors alike, there are also the old-fashioned comforts of safety and cleanliness. You can stroll Toronto's many downtown neighbourhoods,

SPADINA QUAY

with their busy streets and neighbourhood shops, at most hours with virtually no concern for personal safety. As for keeping litter in its place, that just seems to be a habit.

So rapid has been Toronto's ascent to world-class status that it is easy to forget that the city's transformation is built on a solid foundation of growth and development spanning many centuries. Like other great cities, Toronto owes its size and character to a combination of factors including its setting, the values and aspirations of its residents and the events that have befallen it.

EARLY SETTLEMENT

For thousands of years before European explorers came to the area, the routes between Lake Ontario, Lake Huron and Georgian Bay converged at Toronto, which is said to mean "a place of meeting." In 1615, Etienne Brûlé, a companion of explorer Samuel de Champlain, was shown the site when he came to invite the Andaste nation to join in a campaign against the Iroquois.

SOLDIERS AT FORT YORK

Later, after the Dutch had settled what is now New York, they struggled with the French for control of the fur

trade and the Toronto portage became a route for war parties. The rivalry made the surrounding region a no man's land. At last, in 1649, the Huron and their French friends won a decisive victory.

Seventy-one years later, French colonists established a fort at Toronto, one of a network spread throughout the lower Great Lakes region and the Midwest. The Toronto fort was strategically located to allow the French both to tap the rich fur trade between Lake Ontario and Georgian Bay, and to fend off the British, who had established their own posts in upstate New York.

The first French post was abandoned in 1730. A subsequent structure, Fort Rouillé, was destroyed in 1759 by the French themselves to prevent it falling into the hands of the British during the Seven Years' War. Less than twenty years later, the British, having won control of the region, investigated the abandoned site and decided the region would suit an English settlement. For the grand sum of £1,700, 149 barrels of flour and such other goods as blankets and axes, they purchased approximately 400 square miles from the Mississauga Indians, an acquisition known as the "Toronto Purchase."

In 1793, Colonel John Simcoe, a veteran of the American Revolution and the first lieutenant-governor of Upper Canada (now Ontario), chose Toronto as his seat of

NEW SPADINA LRT LINE

operations because of the vantage point it offered for naval defence from the Americans. In addition to building a garrison, Fort York, he laid out a ten-block plan for the town, thereby establishing the user-friendly north-south, east-west grid pattern the city retains today. He also changed its age-old Huron name of Toronto to York.

The only significant test of York's military strength came on April 27th, 1813, when several hundred British, Aboriginal and Canadian soldiers resisted 1,700 Americans and the guns of two dozen warships for over five hours. The British blew up their gunpowder magazine and retreated, leaving so many American casualties behind that the embittered victors looted and burned much of the little town. The British retaliated the following summer by taking and subsequently burning much of the slightly larger, and politically far more important, settlement of Washington.

By then, Simcoe was long gone from York. Little remains of his original townsite, save some of the street names, among them Yonge Street, which Simcoe had the Queen's Rangers lay out in a straight, thirty-mile path north through the wilderness to the limits of the Toronto Purchase. Resolution of the British-American conflict proved a major impetus to the town's growth. Now able to think of Upper Canada as a secure British outpost in the wilderness, English settlers began to arrive in larger numbers.

The second major impetus to the community's growth was the opening in 1824 of the Welland Canal. The canal, which linked Lake Erie and Lake Ontario, made the town an important trade centre along the Montreal-Chicago shipping axis. From a small outpost of some 600 souls in 1813, the settlement had expanded to a burgeoning metropolis of more than 10,000 when it was renamed the City of Toronto in 1834.

GROWING CITY

Within thirty years of its 1834 incorporation, Toronto's population had grown by 30,000. Many immigrants came as a result of the potato crop failures in Ireland, but there were also thousands of escaped American slaves. Many, but not all, of the ex-slaves returned to the United States after the Civil War. A mixture of northern Europeans, mostly Germans, Dutch and Belgians, also came to farm in the surrounding regions or to open businesses serving their compatriots in the agricultural community.

By the 1880s and 1890s the population — now approaching the 200,000 mark — was becoming ever more diverse. The first Asian immigrants came with the building of Canada's railroads. The discovery of fabulous nickel, silver and uranium deposits in northern Ontario in the first

HARBOURFRONT

three decades of the twentieth century set the stage for Toronto's post-World War II emergence as Canada's financial capital. The minerals drew skilled miners from Poland, the Balkans, Silesia and Hungary. As well, industrialization sparked a large-scale internal migration, drawing a flood of rural youth to the big city. By 1910, Toronto had clearly become the pre-eminent centre of industry, trade and commerce in English Canada. By that time, too, commercial activity in the city had moved north and west to the areas that are now the modern, largely high-rise core of the city, and roads and rails stretched along the harbour, giving the central city the layout and something of the look it retains to this day.

After World War II, Toronto and its environs took off, doubling twice in size, from just over 1 million in 1945 to over 2 million in 1971 to 4.1 million by 1995. Skilled labourers, craftspeople and refugees flocked here from Italy, Greece and central Europe. Students and skilled and unskilled workers came from all over the British Commonwealth, the Caribbean and the Indian subcontinent. After various international upheavals, large blocks of new immigrants contributed something of their culture and cuisine along with their numbers: Hungarians in 1956, Czechs in 1968, Chileans, Argentinians and Vietnamese in the 1970s. The bigger it got, the more

SPADINA POLE ART AT KENSINGTON MARKET

Toronto attracted new investment. Money and people poured in from Hong Kong and from Europe throughout the 1990s.

The most extreme and recent change occurred in 1997, when the Ontario provincial government abolished the older suburban municipalities of East York, York, North York, Scarborough and Etobicoke; and with them the two-tier metropolitan form of government that had been widely praised and copied throughout its 43-year history. In place of the municipalities, the province created a single-tier, amalgamated city that it had the decency to continue to call "Toronto."

The new city, which came into being on January 1st, 1999, has a population of 2.5 million, making it the fourth-largest city in North America. As it struggles to reorganize itself, the long term effects of amalgamation remain to be seen. What is clear, however, is that with a population that represents at least 75 different cultures — the largest of which accounts for less than one-fifth of the population, and more than a dozen of which have more than 100,000 members — there is no longer a single majority culture.

No other city in the world can boast such diversity. What really distinguishes Toronto from other places that approach its ethnic variety (New York, for example) is that it has managed to absorb all this growth without losing the characteristics that made it attractive in the first place. It remains a pleasant, clean, safe, civil environment in which to prosper and raise a family.

TORONTO'S TOP ATTRACTIONS

TORONTO'S BEST

THE CN TOWER

In addition to its many neighbourhoods, Toronto is replete with attractions, destination points that merit anywhere from a half-day visit (Casa Loma, Spadina House and the Science Centre) to at least three-quarters of a day (Black Creek Pioneer Village), a full day (the Toronto Zoo) and then some (Ontario Place, the Ex in season and Harbourfront).

CN TOWER

— 301 Front Street West. Open year round from 9 a.m. to 10 p.m. (11 p.m. on Fridays and Saturdays). For information call 416 360-8500.

THE CN TOWER'S SKYPOD

The CN Tower is the city's most popular attraction. When the weather is clear, the view from the top is spectacular. To the north, you can see Lake Simcoe; to the southwest, you can see the mist rising from Niagara Falls. It is an ideal way to get an overview of Toronto — even on days when it is not clear enough to see great distances. All sorts of interesting things present themselves: roofs that have gardens or jogging tracks; the weird cubes almost directly below, atop the Canadian Broadcasting Corporation (CBC) Building (they are studios); the roar of the crowd if a game is on at the SkyDome. But most interesting of all (unless it's winter) is to see how very green Toronto is. Except for the financial district, there seem to be trees everywhere. There are the parks, and the Toronto Islands, of course. There are the Don and Humber Valleys and the many ravines that carry the rivers' tributaries. And then there are the backyards and the streets, all but a few of which are lined with trees. So from atop the CN Tower, a fair portion of Toronto vanishes.

Every year, some two million visitors ride the six elevators that soar 114 storeys (1,136 feet) to the seven-storey LookOut Levels, the fat white donut slung two-thirds of the way up the tower. Access to these observation decks is priced between $10.99 and $15.99. For an additional $7.50, visitors can continue thirty-three storeys higher, to the SkyPod, 1,465 feet above the ground. When the wind is not too strong, the "shorter" ride takes only 58 seconds. When it is windy, the tower sways and a slightly slower system is used. Much of the "donut" is filled with the microwave broadcasting equipment that is the $57-million tower's *raison d'être*, but there is plenty of room for visitors and lots to do. There are indoor and outdoor observation decks and a glass floor you can walk on, if you dare. There is a futuristic laser tag game called Q-Zar and a variety of virtual sports at the Edge Arcade. There is also a surprisingly good revolving restaurant, 360, for which reservations are strongly recommended (416 362-5411), and a café called Horizons. Be forewarned that there is almost always a long wait at the elevators, both up and down.

SKYDOME

—1 Blue Jays Way. Open year round, event schedule permitting. For game information call 416 341-1111 (baseball), 416 341-5151 (football). For the Skydome Tour Experience call 416 341-2770. Tours are $12.50.

The home of the Toronto Blue Jays and Argonauts is right next door to the CN Tower. You probably would have to live on Mars not to have heard the hype about Toronto's

MICHAEL SNOW'S "AUDIENCE" SCULPTURE AT THE SKYDOME

ERIC HINSKE AND CARLOS DELGADO OF THE JAYS AT THE SKYDOME

SkyDome: "the world's first multipurpose stadium with a retractable roof," "the Jumbotron, at nine storeys, the largest video display board in the world" and so on. But whether you are a sports fan or not, it is easy to get caught up in the hype; the great white clamshell is truly an engineering marvel. Its 11,000-ton roof spans 674 feet and reaches a height of 282 feet (31 storeys), making it a highly visible landmark. The roof consists of four panels, two of which slide into one another, then rotate 180 degrees with a third one to fit into the fourth. The panels move at a rate of seventy-one feet per minute, allowing the roof to close or open in a mere twenty minutes. The field itself also changes shape mechanically, allowing a change from baseball to football mode in ten hours. Up to 50,600 people can be accommodated at baseball games, 53,000 at football events and as many as 67,000 at concerts. Tickets for Jays and Argos games may be purchased in person at "the Dome" or by calling the number at the top of this section.

When there is no scheduled event, there are one-hour tours that are well worth taking since they provide a behind-the-scenes view that visitors to the Dome would not otherwise experience. These tours include watching a video of the designers figuring out how to achieve the project's objectives and the chance to sit in the dugouts, run out on the Astro Turf field (held together by eight miles of zippers) and visit one of the private SkyBoxes, which cost between $1-million and $2-million for ten years of use, not including game tickets or refreshments. You also get a look at some of the more than 1,400 artifacts that were uncovered during the archaeological dig that took place prior to construction, for the site was part of the early settlement of the city.

If you are taking in a game with young children in tow, there is an indoor playground on the first level near section 115, should they grow restless. Another way to see a game is to stay at the SkyDome (Renaissance) Hotel in one of the seventy rooms that overlook the playing field (416 341-7100). Or you can grab a burger at the Hard Rock Cafe, located beside Gate 1. During events, the rock music is turned off, and for

a price, you can get window seats overlooking the field (416 341-2381). Nearby, for hard-core devotees of The Great One, is Wayne Gretzky's restaurant (99 Blue Jays Way). If you are not an ardent worshipper, you will want to give it a miss, since you certainly wouldn't go there for the food.

HARBOURFRONT

— Queen's Quay between York and Bathurst Streets. Open all year round. For general information call 416 973-3000, for the box office 416 973-4000.

Harbourfront is an amazing ten-acre complex of theatres, galleries, shops, studios and restaurants located next to the lake and ten minutes from downtown. If you like theatre, dance, music, art, film, crafts, literature, shopping, antiques, ethnic festivals, ice skating or sailing, you will like Harbourfront. In fact, whether you are in town for only

a weekend or for much longer, you and your family could easily spend all your time here, much of it at little or no cost. Only in the cuisine department might Harbourfront be said to fall a bit short. It's not that there aren't a lot of places to eat: eateries range from low-end, independent fast food, like Lakeside Eats, the cafe at York Quay Centre, to mid-priced seaside bars such as the Pier 4 Storehouse and Spinnakers, or the non sea-faring Il Fornello or Bambu with its trendy music, to the pricier Captain John's or the Boat House Grill, and even the haute Chinese of the Pearl (at Queen's Quay), the Westin Harbour Castle restaurants and the nearby Harbour Sixty Steakhouse. It's just that Harbourfront's choices in dining pale in comparison to the choices it offers in most other areas of interest.

Harbourfront stretches along what once was Toronto's main port. The opening of the St. Lawrence Seaway

INSIDE QUEENS
QUAY TERMINAL

and the switch from manually handled shipping crates to large, uniform, machine-manoeuvred containers moved the port eastward starting in the 1950s. By the early 1970s, only the large grain silos remained busy. There were few port activities other than the island ferries and the police and fire boats, and very little industry. In the last days before the 1972 federal election, in a bid for Toronto's affections, the governing Liberals promised to purchase the entire area and make it all parkland.

What happened next was fortunate. Torontonians were happy about having more trees, trying to reconnect the city to the lake and so on, but, they said, why would people come here when so much of the lakeshore already is green and the islands are so close at hand? Why don't we add a bit of spice? Something unique. And so the programming aspect of Harbourfront was born. Since the mid-1970s, Harbourfront has constantly added new events — there are more than 4,000 every year — and new sites in which to hold them.

THE *ORIOLE* AT
HARBOURFRONT

Theatrical presentations range from new Canadian works to pieces linked to the many festivals that explore the cultural aspects of various nations, and are held at the Du Maurier Theatre Centre or in the York Quay Centre. Dance has long been celebrated at the Premiere Dance Theatre, inside the large Queen's Quay Terminal, and now the National Ballet has a new production facility in the Carsen Centre at King's Landing.

Music is everywhere — in various spots in the York Quay Centre, at Cushion Concerts for children on Saturdays and at free concerts for everyone on Sundays at the Du Maurier Theatre; throughout the warmer months at the outdoor Molson Place; and often just out on the lawns. It is embedded in the landscape, courtesy of Yo-Yo Ma and designer Julie Moir Messervy, whose

six-part garden celebrating Bach's First Suite for Unaccompanied Cello is the site of concerts in the summer and of a relaxing stroll year-round. Also on the gardening front are some 24 artists' gardens scattered throughout the area and ranging from the sublime to the ridiculous. Some are new, others date back to 1990 when the program first began. A self-guided tour sheet can be obtained at York Quay.

There is an art gallery in the Power Plant, a building that once provided the juice for chilling the huge terminal warehouse, itself once the world's largest refrigerator, and in the Community Gallery and the Photo Passage, both at York Quay Centre. There is art as well at Kaleidoscope, a craft studio where, for a dollar or so, children of all ages (so long as they have real kids in tow) can make masks, origami figures, funny hats, puppets and just about anything else on weekends and most holidays. Artisans and their wares are on display at the Craft Studio. You can buy the glass, metal, ceramic and other works you see in production next door at Bounty. Both are also in the York Quay Centre.

ALASTAIR MACLEOD AT THE INTERNATIONAL FESTIVAL OF AUTHORS

Harbourfront has also rekindled reading as an art form. Authors from around the world can be heard almost every Tuesday evening, but the highlight of the year is the autumn International Festival of Authors. Now entering its thirtieth year, it attracts just about everyone who is anyone in the literary world.

The main retail centre for Harbourfront is in the Queen's Quay Terminal. Its more than 100 stores are mainly of the upscale variety and feature beautiful clothes and jewellery, fine crafts and household furnishings, an amazing collection of dolls (at Dollina) and the classiest souvenir shop in the city, Oh, Yes! Toronto. To the west, near Spadina Avenue, is The Antiques Market, which offers two hours of free parking on Sundays. Here, somewhere amidst its dozens of stalls, you'll surely find that piece of silverware you've been missing, along with the very large chests, beds and armoires you've always craved. Flea, craft and international markets are also held, often in conjunction with festivals, usually in Ann Tindal Park.

THE POWER PLANT AT HARBOURFRONT

Harbourfront also takes advantage of its proximity to Lake Ontario, hosting marine-related events and offering sailing and boating courses and boat, canoe and skate rentals for use on Canada's largest artificial rink. There are three playgrounds on the site, none large but all unusual and popular, especially the one near York Quay Centre.

Major festivals are held throughout the year, but perhaps the best known is the annual mid-May Milk International Children's Festival, which for a very nominal

INSIDE THE MUSIC GARDEN

sum (about $8.50 for a weekend pass) allows you to choose from among dozens of performances by musicians, dancers, acrobats, actors, storytellers, magicians and others.

Finally, there are HarbourKids Camps, which operate during winter and spring breaks as well as throughout the summer. These are one- or two-week sessions for children from ages four to seventeen focusing on such areas of interest as baseball, canoeing, chess, computers, costume making, film animation, sailing, kayaking and squash (to name but a few). If you are in town for business or if your children aren't keen on spending their vacation poking around the rest of the city, these camps offer an ideal way of planning your time in Toronto to everyone's benefit.

ONTARIO PLACE

— 955 Lakeshore Boulevard West (just south of Exhibition Place). Open from mid-May through Labour Day. For information call 416 314-9900 or 416 314-9811.

Ontario Place might be described as an intellectual's theme park, an upscale, ninety-six-acre futuristic urban playground. What exactly, you might well ask, is its theme? Allegedly something to do with "exploiting advanced technology to shape the society of tomorrow." If this objective is not immediately evident, it matters not. What makes Ontario Place unique is that it offers most of the activities available at traditional theme parks — and adds a few of its own — while eschewing much of the attendant honky-tonk and commercialism. The setting doesn't hurt either. Built on a series of islands and pods that sit above the water on giant stilts, there are lots of trees, views of the city and the lake, cool breezes on even the hottest days and enough space to enable you to step back from the crowds. As well, there is really good music at the Molson Amphitheatre and at other locations on site.

The roughly $25 admission price to Ontario Place entitles you to a "Play All Day Pass," good for all attractions except Molson Amphitheatre concerts. These include the Children's Village, the Children's Festival

Stage, the Lego Pod and the Nintendo Power Pod. The village offers some of the most imaginative playground toys ever created; if you don't have a kid of your own in tow, you might want to borrow one or at least have a look at how much fun children can have. On the stage, there are concerts, puppet and magic shows, storytelling and other performances throughout the day, no reservations required. The Lego and Nintendo centres are located in the weird white steel-and-glass pavilions that stand thirty-six feet above the water, so they are good places to head to, especially if it's raining.

On nice days there is the amazing Soak City featuring water toys and slides for kids of all ages; the Wilderness Adventure Ride, which takes you through the forests and canyons of northern Ontario; water-based rides like the Hydrofuge and Rush River, each of which has three slides; pedal boats and bumper boats, and even canoes; the MegaMaze, actually seven different mazes in which to get lost; and a miniature golf course. The IMAX theatre and

FIREWORKS AT THE HARBOURFRONT CENTRE

ONTARIO PLACE ENTRANCE

CNE BUILDING

Omnimax Theatre are open year-round. There are about a dozen fast-food outlets (only one of which is operated by a major chain) and about half a dozen full-service restaurants to choose from. None are really inexpensive, but they aren't rip-offs either; the food is not gourmet calibre, but it serves its purpose.

THE CANADIAN NATIONAL EXHIBITION

— Exhibition Park (Lakeshore Boulevard between Strachan and Dufferin). Grounds open all year round; CNE for 18 days in August until Labour Day. For general information on the Ex, call 416 263-3800. For information on activities through the rest of the year, call 416 393-6000.

The Ex has its origins in the great agricultural and industrial fairs of the nineteenth century. Thousands flocked to inspect and enjoy the produce, livestock and other hallmarks of rural culture like fiddling, quilting and floral displays. It was here, too, that electric streetlights and

RIDES AT THE CNE

streetcars first were shown off, where cinema made its Toronto debut, where the proof of Human Progress was proudly displayed. Through the years, air shows, stomach-wrenching rides on the midway and cotton candy have perhaps overshadowed, if not quite replaced, the rural origins of the fair, to say nothing of the faith once placed in progress.

Today there are many permanent buildings with year-round uses on the site. The grounds are home now not only to the Ex, the large annual fair,

but to events like the Royal Agricultural Winter Fair, the Home Show, the Boat Show, the Car Show, major crafts fairs and other exhibitions. Canada's Sports Hall of Fame, opened in 1955, operates year-round and is free (except during the Ex, when admission to the grounds is charged). The former Arts, Crafts and Hobbies Building is now home to Medieval Times, a dinner theatre in which the play features knights in shining armour jousting on horseback.

PRINCES' GATES

DUFFERIN GATE (BELOW)
NATIONAL TRADE CENTRE (BOTTOM)

In the early 1990s, local politicians flirted briefly with replacing some of the CNE's buildings with more profitable ventures, as befits such a valuable site. Fortunately, they were largely unsuccessful. Torontonians made it clear they did not want to lose the fire hall and police station, the Music Building (originally the Railways Building), the Ontario Government Building, the Automotive Building, all built before 1930, or even the more recent, very fifties-style Shell Tower. As a result, many of the buildings have been designated as heritage sites. These monuments of an earlier time, along with such favourites as the Princes' Gates — opened in 1927 by His Royal Highness Edward, Prince of Wales, and his brother, Prince George — will remain.

The National Trade Centre (NTC) is a relative newcomer to the CNE grounds, and is the largest trade show facility in Canada. Part of its vast exterior mirrors the Automotive Building opposite, while the rest dazzles the eye with round towers punctuating a glass facade. The NTC is a fine example of how new construction can both pay homage to existing structures and make a unique architectural statement. Also on the site, but only coincidentally, is the Officers' Quarters of Stanley Barracks, a fine stone structure built in 1841 as part of the fort that replaced the original Fort York.

FUN AT THE SCIENCE CENTRE

ONTARIO SCIENCE CENTRE

— 770 Don Mills Road. Open every day except December 25 from 10 a.m. to 6 p.m. For information call 416 696-1000.

"It must be fun!" wrote the centre's architect, Raymond Moriyama, back in 1964 during the planning phase of this Ontario centennial project. And fun it is! One of the city's most-visited attractions, the Science Centre can only be described in superlative terms. It succeeds admirably in providing people of all ages with some of the sense of wonder and pleasure that motivates professional scientists. For a family of two or more with a desire to do everything — including seeing two Omnimax shows — the $25 family pass is your best bet. Parking is $7.

Its more than 800 exhibits invite you to twirl knobs, push buttons, fiddle with instruments and test your skills using gizmos related to astronomy, biology, chemistry, communications, ecology and physics. Favourites include the real rainforest in the Living Earth area and the pitching cage at the Sport exhibit. Demonstrations at various locations throughout the day include the popular laser show, the electricity demonstration and the changing programs in the mini-planetarium, Starlab. Special exhibitions range widely, from explorations of human nature to travels through Siberia. Often these are augmented by lectures so popular they bring to mind the days before radio and TV, when public talks were the main way the latest in scientific discoveries were conveyed to the masses. The centre's shop, an outlet for the small chain called Mastermind, offers a wide selection of books, software, educational toys and science kits.

ONTARIO SCIENCE CENTRE AND GROUNDS

The centre is vast: five levels cascade down the Don Valley, providing low-tech views that contrast comfortably with the exhibits and the building itself, and more than enough opportunity for walking — and the new Timescape

exhibit, installed along one of the longest parts of your trek, unearths the mysteries of time by presenting materials (stones, fossils and the like) from millions of years ago to the present. If there are any drawbacks to the centre, it's that its success is overwhelming. The only way to avoid crowds is to arrive the moment the place opens (10 a.m.). Weekdays are no better than weekends; as many as ten thousand children a day come on school trips. Although even toddlers seem to have a good time, getting the most out of the exhibits requires at least a Grade 3 or 4 reading ability. The weakest link is in the food department: only vending machines and a fairly institutional-type cafeteria, with nowhere to eat nearby.

AN EXHIBIT AT THE SCIENCE CENTRE (ABOVE); LASER SHOW AT THE ONTARIO SCIENCE CENTRE (MIDDLE) CHEETAH AT THE TORONTO ZOO (BELOW)

TORONTO ZOO

— Eastern edge of Toronto in the Rouge Valley Park, on Meadowvale Road, north of the 401, the largest urban park in North America (11,600 acres/4,700 hectares). Open every day except December 25; hours vary seasonally. For information call 416 392-5900.

Have you been meaning to go to Africa but lacked the time? Then head to the African Pavilion at the Toronto Zoo

to catch perennial favourites like gorillas and chimpanzees, as well as a host of lesser-known species. Along with the fauna, there is an array of indigenous flora, through which many of the animals appear able to wander at will, particularly the birds, who fly freely

ZOO INHABITANTS

around the verdant enclosure. In the areas adjacent to the pavilion are ostriches, African elephants, white rhinos, cheetahs, a variety of antelopes, hyenas, big cats, giraffes and many more.

The Toronto Zoo, designed in the 1960s and completed in the early 1970s, was among the first in the world to group its collection of five thousand animals according to their region of origin rather than by type. You will find monkeys, snakes, rodents and so on, not only in the African Pavilion but, where appropriate, in each of the four other pavilions: the Americas, the Malayan Woods, Australasia and the Marco Polo Trail (next to which you can test your camel-riding skills).

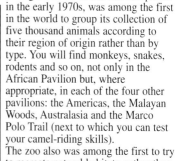

The zoo also was among the first to try to recreate natural habitats, rather than use small enclosures, for its collection. Thus, it sometimes appears as if you could reach out and touch the animals on display; although it also sometimes means you can't find the animal at all!

In other words, this zoo was designed primarily for animals rather than for people. As well as showcasing its collection, it is also an international leader in research and species survival projects. The zoo is huge, spread over 710 acres (287 hectares), making it humanly impossible to cover it entirely in one visit. You will have to pick your

priorities. Excellent maps and signage help enormously in this task, as does the posted schedule of feeding times and other events, such as meeting the keepers of various animals. There is an open-air tram, the Zoomobile, that takes you directly to some of the more distant pavilions.

You will want to pack a picnic unless fast food is your fare of choice, since that's the only food available to the human animals at the zoo. Throughout the summer, the zoo is pretty crowded, so be prepared to contend with the herd. If you can get there on a weekday at any other time of year, you will have a much more enjoyable experience. Admission prices range from $6 to $17 (free on December 26th). Parking is $7 (free from November 1st through February).

CASA LOMA INTERIOR

CASA LOMA AND SPADINA HOUSE
— 1 Austin Terrace and 285 Spadina Road, respectively. Casa Loma is open daily from 10 a.m. to 4 p.m. Spadina House is open from 9:30 a.m. to 5 p.m. on weekdays, noon to 5 p.m. on weekends. For information on special events call Casa Loma at 416 923-1171 and Spadina House at 416 392-6910.

You could be forgiven for wondering whether the Disney-esque castle perched on the escarpment above the Spadina-Dupont area is a set for some movie in progress. But it is not. It is the turreted fantasy of industrialist Sir Henry Pellatt made manifest. The $3.5-million, ninety-

CASA LOMA

eight-room folly, built between 1910 and 1913, was his home and at least in part his undoing. Within ten years of its construction, Pellatt, a pioneer of electrification, philanthropist and soldier, had lost two wives, his business and his belongings. By his death in 1939 he dwelt alone in a single room in a grim industrial suburb.

INTERIORS AT CASA LOMA

The castle, designed by John Lennox, architect of Old City Hall, is now owned by the City of Toronto, and since 1937 has been operated by the Kiwanis Club of Casa Loma. Visitors are welcome to wander the castle, the huge stables and the grounds (entry from $6 to $10;

GARDENS AT CASA LOMA

CASA LOMA
GARDENS

audiocassette tours are available in seven languages). In the late eighties, the Toronto Garden Club restored the gardens, which are now magnificent (and open free on Tuesdays from 4 p.m. until sunset).

In the main, Casa Loma has been kept much as it was, although the original $1.5-million worth of real and pseudo-baronial furniture was sold to help pay Sir Henry's debts. During the Christmas season, visitors can partake of an array of entertainments — music, drama, puppetry — designed mainly for children. Proceeds from visitors go to maintain the buildings (Sir Henry spent about $25,000 per year just on heating) and to the Kiwanis's many good causes. Throughout the year, there are special fundraising events, many of them open to the public. For instance, in mid-November, the National Ballet School runs its Sugar Plum Fair, featuring fine crafts to benefit its scholarship fund.

Just to the north and east of Casa Loma is Spadina

SPADINA HOUSE

House. The third house in the city to bear this name (which is supposed to be pronounced spa-DEE-na, but usually is comes out as spa-DIE-na), it was built in 1866 by James Austin (hence Austin Terrace), one of the founders and the first

SPADINA HOUSE INTERIORS

president of the Dominion Bank, and remained in the family until the 1970s. Today it is the grandest of several nineteenth-century homes owned and operated by Heritage Toronto (see the listings for the others), and the only one to contain its original furnishings, fixtures and works of art. Except for the six acres of grounds, which like those at Casa Loma are maintained in their Victorian and Edwardian splendour by the Toronto Garden Club, there is no idle wandering around here. Supervised tours are included with the price of admission (adults $5, less for seniors and children; discounts available for same-day visitors to Casa Loma and vice versa).

CIVIC CENTRE: CITY HALLS NEW AND OLD AND OSGOODE HALL
— *Queen Street West between Bay Street and University Avenue.*

No other building in Toronto captures the city's optimism as well as the "new" City Hall, so called to distinguish it from the Old City Hall (just across the street), which it replaced in 1965. As with two of the city's previous city halls, the design was the product of a competition, this one the work of the Finnish architect Viljo Revell. From the air, the domed council chamber and curved towers resemble an eye, a symbol in Finland for the tradition of democratic rule. From the ground, the complex often is

described as a clamshell hugging a flying saucer.

The civic pride engendered by new City Hall's design is reflected inside by the constant parade of visitors. In the lobby is a large, detailed model of downtown Toronto, which is very useful for orienting yourself. Helpful, too, are the racks of pamphlets about sights and special activities in and around Toronto, and City Shop, a bookstore that sells excellent guides, maps and souvenirs. Another favourite feature is Metropolis, one of several works by local artists, many with a local theme, that are displayed throughout the building. Metropolis is David Partridge's riveting three-dimensional wall sculpture made entirely of nails of different sizes and materials. The piece

CITY HALL AT NIGHT (ABOVE) AND DURING THE DAY (BELOW)

OLD CITY HALL is meant to represent the way cities grow from dense cores to spread-out suburbs, but its major attraction seems to be that a coin inserted at the top can find its way down to the bottom.

Popular as the new City Hall is, it is the large outdoor square it embraces — Nathan Phillips Square, named for the mayor responsible for the building's construction — that attracts crowds. Even on the coldest winter days, skaters flock to the ice rink, which is transformed into a cooling fountain in the summer. Throughout the warmer months there are concerts and other performances almost daily. There is a farmers' market

CLOCK TOWER OF OLD CITY HALL

every Wednesday, a weekend art show in midsummer and a host of other special activities for visitors of all ages. Also in the square is the Peace Garden, a small stone cube that has one corner broken away in remembrance of war's destruction. The piece was built by the city in 1984, Toronto's sesquicentennial, to express the desire of all Torontonians for world peace. Perhaps the most famous work, however, is Henry Moore's Three Way Piece No. 2, commonly called "The Archer" by Torontonians. The piece was selected by architect Viljo Revell, who was a friend of the English sculptor, but despite a generous budget for art work for the new building, council believed that an abstract piece would be unacceptable to taxpayers and decided not to purchase it. Following that decision, the mayor who succeeded Nathan Phillips, Phil Givens, led a successful campaign to raise the necessary funds by private subscription.

Just east of Nathan Phillips Square is Toronto's Old City Hall. The Toronto architect responsible for this building ensured he would be remembered by having "E.J. Lennox Architect A.D. 1889" carved under the eaves on all four sides of the building. He managed to incorporate not only the grimacing faces of the municipal politicians of the day, but also his own likeness in the carved stone work above the main entrance. In its heyday, the intricate stone work, generous proportions, stained glass, handsome council chamber, well-chosen furnishings and airy atmosphere engendered as much pride in Toronto's citizens as the new City Hall does today. The 300-foot-high clock tower, which appears from the south to cap Bay Street and is still prominently visible from many parts of downtown, was designed to be more than a landmark; it was an essential component of the building's advanced ventilating and heating system. Today, the Old City Hall is used exclusively for its courtrooms and is visited primarily by

HENRY MOORE SCULPTURE

those on court business.

West of Nathan Phillips Square is the grandly classical Osgoode Hall. Built originally as a sort of union hall for the Law Society of Upper Canada and named for the province's first chief justice, William Osgoode, it now houses the Ontario Court of Appeal, as well as continuing to serve its original purpose.

No fewer than three firms had a hand in its design prior to 1860, and another six have had a go at it since then — all of them extremely prominent, and therefore, one would think, somewhat egotistical. Yet their work has harmonized to create an exquisitely elegant, if somewhat forbidding building, and its library (which is open to the public) is widely considered one of the most elegant rooms in Canada. In another of its elegant rooms is one of the best kept secrets in the city: The Restaurant at Osgoode Hall. Open from noon to 2 p.m. on weekdays, it serves up fine French fare and has an excellent wine list. Reservations are a must (416 947-3361).

The fence surrounding Osgoode hall and the gate on Queen Street were constructed not to intimidate the public, but to keep out wandering cows. Functionally and architecturally, these three buildings beautifully reflect the growth of the city from a straight-laced, austere provincial capital to a somewhat overstuffed, rapidly growing Victorian centre of trade and commerce, to a worldly but community-oriented modern city.

OSGOODE HALL

MUSEUMS AND GALLERIES

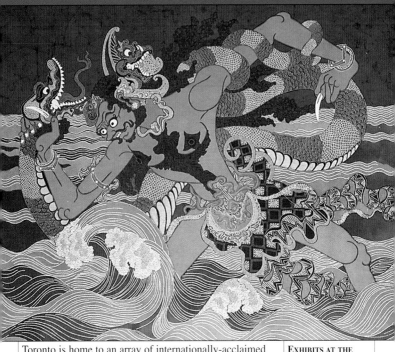

Toronto is home to an array of internationally-acclaimed public museums and galleries. There are the large and eclectic collections of institutions like the Royal Ontario Museum (ROM), which features natural, archaeological and social history, and the Art Gallery of Ontario (AGO), which houses fine art from diverse periods and cultures. Then there are the smaller and specialized offerings of the Bata Shoe Museum, the Gardiner Museum of Ceramic Art and the Textile Museum of Canada. Specialization is also the hallmark of a large number of quite small, lesser-known institutions that contain materials representing such things as police work and firefighting, hockey and other Canadian sports, cars, interior and industrial design, television, medicine and even contraception. Toronto's diverse cultures are displayed at several excellent small museums or institutes, while Toronto's own history is well-represented at Black Creek Pioneer Village, Fort York and numerous period homes throughout the city. Here we will cover the best of the well-known institutions, but be aware that in its quiet, non-assuming way, Toronto has been building a large collection of easily seen art all over town. Dozens of corporations have put paintings, sculpture and specially-commissioned work of all kinds in and around their buildings, and hundreds of pieces have been placed in libraries and other public buildings, at intersections, in

EXHIBITS AT THE TEXTILE MUSEUM OF CANADA

ROM ENTRANCE

**EARTH SCIENCES
GALLERY**

parks, on streets and bridges, and in the changing display at the city's downtown, outdoor sculpture garden. So while a visit to a gallery or museum will be well-rewarded, so too, will a thorough look at all you pass as you traverse the city.

ROYAL ONTARIO MUSEUM (ROM)

The ROM has never aspired to modesty. Until 1955, it was actually five museums, each with its own entrance and director. They covered the subjects of archaeology, paleontology, mineralogy, zoology and geology. The original building, now best seen from the south, is an exuberant pre–World War I Romanesque concoction rich with a veritable tapestry of carved arches and stonework. The first major addition came in the 1930s, a flattened art deco-ish version of the Romanesque structure, which formed what is now the east wing facing Queen's Park, through which one enters today — though not for long as still more changes are in the works. During the course of constructing that addition, the four mid-nineteenth-century "totem" or, more accurately, crest poles from British Columbia — three by the Nisga'a nation, one by the Haida — that now grace the main stairwell inside were lowered into place from above. The tallest one is a mere six inches (15 cm) from the ceiling! Subsequent additions over the past two decades have filled in the courtyards and made the ROM one of the biggest museums in North America.

In 2004, the ROM will again be under renovation, and it is possible that what you read below will not be entirely

accurate as the museum readies itself for the construction activity. The impending changes will be major, including, for example, a complete reorientation that will see the museum's main entrance relocated to Bloor Street. Called "Renaissance ROM", the 40,000 square feet of additional or reallocated space will permit the ROM to finally display its fabulous collections of musical instruments, and of textiles and costumes. Its Canadiana galleries will be expanded and there will be a new First Nations gallery, as well as a new, direct connection to the subway system. The most obvious change will be the huge glass pavilion that will serve as the

new entrance. The project is being designed by Daniel Libeskind, architect of Berlin's internationally-acclaimed Holocaust & Jewish Museum and a finalist for the work at New York's World Trade Center site.

Before you get to the five-million-odd objects in the over 40 galleries that make up the ROM's collection, you pass beneath the impressive mosaic ceiling and floor of the entry rotunda. Look up and see, set in the coruscating gold and bronze of over a million Venetian glass mosaic tiles, images of other civilizations and cultures; at your feet, a marble sunburst heralds one's passage into the ROM proper. The ROM's collection is not easily defined by categories. Broadly speaking, it has a life and earth sciences component, a Canadiana component, and an ancient civilizations and European component. Within each, there are comprehensive exhibits of fairly narrowly defined aspects, and modest collections of broadly defined aspects.

ROTUNDA MOSAIC AT THE ROM (TOP) ANCIENT EGYPT GALLERY (MIDDLE) MOSAIC OF ARTEMIS (BOTTOM)

To help you get an overview of the museum's collections, and to help you decide how much of the place to tackle, the Samuel Hall/Currelly Gallery provides a foretaste of the collections with cases displaying artifacts and specimens keyed to the museum's floor levels. This space used to house the museums's collection of armour (now on the third level), as can be seen from artist Sylvia Hahn's large murals of medieval life. For the jousting scene, she gave the spectators the faces of museum staff members at the time (1943). The grey-haired gent, second from the right, is C.T. Currelly, first director of the Royal Ontario Museum of Archaeology. Briefly, the street level (main floor) contains the ROM's magnificent Chinese collections, its Korean collection — the largest in North America — and its deservedly popular mineral collection in the (S.R. Perren Gem and Gold Room).

The level somewhat confusingly called "1B" is the Canadian Heritage floor, which contains materials from Canada's indigenous peoples to contemporary art works, the latter in the

43

TOTEM POLE

BYZANTINE CROSS

DINOSAUR GALLERY

Roloff Beny Gallery. But a huge stock of Canadiana, including everyday household items and fine antiques and paintings, is located off-site altogether, in the Sigmund Samuel Building just to the south of the ROM.

The museum's second floor is devoted to life sciences, and the third to various aspects of Mediterranean civilization. Several rooms throughout the building are used for special exhibits, sometimes blockbusters like "Egyptian Art in the Age of the Pyramids" or "Arts of the Sikh Kingdoms", or to show off parts of the vast collections normally held in storage for lack of exhibition space. For instance, the ROM's textile collection, which ranks fifth in the world and contains woven, dyed, printed and hand-worked pieces from near and far, is rarely seen. Nor is its wealth of hundreds of musical instruments.

Highlights of this profusion are found scattered throughout the building. One of the most popular parts of the Life Sciences collection (second level), for example, is the several rooms of reconstructed dinosaurs or skeletons happily stationed amidst what seems to be their original habitat. Its thirteen full skeletons span the Jurassic and the Cretaceous periods, and there is much to be gleaned from accompanying flora. Nearby are rooms filled with invertebrate fossils — from Australian bacteria that are 3.5 billion years old, to the assorted aquatic animals found in British Columbia's Burgess Shale that are a mere 535 to 515 million years old, to a glimpse of Toronto life as it would have been 440 million years ago. There is a gallery explaining evolution, and others filled with displays of mammals, birds, insects and reptiles, and a marvellous bat cave (with some 2,500 simulated bats!) that accurately replicates Jamaica's St. Clair cave. Throughout these displays, the emphasis is on explaining connections between and among living things, on providing a context in which to understand how and why different forms of life have flourished or declined.

In the significant Mediterranean World collection (third floor), you can see materials spanning Mesopotamia

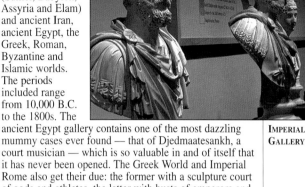

(Sumer, Babylon, Assyria and Elam) and ancient Iran, ancient Egypt, the Greek, Roman, Byzantine and Islamic worlds. The periods included range from 10,000 B.C. to the 1800s. The ancient Egypt gallery contains one of the most dazzling mummy cases ever found — that of Djedmaatesankh, a court musician — which is so valuable in and of itself that it has never been opened. The Greek World and Imperial Rome also get their due: the former with a sculpture court of gods and athletes, the latter with busts of emperors and citizens. You can sail to Byzantium to take in the Joey and Toby Tanenbaum Gallery of Byzantine Art or stroll through a sampling of an entire — but small — Islamic city, including a mosque, shrine, house, garden and market. The Samuel European galleries fill in the picture north of the Mediterranean from the Middle Ages to the 20th century. The arms and armour gallery that takes you from chain mail to machine guns is always a hit. Medieval Europe's religiosity is well represented by pieces depicting saints, and containers for holding saintly relics. The Judaica Gallery showcases Jewish ceremonial art from the 1500s onward. Nearby is a variety of reconstructed rooms, each

IMPERIAL ROME GALLERY

filled with a veritable antiques road show of the furnishings and art of different periods of European history. Also on this level is a deluxe and extensive collection of Art Deco furniture donated to the ROM by Sylvia and Bernard Ostry.

It is on the ground (street level) floor, however, that you will find what are probably the ROMs most noteworthy and certainly unique collections: its various Chinese displays. To reach these, you pass first through the aforementioned Samuel Hall/Currelly Gallery, and then

TANG DYNASTY CAMEL (MIDDLE) MING TOMB (BOTTOM)

CHINESE POTTERY

through the John David and Signy Eaton Court. The latter contains Chinese religious stone sculptures, but its primary use is as a venue for special occasions, gala openings and concerts. From there, you enter the T.T. Tsui Galleries of Chinese Art. Named in recognition of a generous donation by a Hong Kong businessman and collector, the pieces in this area are arranged a series of court-like areas and halls designed to evoke classical Chinese architecture and spanning more than 6,000 years of Chinese history, from 1500 BC to AD 1900, from the Stone Age through the Qing dynasty. There is a tale to this collection's existence. Many of the pieces were supplied by George Crofts, an Anglo-Irishman who worked as a fur trader from the turn of the century through China's major

ZHOU DYNASTY DRAGON

upheavals in the 1920s. Throughout this period, Crofts managed to acquire pieces ranging from the Imperial wardrobe to a massive Ming temple and accompanying tomb sculptures, complete with stone arches and, most amazingly of all, a procession of early 6th to late 7th century AD ceramic figures of soldiers, musicians, ox drawn carts and assorted attendants that once lined the avenue leading to the burial plot, the Bodhisattvas. For all those years, Crofts' name was kept secret so that rival dealers would not discover his identity.

From the Tsui Galleries, you pass into the Chinese Tomb area. Popularly known as the Ming Tomb, the collection actually ranges from the Yuan dynasty (14th century), to the Ming (15th to 16th centuries), to the Qing (17th to 20th centuries). The pieces formerly were displayed outdoors, but at the conclusion of the ROM's most recent construction project, only *shi shi*, the ROM's Chinese stone lions, were left to face the elements. Dating

BUDDHA AT GALLERY OF KOREAN ART

from the 1600s, the lions are thought to have once guarded the main gateway to the Su Wang Fu, a magnificent palace in Beijing destroyed during the Boxer Rebellion of 1900. Today's nasty pollution requires that even these hearty beasts — who after 300 years of guard duty spent an entire year journeying to Canada — must be encased in plastic to protect them.

Finally, in the Bishop White Gallery of Chinese Temple Art (named for Bishop William Charles White, a Canadian Anglican bishop who was stationed in Henan province from 1901 until 1934, when he became the first curator of the ROM's Chinese collections), enormous thirteenth-century wall paintings of Buddhist and Taoist gods serve as a backdrop to towering Buddhist sculptures. On a smaller scale, the collection includes hundreds of intricate jade and ivory carvings, delicate perfume bottles, fine porcelain dating back almost 1,000 years and many other treasures. Taken together, these collections represent one of the largest and most important ensembles of Chinese artifacts outside China. The only drawback to this fabulous

collection is that too little information is provided about many of the pieces.

In addition to its collections, the ROM is a major centre of research. Consequently, there are many public lectures and tours that more rigorously supplement the information in the galleries. Funding cutbacks over the past decade have inspired the ROM to recreate itself. From a purely erudite and somewhat stuffy shrine to the past, it has become a mecca for community and social events, a venue geared to all ages and filled not only with surprising artifacts, but with diverse activities. During the warmer months (May through September) the ROM offers walks, many of them free, through Toronto's diverse neighbourhoods. There are also special events for children, concerts in some of the acoustically fine courtyards and one- and two-week summer day camps. On the third Friday evening of every month, the ROM even caters specifically to singles! Also contained in the ROM is the Discovery Gallery, which enables anyone over age seven to handle objects from the collections and to view them using microscopes, magnifying glasses or other appropriate forms of technology. During some hours, museum staff

DISCOVERY GALLERY

take pieces from this gallery around on small carts, so that while viewing, say, the mammals, you might get to handle skins from different animals as well as obtaining additional information about the display. The museum has four shops: one devoted to relevant books and the ROM's own publications, another to replicas of works in the museum, a third to products for children (in the basement), and the largest to an array of gift items. There is a cafeteria, but better yet (and far more expensive) is the Jamie Kennedy at the ROM Restaurant, named for and run by one of Toronto's most highly respected chefs.

THE ART GALLERY OF ONTARIO (AGO)

From its modest beginnings around World War I as the Art Gallery of Toronto in the old house

AGO ENTRANCE

THE MARCHESA CASATI BY AUGUSTUS JOHN AT THE AGO

known as The Grange, which is connected to the south side of the modern museum, the AGO has grown gradually to a museum comprising 50 galleries with a collection of more than 24,000 pieces. Thanks to the sensible approach of the architects who undertook the AGO's most recent enlargement (from twenty galleries to fifty) in 1990, viewing these works is a comfortable and rewarding experience — which unfortunately was not the case after the expansion in the 1970s. So if you visited before 1992 and found the AGO confusing and cold, you will be more than pleasantly surprised when you return. The rooms are now sized according to the works they contain, and the walls are painted deep, rich colours — evocative of the drawing rooms in which the paintings originally might have hung. The lighting provides a sense of intimacy and privacy that invites you and other patrons to view the art rather than each other, and the classical detailing and proportions of the gallery's core, the Walker Court (also the core of the original 1918 structure), have been fully restored after being obliterated in the 1970s.

Despite its increased size, the AGO remains easily "do-able" and quite simply organized. Turning left after entering from the lobby will take you down a long ramp, past Jackman Hall past the business areas of the institution and to the Hands On Centre, where children can express their artistic sensibilities. More likely, you will choose to go up the ramp to the second level, and directly to the Moore Sculpture Centre. The remainder of this upper level is devoted to special exhibits, to twentieth-century pieces requiring large rooms, to the AGO's Inuit collection and to pre-1960 Canadian pieces.

You can return to the street level via the ramp or stairs at the westerly end of the building. Here the rooms are more warren-like and intimate, the special exhibit areas (usually) smaller, the many smaller rooms providing substantial wall space for smaller prints, drawings, photographs and paintings from the AGO's collection of European and Canadian works. These spaces encircle the aforementioned Walker Court, which lets out, on the south side of the building, to the Grange via a light-filled long atrium that contains the museum's superb restaurant, The Agora, and is also the site of concerts.

Of the AGO's many collections, three in particular make it worth a trip from anywhere in North America, if not the world. The first is its trove of Henry

Moore's works — the largest and most important single collection of his work in the world. The second is its small, but very fine group of Inuit sculpture and prints, the work of the people of Canada's western Arctic. The third is its large selection of twentieth-century, pre-1960 Canadian painters, most notably the Group of Seven — those would-be renegades who in fact were immediately embraced by critics, their peers and the public alike as superb imagists of the Canadian wilderness — and British Columbia's Emily Carr, with her vivid explorations of the West Coast.

HENRY MOORE SCULPTURE

The presence of the AGO is signaled from afar by the neo-constructivist tower built as part of the gallery's most recent and largest expansion in 1992. If you approach from the north or east, Henry Moore's *Two Forms* will catch your attention and that of any children accompanying you; it has been scientifically proven to be impossible for anyone under ten to refrain from climbing on this lovely, sensual sculpture. The Moore piece is a good introduction to what is housed within, for the artist bequeathed some 800 pieces, including bronzes, woodcuts, etchings, drawings, lithographs and maquettes to the AGO. The son of a coal miner, Moore's (1898-1986) use of elemental forms evocative of England's windswept dales makes his work as accessible to art illiterates as to aficionados of all ages. Moore believed strongly that art is international,

STUDY IN MOVEMENT BY EMILY CARR AT THE AGO

and that his exploration of the essence of shapes, whether human or geological, could speak to all. And indeed, one often will see children experimentally arranging their limbs to mimic his sensual forms. The artist had a hand in the design of the space that contains his sculptures, and the calm, natural light he insisted on is ideal for their contemplation and enjoyment. Around the corner from Moore's work is a small corridor containing examples of the works of a number of his British colleagues — Barbara Hepworth and Ben Nicholson among them — who worked from time to time in an idiom in sync with Moore's own.

The AGO's second unique collection located in the northwesterly corner of the second floor, its Inuit works, are also by people who express their perception of the world through elemental shapes, somewhat as Moore did. A piece like Hepworth's *Hollow Oval* from 1965 or *Holed Stone* from 1959, or Moore's *Working Model for Oval with*

HENRY MOORE SCULPTURE GALLERY

Points from 1968, bear a more than passing resemblance to Inuit artist Jessie Ishulutaq's *Fantastic Flying Caribou* of 1989, although the latter is carved from whale bone and antler rather than stone. Very few of the AGO pieces date from pre-historic times, or from the initial period of contact with Europeans. Rather, the bulk of the collection is from the years after 1950. Before then, Inuit pieces were almost always very small — a necessity for a nomadic people — and had either ritualistic significance or were toys. Later nineteenth- and early twentieth-century pieces were designed to be sold to visitors as souvenirs, or were models of the objects of everyday life. Only since about 1950 have the Inuit carvers of Canada's western Arctic used their skills to explore their subjective views of the world, and to communicate these views to a larger world.

Perhaps it is stretching things a bit to find that there are again similarities with Moore and the Inuit in the third of the AGO's notable collections. After all, the Group of Seven worked exclusively in two dimensions, primarily in oil, rather than in stone or bone. Yet there can be little doubt that what grabbed the imagination of these artists — Franklin Carmichael, Lawren Harris, A.Y. Jackson, Frank Johnston, Arthur Lismer, J.E.H. MacDonald, Tom

THE WEST WIND BY TOM THOMSON AT THE AGO

Thomson, F.H. Varley and the others who joined with them on occasion — were the elemental shapes, the massive strength of the Canadian landscape itself. Well-known pieces, like Lawren Harris's *Beaver Swamp, Algoma*, from 1920 and *Lake and Mountains* from 1928 or Tom Thomson's 1917 *The West Wind* are

hung here. But most unusual and rewarding is the AGO's vast supply of small (usually 8 by 10 inch) sketches or studies of these artists' larger works. Generally in oil, like the final pieces, these little works are housed in tiers of drawers and on special display panels in the middle of the exhibit. No other collection of these prolific artists shows so clearly how they worked.

The remainder of the AGO's collection includes examples of virtually all of Western art's most famous practitioners: Rembrandt, Degas, Rothko, Gauguin, Fragonard, Picasso, Durer, Gainsborough, Brancusi and Lorrain, to name but a few. In the main, however, there is but one piece by each of these, and generally it is not of these artists' highest quality. So unless you are keen on a whirlwind art history lesson, these are not the areas in which you will want to linger. The collection of pieces by other Canadians working in the European tradition is of somewhat greater interest and

ELM TREE AT HORTON LANDING BY ALEX COLVILLE AT THE AGO

BLUE NUDE BY **HENRI MATISSE** VISITS THE **AGO**

spans the country and its history: Quebec's Joseph Légaré, with his almost journalistic capturing of significant nineteenth-century events, such as the 1845 conflagration near Quebec City; Nova Scotia's Alex Colville, with his disquieting depiction of seemingly mundane activities; Cornelius Krieghoff's somewhat saccharine portrayal of nineteenth-century rural Quebec, Paul Kane's images of the then-unknown west, and other lesser knowns like Lucius O'Brien and Paul Peel. There is a room devoted to two Toronto favourites — "the girls" as the sculptresses Florence Wyle and Frances Loring were called, and a fair sampling of moderns such as Harold Town, Kenneth Lochhead, Jock Macdonald, Jack Bush, Michael Snow,

EATING AT THE AGORA

Guido Molinari and Jean-Paul Riopelle. And, evocative of the Inuit work, there is a single case containing the Charles Eden Shaw collection of some 50 soft black slate (argillite) miniature totem poles carved at the turn of the last century, probably by two Old Masset villagers of British Columbia's Queen Charlotte Islands. As well, the AGO has assembled a fine contemporary collection that takes in the United States and Europe, including the largest set of American Expressionist Robert Motherwell's works on paper in the world. The AGO's photographic resources are likewise diverse, with calotypes by British photographers Linnaeus Tripe, heligravures by Édouard Baldus, and

L'INCENDIE DU QUARTIER SAINT-JEAN VU VERS L'OUEST BY JOSEPH LÉGARÉ AT THE AGO

motion study images by Étienne-Jules Marey. The gallery also boasts the largest collection of art films in Canada.

Like most galleries, the AGO organizes special exhibits to augment its permanent displays. Some of these are drawn from its own collections — for example, the almost-annual, end-of-year favourite, The Magic Toy Shop, a selection of pieces from the Trier-Fodor Foundation gift to the museum. Other special shows are relatively modest exhibits that are excellently curated. Occasionally, the AGO gets into the blockbuster game. Upcoming shows include the drawings of Raphael and His Circle, etchings by Rembrandt, works of Goya, and Italian drawings from the Renaissance to the Enlightenment. Special tickets are usually needed for such shows, during which the gallery — or at least the special exhibition portions of it — is jammed to the rafters.

In addition to viewing the art, there are numerous other activities available. You can visit The Grange or take in a film. The Toronto Film Society makes its home at the gallery and runs numerous festival series (Film Buffs [sic]

Mondays, Classics of World Cinema and so on) throughout the year (call 416 363-7222). There is the Hands-On Centre for Children, which, as the name implies, provides interactive activities for budding young masters. The gallery's many educational activities (courses, lectures, films and performances) are considerably augmented by its Edward P. Taylor Research Library and Archives, which is open to the public on Wednesday and Friday afternoons. The library contains over 100,000 volumes on Canadian, Inuit, international and contemporary art. The archives and special collections, which require an appointment for viewing, include illustrated Victorian books and writings, as well as memorabilia of members of the Group of Seven. The Marvin Gelber Print and Drawing Study Centre, open the same hours as the library, holds some 14,000 works on paper, which can be viewed in the study room. The cafeteria — not to be confused with The Agora, the fine restaurant in the atrium — is located beside the gift shop. And finally, there is the very large and fine gift shop. It carries not only the standard museum fare such as Monet calendars, but much, much more. Its book collection is very extensive and is probably one of the best in the country on Canadian arts and artists. The gift shop also features a wide and ever-changing selection of Canadian-crafted jewelry, household items and assorted objets d'art. *Hot off the press*: In 2005, the AGO will close for two years as it again expands. The new space is being designed by Toronto-born architect Frank Gehry, best known in the museum world for Bilbao's Guggenheim. When it reopens in 2007, in addition to its new design the AGO will boast a greatly enhanced collection — the gift of press baron and philanthropist Sir Kenneth Thomson, who will be donating virtually his entire, highly-rated holdings to the museum. Included in the donation, for example, is Rubens' *Massacre of the Innocents*, for which Thomson paid $117 million. Thomson is also providing about 40 percent of the money required for the new addition.

HARLEQUIN AT THE
GARDINER MUSEUM

THE GARDINER MUSEUM OF CERAMIC ART

A bijoux museum displaying North America's largest collection of European porcelain and other clay-based articles of the past five millennia, the Gardiner is located directly opposite the ROM. Both the building and much of its permanent collection were the gift of George R. Gardiner and his wife Helen. Pieces from virtually all the well known ceramic centres of Europe — Sèvres, Saint-Cloud, Plymouth and Bristol, Vienna and Meissen among them — along with a sampling of blue and white Chinese porcelain are displayed on the second floor. Here you will find seventeenth-century English Delftware and slipware, Italian Renaissance majolica and remarkably Picasso-

esque tin-glazed earthenware intended for everyday use, soft-paste porcelain from Chelsea, and hard-paste porcelain from the Meissen factory and its rival, the Viennese Du Paquier factory. Of special interest are the tiny figurines depicting the stock characters of the Commedia dell'arte. Information on each piece, the factories that made them and the processes employed, is clear and thorough. Here, too, is A la Carte at the Gardiner, a deeply comfortable small restaurant offering a gourmet lunch from 11:30 a.m. to 2 p.m. on weekdays. On the ground floor is the museum's fine collection of ancient American ceramics, some dating as far back as 3,000 BC, and its smaller selection of fifteenth- and sixteenth-century Italian majolica. Two galleries on this level are devoted to temporary exhibits. Here, too, is a small shop filled with the work of modern potters, many of them local. There are guided tours on Tuesdays and Thursdays at 11 a.m. and Sundays at 1 p.m. Also, on Sundays between 1 and 3 p.m., visitors can try their luck at a potter's wheel or at hand building in the museum's well-outfitted studio, the Clay Pit, for a small fee.

BATA SHOE MUSEUM

If you're like most people, your initial reaction to the very idea of a museum devoted to shoes will be a snort of derision: "What's this? A foot fetishist's wonderland?" But

hold the snort. The odd little Bata Shoe Museum — the building is even shaped like a shoe — is actually a delight. The All About Shoes exhibit gets you from the earliest sandals to the latest in haut monde in a room so well laid out that your feet don't even get tired. Adults will learn a lot wherever they tread and will no doubt get a charge from the footwear of the rich and famous: Elvis's blue suede shoes and Elton John's sneakers, for instance. Some visitors will enthuse over the workwear collection of boots specially designed for everything from mining to rice harvesting, while others are sure to delight in the Gentle Step, an overview of the changing role of nineteenth-century women and the variations in shoes (and costumes) that reflected these developments. Special exhibits are well-designed, informative and

BATA SHOE MUSEUM

always pun-filled. Little Feats, for example, displayed children's shoes from around the world, while One, Two Buckle My Shoe, drew on children's literature ranging from classic fairy tales to contemporary urban stories to depict the ever-present role of feet, footwear and shoemakers. Another, called Loose Tongues and Lost Soles, focused entirely on humorous foot-related sculptures and works on paper, ranging from caricatures by Daumier to cartoons from the *New Yorker*.

TEXTILE MUSEUM OF CANADA

Perhaps because few would find it kinky to collect fabric, the Textile Museum generally lacks the humour of the Bata, although a recent show on modes of dress was called "Moral Fibre." Lacking also the financial backing of the shoe-wealthy Batas, it is housed in a non-descript building behind City Hall rather than in a Cinderella-inspired slipper. Apart from these distinctions, however, the Museum for Textiles competes very effectively as an internationally-known centre for the collection, display and documentation of its chosen subject. It contains over 10,000 pieces of ethnographic and historic textiles — including woven, knotted, hooked and tied, dyed and natural wools, silks, cottons and grasses, the well-stocked H.N. Pullen library (over 3,000 items), and a lovely gift shop filled with woven and reading materials from around the world. In addition to its own vast collection, only a small portion of which can be displayed at any one time in this 4,000 square foot facility, the museum hosts traveling exhibits. Recent visitors have included the hooked mats of the Grenfell Mission — a selection of the nearly forgotten, but once immensely popular work (it was carried by Eaton's) of women from Newfoundland and Labrador. Another was an amazing display of European lacework spanning several centuries.

AFGHANISTAN EXHIBIT (ABOVE) AND MOCHE FRINGE (INSET) AT THE TEXTILE MUSEUM OF CANADA

HISTORY ON DISPLAY

Toronto displays its heritage at numerous sites throughout the city. There is, of course, its sizable collection of historically and architecturally noteworthy buildings — even whole neighbourhoods, such as Cabbagetown. There is Toronto's First Post Office, and several restored nineteenth-century schools. For devotees of soldiering, there is Fort York, site of the garrison first established by the British in 1793. The fort is operated by Heritage Toronto, which gives tours several times a day through tiny barracks that once housed over 100 people. The highlight for many visitors occurs on July 1 (Canada Day), and August 1 (Simcoe Day), when cannons boom, and mock soldiers are put through their paces. There is the Riverdale Farm in the Don Valley, which houses livestock representing heritage breeds, and the nearby Brickworks and Todmorden Mills, both of which hark back to nineteenth-century industries. There are fine homes like Spadina House, Casa Loma and the Grange, as well as more modest abodes like Colbourne Lodge and Mackenzie House. All these demonstrate life in the periods in which they were built. The granddaddy, though, of these living-

THE FORT YORK GUARD

55

INTERPRETERS AT BLACK CREEK

museum, type sites is the 40-year-old Black Creek Pioneer Village.

BLACK CREEK PIONEER VILLAGE

If you are not already a fan of the "living history" style of presenting life in earlier times, Black Creek may convert you. With the exception of some remnants of the Stong farm once located here (the piggery, the barn and two homes), most of the 40-odd buildings on the site were rescued from decay somewhere in southern Ontario; the rest, like Roblin's Mill, were built from scratch.

Visitors can get a good idea of how a variety of household and farm implements were made and used: the harness maker makes and repairs leather items, the blacksmith shoes the village horses, the cooper produces barrels and buckets, the seamstress sews the villagers' costumes, the broom maker makes brooms from corn grown behind the shop, the cabinet maker makes furniture and the tinsmith produces various housewares. In addition to the horses, who haul around a hay wagon you can catch to cut down on walking (or just for fun), there are chickens in the coop, hogs in the piggery and cows in the pasture.

MILL AT BLACK CREEK

You'll also find a printing press, a cider mill, a grain mill, a small school, a church, homes reflecting various degrees of

wealth, and even a Masonic Lodge. The restaurant is not bad, and there are usually freshly baked pies and bread. There are several vegetable gardens, a garden devoted to dye plants used by the weaver, a well-researched medicinal herb garden, a kitchen and folk-remedy herb garden, and a Pennsylvania German square garden. There are weekend and month-long special events, such as the Spring Fair, corn roasts, apple-baking contests, pumpkin parties, craft demonstrations and sales, theatrical and musical performances and, from mid-November until December 24th, special Christmas activities. Of course, it is true that no animals actually meet their demise in the slaughterhouse, and there is little to indicate that life in the times depicted was nasty, brutish and short, but despite these gaps, Black Creek does a good job of providing a highly enjoyable and informative outing for the whole family.

INDEPENDENT GALLERIES

CHRISTOPHER HUME

In the beginning, there was Yorkville. It was the 1960s, and Toronto was just waking from its long provincial slumber. Though it soon would be gentrified beyond recognition, Yorkville suddenly found itself the front line in the War of Love. As the hippies arrived in the Victorian enclave near Bloor Street and Avenue Road, so did artists and art dealers.

ABOVE: *THE POWER PLANT* BY **TIM HAWKINSON**
BELOW: *MOUNTAIN VALLEY, SPRING #2* BY **ANNE MEREDITH BARRY**

YORKVILLE

Walter Moos was the first, setting up shop on Yorkville Avenue in 1961. He would later move further downtown, but his appearance was enough to start the ball rolling. And though the counterculture has long since disappeared from the scene, Yorkville still boasts more than a dozen art galleries. The dealers here tend to be high-end types, their stables filled with senior artists from Canada and the world. The following are among the most prominent.

Many of Canada's leading contemporary artists, including Betty Goodwin, Joanne Tod and Tony Scherman, exhibit at the Sable-Castelli Gallery, 33 Hazelton Avenue. Its success comes from dealer Jared Sable's skill at treading the fine line between intellectual respectability

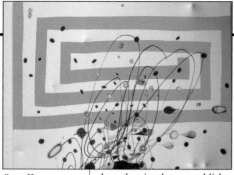

OPEN HOUSE BY DAVID CRAVEN AT THE SABLE-CASTELLI GALLERY

and commercial appeal. The Mira Godard Gallery, at 22 Hazelton, is a Yorkville fixture. Godard represents some of the country's best-known artists: Christopher and Mary Pratt, Joe Fafard, and Edward Burtynsky. Although no hotbed of artistic ferment, this is where the visual-arts establishment struts its stuff.

HARBOURFRONT AND THE SURROUNDING AREA

Off the beaten track, the Power Plant, at the Harbourfront Centre, 231 Queen's Quay West, has emerged as the premier showcase of the most contemporary of contemporary art from Toronto, Tokyo, London and New York. Dramatically housed in a former generating station, this noncollecting gallery finds itself looking sometimes down and dirty, sometimes very slick, but rarely dull. Before reaching the Power Plant, art lovers will have travelled through the gallery-rich district along Spadina Avenue and Richmond Street. Running the gamut from up-market to low-rent, this is home to the good, the bad and the ugly of the Toronto art scene.

The city's original artist-run gallery is A Space, at 401 Richmond Street West. Around for more than thirty years, it has become more a soapbox than a showcase. Post-feminist, pre-millennial, pan-sexual: the revolution is in

full swing here. In the same building is a mix of nonprofits sharing floor space with commercial galleries like Wynick/Tuck Gallery, which carries some big names in the world of art: Kim Adams, Greg Curnoe and Lawrence Weiner.

WEST END

Further west at 788 King Street West is Art Metropole, a gallery, book and multiples shop. This is a great place to buy cool artist-made multiples, jacket crests by General Idea and felt postcards by Joseph Beuys.

A few doors down you'll find Toronto's, if not Canada's, most idiosyncratic gallery, the Ydessa Hendeles Art Foundation, at 778 King Street West. Hendeles has transformed a two-storey

VAULT AT SANDRA AINSLEY GALLERY

commercial building into a shrine for leading-edge work from Europe, the United States and Canada. Named by Artnews as one of the top 100 art collectors in the world, Ydessa Hendeles is as likely to show film-based work by Douglas Gordon and sculptures by Maurizio Cattelan, as she is to display her own outstanding collection of teddy bear photographs. A word of warning: The foundation is only open Saturdays, from noon to 5 p.m.

Deep in Toronto's west end, near College Street and Lansdowne Avenue, is the Morrow Avenue complex, a cluster of galleries gathered around a renovated industrial courtyard. The Olga Korper Gallery, at 17 Morrow, is dedicated to the conceptual and sculptural. It is stunning even at its most minimal. By contrast, the Christopher Cutts Gallery, at 21 Morrow Avenue, is given over to both abstract and figurative painting, and Peak Gallery to emerging local artists.

WEST QUEEN WEST

It's been said that artists are the first sign of a neighbourhood's gentrification. This has never been more true than along West Queen West. Once filled with film studios, fleabag hotels and greasy spoons, the area has quickly developed into the city's hippest district with juice bars and galleries among second-hand appliance stores.

GARDEN LILIES BY MARY PAVEY (BELOW) AT GALLERY ONE

From Bathurst Street onward there are at least twenty galleries that change regularly with each new crop of art grads. Among the fray is dealer Katharine Mulherin who operates three galleries along the strip, at 1040, 1080 and 1086 Queen Street West. Mulherin has dominated the neighbourhood since 1998 when she opened her first gallery and started showing work by people she knew. Her stable now includes top painters Dana Holst, Michael Harrington and Eliza Griffiths.

There are dozens more galleries in the vicinity, including the worthwhile but hard to find Paul Petro Contemporary Art at 980 Queen West (there is no sign out front — look for a baby blue doorway), and the tiny Zsa Zsa Gallery at 962 Queen West. DeLeon White Gallery, at 1096 Queen West, is the chicest on the strip. Specialized in environmental art, they have taken full advantage of the gallery's high ceilings and garage door entrance with massive installations by Doug Buis and Peter von Tiesenhausen.

ARIA BY DORIS SUNG AT A SPACE

EAST END

The latest art district to emerge is at the Gooderham and Worts distillery, a stunning 5.2-hectares of interconnected historic buildings located at the edge of Lake Ontario. This site is being billed as the city's newest centre for arts and entertainment. The redevelopment officially opens May 2003, but high-end tenants have moved in to spacious galleries, including Canada's leading photography dealer Jane Corkin of the Corkin/Shopland Gallery at the Barrel Wash House, 22 Mill Street. At 55 Mill Street is the Sandra Ainsley Gallery, specialists in contemporary glass art. Fans of Dante Chihuly should not miss this one.

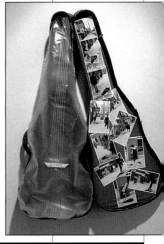

THEATRE AND DANCE

VIT WAGNER AND JON KAPLAN

LION KING AT THE **PRINCESS OF WALES**

The live performing arts rank as Toronto's greatest cultural asset. From theatre and dance to classical music and opera, the city resounds with opportunities year-round.

DRAMA

In the past fifteen years, Toronto has grown to become the third-largest centre for live theatre in the English-speaking world, after New York and London. The commercial scene is dominated by Mirvish Productions, run by the father-

THE ROYAL ALEX

and-son team of Ed and David Mirvish, who have mounted world premieres, such as a musical adaptation of *Jane Eyre*, but are mainly involved in bringing popular Broadway and West End shows, from *Les Misérables* to *The Lion King*, to Toronto. The mega-musicals are housed in the spacious and comfortable Princess Of Wales Theatre, while the more cozy and historic Royal Alexandra Theatre is home to the ABBA-

inspired musical *Mamma Mia!* Recently, the Mirvishes have put the shows from their subscription season — including Broadway hit *The Producers* —in other restored landmark theatres such as the Canon and the Winter Garden.

The home-grown treasures of Canadian theatre are to be found at the city's many alternative or not-for-profit houses. Of these, the Tarragon Theatre is without equal as a purveyor of original Canadian scripts, having served as a welcome home to some of the country's finest playwrights, including Judith Thompson, Jason Sherman, John Murrell and Montreal's universally acclaimed Michel Tremblay. Another stalwart, the Factory Theatre, is most closely associated with the work of playwright George F. Walker, whose scripts have been produced throughout the United States, while Theatre Passe Muraille has a long-standing tradition of experimental, collective creations. Also of note is Buddies in Bad Times Theatre, which produces more gay and lesbian plays than any other theatre on the continent. For family fare, check out the Lorraine Kimsa Theatre for Young People, whose repertoire ranges from adaptations of Dickens and other masters to world premières by Canadian writers whose work mirrors the city's multicultural fabric.

CLEOPATRA (ABOVE) AND *CHAPLIN* (BELOW) AT THE SHAW FESTIVAL

And this sample only scratches the surface. There are scores of companies in the city, including Necessary Angel, Theatre Columbus, Nightwood Theatre, Crow's Theatre and Theatre Smith-Gilmour, which produce one or two shows a season in rental spaces around the city. The Canadian Stage Company, Toronto's largest not-for-profit producer, offers a full, September-to-May subscription season at the St. Lawrence Centre and its own theatre, with programming that includes new Canadian work alongside revivals by well-known foreign writers such as Tom Stoppard and composer Stephen Sondheim. The company's annual Dream in High Park outdoor production, running throughout July and August in a grassy amphitheatre, is one of the calendar's most popular and populist events, with families gathering as early as two hours before show time to secure a clear view and enjoy a picnic

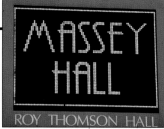

CanStage's *Picasso at the Lapin Agile* (MIDDLE) AND *Cleopatra* AT THE SHAW FESTIVAL (BELOW)

dinner.

Two other summer attractions, the Toronto Fringe and SummerWorks festivals, are browsers' delights. Most shows are an hour long, and although line-ups are common for word-of-mouth hits, prices are low (less than $10). Venues are spread out over an area roughly bounded by Bloor and Queen, to the north and south, and Bathurst and St. George, to the west and east.

Harbourfront Centre, which operates three theatres and a variety of other performance facilities on the shores of Lake Ontario, is festival central. Harbourfront facilitates the World Stage in April, Toronto's main window on the international theatre scene. May's annual Milk International Children's Festival offers scores of performances and free outdoor events.

Also based at Harbourfront is Soulpepper Theatre, which has proven itself to be a leading producer of classical repertoire, from Shakespeare and Molière to Chekhov and Beckett. Its summer season features some of Canada's finest actors.

The Stratford Festival and Shaw Festival are two of North America's leading classical repertory companies. They're also less than two hour's drive from Toronto. The Stratford Festival, a jog off Highway 401 en route to Windsor

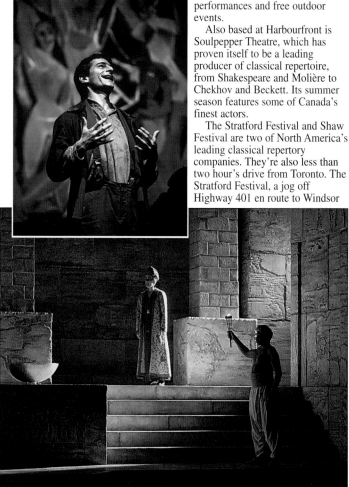

and Detroit, is the continent's leading Shakespearean interpreter. Since its inaugural season in 1953, when Alec Guinness kicked things off in the role of Richard III, Stratford has presented an expanding program of Shakespeare and other giants of the theatre — from the Greeks to Tennessee Williams — during a season that runs from May to November. The Shaw Festival, off the Q.E.W. in Niagara-on-the-Lake, was founded in 1962. It specializes in the work of Bernard Shaw, with nods toward other modernist visionaries, from Henrik Ibsen to Luigi Pirandello, and has recently begun staging newer plays as well. Both festivals balance their emphasis on the dramatic classics with lighter fare, including musicals.

HIGHER BY THE **DANNY GROSSMAN DANCE COMPANY** (MIDDLE) **PREMIERE DANCE THEATRE AT HARBOURFRONT**

DANCE

Harbourfront is also a hive of dance activity, much of it on the cutting edge, with the Premiere Dance Theatre serving as host to both visiting and resident productions. Among the Canadian companies to watch for are Danny Grossman, Desrosiers and Toronto Dance Theatre.

For classical dance, there is the Hummingbird Centre for the Performing Arts, Toronto's oldest modern-style auditorium and home to the world-renowned National Ballet of Canada. Traditionalist in orientation, the company has produced several leading lights of the international dance scene since it was founded in 1951, including such graceful luminaries as the now-retired Karen Kain. Its annual production of *The Nutcracker* is a seasonal favourite.

SYMPHONY, CHAMBER MUSIC AND OPERA

JON KAPLAN

TAFELMUSIK

ROY THOMSON REVAMPED

Toronto classical music groups score big with their audiences, since concertgoers can hear anything from A (Tomaso Albinoni) to Z (Alexander Zemlinsky) — including pieces by Bach, Mozart, Schubert and Tchaikovsky. With dozens of companies large and small from which to choose, music buffs are offered several events nearly every night of the year.

ORCHESTRA

The big kid on the block is the Toronto Symphony Orchestra, which has toured the world. Its home base, in one of Toronto's theatre districts, is Roy Thomson Hall, which resembles nothing so much as a glass-faced volcanic dome. Renovated in 2002, Thomson Hall now boasts superior acoustics for all sorts of performances. The symphony's extensive series of concerts begins in September and runs through June, featuring the standard rep as well as pieces by lesser-known composers such as Schreker, Ligeti and Pärt. The company — which has been led by such luminaries as Seiji Ozawa, Andrew Davis and Jukka-Pekka Saraste — also prides itself on regularly programming world-première commissions by Canadian composers, including Brian Cherney's *La Princesse lointaine* and Eric Morin's *Museum Music*. World-renowned soloists like clarinetist Sabine Meyer, pianists Emanuel Ax and Radu Lupu, and cellist Yo-Yo Ma are regular guests with the symphony.

One of the little joys provided by the TSO is its pre-show Evening Overture series, which precedes several concerts. Ticket-holders for the series have a chance to listen to musicians discuss the upcoming concert or hear chamber music by composers whose symphonic works will be played later. It's an instructive introduction to the music as well as a fascinating way to compare how artists create on both a small and a large scale.

The TSO also holds a number of special events during the season, featuring performances of Handel's perennial Christmas favourite *Messiah*, solo performances by such guest artists as violinist Itzhak Perlman and soprano Kathleen Battle, a series of pop concerts for the family and several concerts aimed at youngsters from five to 12.

Another classical group with an international reputation is Tafelmusik, a baroque orchestra led by concert master and first violinist Jeanne Lamon. Playing on period instruments, the group offers a season of music that focuses on the works of Vivaldi, Handel, Bach, Mozart and Purcell. No scratchy, out-of-tune academic recreations here — Tafelmusik plays with a warmth and a skill that sweeps listeners along. Performing in the acoustically superb Trinity-St. Paul's Church, the orchestra offers thematic programs (an evening in Venice, for instance, featuring music by Cavalli, Gabrieli and Vivaldi) or full-scale choral works (Bach's *Mass in B Minor* or its annual *Messiah*, including a singalong performance) with its own chamber choir led by Ivars Taurins as Mr. Handel himself.

For modern classical sounds, check out Alex Pauk's Esprit Orchestra, devoted exclusively to contemporary music.

TORONTO MENDELSSOHN CHOIR	**CHOIRS**

The most venerable of local singing groups is the Toronto Mendelssohn Choir, founded in 1894 and now comprising of over 150 volunteer singers. Led by Noel Edison, the group performs frequently with orchestras around the country and also offers its own concert series, ranging from carol works and the inevitable *Messiah* at Christmastime to pieces by Handel, Mendelssohn and Stravinsky. Hearing the full-voiced choir in the Hallelujah Chorus makes for a stirring evening. The group has its junior associates, the Toronto Mendelssohn Youth Choir, which provides a fine training and performance opportunity for young singers.

Also worth checking out are concerts by the Amadeus Choir, the Elmer Iseler Singers, the Toronto Children's Chorus, and the Canadian Childrens' Opera Chorus, all over 20 years old, and the newer Orpheus Choir, which focuses on some of the more unusual choral repertoire.

OPERA ATELIER

CHAMBER ENSEMBLES AND RECITALS

Toronto has dozens of smaller groups who make beautiful music throughout the year. Only a few seasons old, the Aradia Ensemble under Kevin Mallon began as a baroque group but has since branched out. The Toronto Consort, led by David Fallis, offers an unusual series of medieval and Renaissance music. The group has performed such rarities as Monteverdi's *The Coronation of Poppea* and an evening devoted to the love story of Tristan and Isolde. Music Toronto mounts a chamber-music series devoted largely to recitals by string quartets and pianists, with the occasional vocalist included as well. The Aldeburgh Connection, run by Stephen Ralls and Bruce Ubukata, highlights Canadian singers in performances that range from Schumann and Schubert — there's an annual Schubertiad evening — to Britten and Grieg. The Off Centre Music series, founded by Inna Perkis and Boris Zarankin, recreates a nineteenth-century musical salon evening, complete with soloists and the occasional bit of poetry. New Music Concerts is Canada's oldest presenter

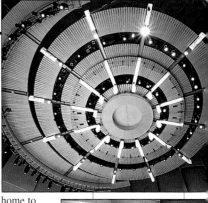

of contemporary music.

Several venues offer their own classical-music performances, usually as one-time events. Roy Thomson Hall has brought in Amsterdam's Royal Concertgebouw Orchestra, violinist Midori and pianist Evgeny Kissin and sponsors an international vocal series with such guests as baritone Bryn Terfel, soprano Renee Fleming and mezzo Cecilia Bartoli. The Glenn Gould Studio, a recital and recording hall that's part of the Canadian Broadcasting Corporation, is home to chamber music and vocal recitals by performers such as Canadian pianist Angela Hewitt and tenor Michael Schade.

OPERA

The two main players here are the Canadian Opera Company and Opera Atelier, each with its loyal followers. The COC — which performs at the Hummingbird Centre but gets its own home in 2005 — stages six English-surtitled productions a year, everything from the standard Puccini, Verdi and Rossini to more exotic works by Janacek, Britten and Monteverdi. Audiences eagerly anticipate a new production of Richard Wagner's *Ring Cycle*, set to begin in 2004. General director Richard Bradshaw has a canny way of giving even well-known pieces a new twist, such as a staging of Wagner's *The Flying Dutchman* that draws on German expressionist films of the twenties. He also has a keen eye for up-and-coming European singers, often providing them with a North American debut, and he regularly draws on artists from other disciplines — stage directors Robert Lepage and Robin Phillips, film directors Atom Egoyan and Francois Girard — to guide productions. Bradshaw, who conducts half of the season's presentations, also commissions new Canadian operas, such as *The Golden Ass*, with music by Randolph Peters and a libretto by celebrated Canadian author Robertson Davies.

CEILING AND SEATING IN ROY THOMSON HALL

Opera Atelier, founded by Marshall Pynkoski and Jeannette Zingg, has travelled the world with its presentations, many from the baroque period. Beautifully costumed and drawing on dance as much as on singing, works such as Purcell's *Dido and Aeneas* and Rameau's *Pygmalion* are a delight to the eye and the ear. In recent years, the company has included later compositions by Mozart and Gluck in its season.

Current classical-music performances are listed in the Thursday What's On section of the *Toronto Star* and in *NOW* Magazine. The most complete information is in the monthly publication *WholeNote*. Its articles are rather lightweight, but the extensive calendar section includes everything from a solo flute concert in a small church to an orchestral gala at Roy Thomson Hall.

GLENN GOULD

JOHN MILLER

GLENN GOULD AT THE PIANO

Glenn Gould is this city's most famous citizen — a fact that will surely puzzle Torontonians and likely lead to an argument if you say it. But remind your friends that more books are written in more languages about Mr. Gould than about any other Canadian. Tell them that interest in his unique (some would say eccentric) life and artistry grows stronger year after year around the globe. If you doubt this, check with The Glenn Gould Foundation whose website, www.glenngould.ca, is a great place to prepare yourself for your G.G. excursion around the city; their phone number is 416 962-6200.

You might also consider that Gould's music is not just of interest to humans. Extraterrestrials have a chance to hear Gould in a performance of Bach's The Well-Tempered Clavier (book 2), Prelude and Fugue in C. No. 1 on board NASA's two Voyager craft launched in 1989 and aimed well beyond our own solar system. Not until 40,000 years have passed will the golden-plated copper discs with the music of Gould, plus 189 other sounds of our earth, approach any other planetary systems!

But you are in an earthly dimension in Toronto, the city which Gould loved above all others, so your tour must either begin or end at the corner of Front Street West and John Street, where you almost meet the man himself and can have your picture taken on his sidewalk bench. This life-sized, bronze sculpture by Ontario artist Ruth Abernethy recreates a famous photo snapped just north of the city by Gould's favourite photographer, Don Hunstein.

The sculpture, unveiled during an international Gould festival in 1999, is a gift to the people of Canada from Toronto philanthropist Clarice Chalmers to honour her husband Wallace Gordon Chalmers, a member of this city's distinguished family of cultural donors.

Nearby is the Canadian Broadcasting Centre's Glenn

Gould Studio, so named because it is a state-of-the-art broadcast facility and not just a performance venue. Gould was strongly against live performances, but his estate consented to sharing his name with this CBC facility because sound emanates from here to Canada and the world via broadcasting, which Gould loved.

YO-YO MA AND FRIENDS WITH GOULD STATUE AT THE CBC

Check out the photographs and album covers in the Studio lobby and take a moment to see his boyhood instrument, the Chickering piano against whose sensitivity the pianist was said to measure every other instrument he owned or played. Here also are the photographs of the Laureates of the Glenn Gould Prize, awarded triennially to renowned figures whose musical genius, like Gould's, has been disseminated through communication technologies.

Another famous Gould piano — the Yamaha instrument on which he recorded his 1981 interpretation of the Goldberg Variations, a year before his death — is on display in the lobby of Roy Thomson Hall. Occasionally, visiting amateur pianists are allowed to play this keyboard.

Glenn Gould was buried in Mount Pleasant Cemetery in October, 1982. To find the site it is best to stop by the office in the eastern section of the cemetery, off Mount Pleasant Boulevard. Gould's grave, with its simple but famous marker carved with the opening bars of the Goldbergs, is at Section 38, Plot 1050, Row 1088. Close by are a large stone marker unveiled during another Gould Gathering as well as an Alaskan Sitka spruce tree planted by Glenn's father, Herbert, in 1992. This tree is the only one of its species in the entire cemetery; what makes it appropriate to mark the Gould family plot is that its wood is used to make the sounding boards of pianos.

You might also want to see the two buildings which Glenn Gould called home — 32 Southwood Drive, his boyhood residence in the Beaches, and 110 St. Clair Avenue West, the apartment building he lived in as an adult. Both dwellings have historical plaques on their front lawns saying that Glenn Gould lived there.

Toronto also has Glenn Gould Park on the northwest corner of Avenue Road and St. Clair, not far from the apartment building. The nearby Fran's Restaurant, where the pianist ate many of his late-night meals and delighted in rice pudding with raisins, is now unfortunately closed.

Finally, if you want Glenn Gould books or records, you should visit L'Atelier Grigorian, a record store on Yorkville Avenue just west of Bay Street which Gould devotees regard as the world headquarters of Gould memorabilia. The amazing Gould specialists on staff ship packages around the globe and take payment in Canadian dollars — two points which international collectors and travellers especially appreciate.

NIGHTLIFE

ADAM STERNBERGH

THE GYPSY CO-OP

In Toronto, nightlife revolves around neighbourhoods: when making plans to go out, you are just as likely to choose as the destination an intersection as a specific club or bar. It all depends on what you're looking for.

LITTLE ITALY

College Street, smack-dab in the middle of Little Italy, has, in recent years, seen intimate trattorias and atmosphere-rich cocktail spots replace the old guard of tailors and barber shops. Bar Italia (582) is the nexus of the action here — a spare, casually swank restaurant and bar with cream-coloured booths. Steps away, you'll find any number of laid-back pit stops to linger over drinks: the College St. Bar (514) and the Midtown (552), with their neighbourhood pub feel and beers on tap, both offer relaxed environs to while away the hours. A more lively

crowd gathers at Ciao Edie (489), a retro-flavoured basement bar stacked to the rafters with vintage lamps and lithe scenesters. Romantics can enjoy red wine in glass tumblers over candlelight at Kalendar (546), or trek a little further west to the shimmering Souz Dal (636),

purveyors of grade-A martinis. In the summer, this neighbourhood is patio central. Stroll along this stretch to see and be seen on a hot summer night. Those seeking a hipper vibe should head a few blocks east to the Lava Lounge (507), a groovy habitat complete with beaded curtains and the eponymous lamps, where you're likely to stumble in on anything from swing bands to Latin combos to cutting-edge DJs weaving a backdrop of chilled-out tracks.

RICHMOND-ADELAIDE
If your perfect evening out includes ringing ears, serpentine line-ups and warehouse-sized dance floors, hop in a cab to Richmond Street West or Adelaide Street West, home of the superclubs. For all-night hedonistic partying, the best bet on the strip is System Soundbar (117 Peter). The two-room dance club packs in a mixed crowd each week, and regularly plays host to international DJ superstars. Just a few blocks over is the Fluid Lounge (217 Richmond), an upscale spot for the older, ponytail-and-pinkie-ring set. Joker (318 Richmond) is hard to miss: a huge, lavishly overdesigned club that's part dance emporium and part funhouse. Limelight (250 Adelaide) is the McDonald's of the megaclubs, with an always-crowded jam of college kids and suburban field-trippers. Just don't wear anything you mind getting wet, either from spilled drinks or the crush of sweaty bodies. For a more laid-back alternative, seek out The Apothecary (340 Adelaide), a white-and-pale-wood oasis of cocktails and cool in a neighbourhood where the nightspots are usually as subtle and enticing as a car alarm.

DINNER THEATRE AT THE LIMELIGHT

THE LEFT BANK ON QUEEN STREET

QUEEN STREET WEST
Queen Street West is a one-time bohemian staple that's seen the megastores move in and the hipsters move out. Still, the Rivoli (334) retains its cachet as a mainstay for either dinner or drinks, and it's the city's best venue for live bands and cutting-edge alternative comedy. Nearby, both the Horseshoe (368) and the Cameron (408) also feature great local bands. The Horseshoe is a raucous jeans-and-draught pub while the Cameron is favoured by

black-clad clientele. The Gypsy Co-op (815) is everything the name implies: a comfy and eclectic mix of pool and board games and overstuffed, tattered couches. The NASA Dance Pub (609 Queen West) is a small but busy little dance bar, featuring DJs spinning a wide variety of dance music, from underground hip hop, to deep house, to drum'n'bass. For dancing, Element Bar (553 Queen West) features two floors of fun and attracts a young crowd ready to party. The music tends to be mainly house, although it also hosts hip hop and techno on some nights. Queen West also serves as the long-standing haunt for the city's Goths — you'll find them at Velvet Underground (508) and Savage Garden (550), a gritty, dark, industrial dance bar. More mainstream crowds favour the dependably packed-to-the-rafters Left Bank (561), a cavernous cathedral of rococo flourishes and Top 40 hits.

DOWNTOWN AND MIDTOWN

Visitors to the city can enjoy a picture-postcard view to go with their drinks. The grand poobah is Horizons, in the CN Tower (301 Front St. W.): it offers the best sight lines, but also the longest wait to get in. The Roof Lounge at the Park Hyatt Hotel (4 Avenue Rd.) has an outdoor patio for the summer and was, at one time, the favourite watering hole for Toronto's literati. Swanky Canoe (66 Wellington St. W.) sits atop the fifty-four-storey TD Tower; here barflies can enjoy tinkly recorded jazz and a view that stretches down along the lakeshore.

TORONTO SKYLINE AT NIGHT

Church and Wellesley is the heart of Toronto's gay community. The drinks menu at Byzantium (499 Church St.) is headed by a quote from Dorothy Parker: "Martini, martini, the drink I love the most. Two and I'm under the table, three and I'm under the host." Here you'll find a veritable buffet of martini choices: 21 variations on the menu alone. Woody's (467 Church St.) is more of an old-school gay hangout, complete with beefy men on both sides of the bar and porno films on suspended TV screens. Close by is the Buddies in Bad Times Theatre (12 Alexander St.), which on weekends opens up its main floor as Tallulah's Cabaret. Friday night is ostensibly for

THE VELVET UNDERGROUND

lesbians, while Saturday is for men, but both nights find shorn heads of either gender mixing it up in the near-pitch darkness. Comedy fans can head downtown to The Second City's sparkling new digs (56 Blue Jays Way) which they occupied just in time to celebrate their 25th anniversary. The launching pad for such talent as Dan Aykroyd and Mike Myers, Second City features crowd-pleasing sketch and improv shows. Stand-up finds a home at the Laugh Resort (370 King St. W. in the Holiday Inn), also downtown,

and Yuk Yuk's (224 Richmond St. W.), the flagship for North America's largest comedy chain. Both offer a reliable mix of ascending comics and surefire headliners.

For jazz, head to the legendary Top o' the Senator (253 Victoria St.), a swish and cozy club above the Senator restaurant. It usually nabs any top names passing through town. Or check out either Sherbourne Street's Montreal Bistro and Jazz Club (65) or Queen Street's divey but charming Rex Hotel (194) for the best local and visiting talent.

THE LAUGH RESORT

OTHER NEIGHBOURHOODS

Other worthwhile destinations are tucked away in the city's nooks and crannies. The Comfort Zone on Spadina (486) is the place to go after all the other clubs have shut down — a corral for the city's herd of underage ravers, who can often be spotted blinking against the sun as they emerge, sweat-drenched and smiling, well into Sunday afternoon. A couple blocks west, Sneaky Dee's on College Street (431) is a famously grotty, punk-flavoured beer hall, with an agile mix of alternative and rap offered on the second floor. Guvernment (132 Queen's Quay East) is a kaleidoscope of a dance club down by the water, where see-and-be-seen types get in a little grooving while scoping the other attendees. Boasting the best sound system in the city, the Guvernment is a maze of rooms and different vibes, and is one of the few remaining true "super-clubs" in the world.

For a quieter evening, there's the sophisticated elegance of the Rosewater Supper Club (19 Toronto St.), located downtown and housed in the stately shell of an old gas utilities office building. Serious Billiards fans should seek

SECOND CITY

out Academy of Spherical Arts (38 Hanna Ave.), where aficionados can shoot stick on 15 antique tables, then sip cognac and puff on a premium stogie while relaxing in a leather wingback chair.

For more information on these and other destinations, see the listings in this guide and check local weekly newspapers Eye, NOW and Xtra.

DINING

KAREN BROWN

THE TORCH GRILL

CATCH OF THE DAY IN CHINATOWN

Toronto's astounding ethnic diversity and Bay Street megabucks have together spawned some of the most varied and innovative dining rooms in the world. Recent waves of immigrants have introduced esoteric flavours from Sri Lanka, Ethiopia, Spain, South America and the Middle East. You can discover these throughout local neighbourhoods as well as right downtown. Tiny places pop up and disappear just as quickly as the fortunes of their proprietors. It's always a wise idea to phone ahead, even when reservations aren't called for.

ASIAN FOOD

Toronto has two Chinatowns in the central city. The older one downtown occupies Spadina Avenue between College and Dundas Streets and extends in both directions along Dundas Street West (see also Chinatown, p. 168). No matter what the time of year, greengrocers hawk their miraculously fresh produce outdoors on the wide sidewalks, and local chefs purchase vegetables, live crabs and even fish for their aquariums from the same

delivery trucks that serve the stores. A few restaurants have been here since the Flood, but during the past two decades, Vietnamese immigrants have invigorated the scene with their own vibrant food culture.

Champion House on Dundas West is justly famous for its wonderful Peking duck, and its menu offers a full page of creditable vegetarian dishes. It's generally agreed by critics and eager crowds that Lee Garden on Spadina not only has the spiffiest dining room but also serves some of the most refined Chinese food in the quarter. The whole steamed bass with ginger and scallions is out of this world, and anything made with their black bean sauce tastes remarkable. The nearby Happy Seven fills its modest room throughout the week with casually dressed families who recognize a bargain, and perfectly cooked fish, when they see them. If I had to pick my favourite Vietnamese spot on Spadina, it would be Pho Hung. Despite the soup-kitchen ambience, even the humblest rice and fish preparations sparkle with fresh mint and coriander, and robust soups gladden the most jaded palates. For a nominally larger fee you can experience upscale Vietnamese dining (with a French influence) at Indochine Noodle Café off Yonge just north of Bloor.

Toronto's other official Chinatown is located on Gerrard Street East, east off Broadview. You can't go wrong dropping in anywhere for an inexpensive meal-in-a-bowl of rice noodles and vegetables with meat or fish in a light broth. On a fine day, you can purchase a couple of steamed spring rolls filled with fresh, minced vegetables, sprouts and perhaps some shrimp to nibble in nearby Riverdale Park. Travel by car out to the boonies and you'll be rewarded with some exceptionally fine Szechuan fare at Chung King Garden Market Village (4394 Steeles Ave. E., 905 513-8788) or get lovely seafood and Cantonese classic dishes at Dragon Dynasty (2301 Brimley Rd., 416 321-9000). In fact, if you cruise the uncharted territories (i.e., malls) around Markham and Thornhill, it won't take long to discover your very own culinary prizes that the wave of Hong Kong immigration has brought.

RACK OF SPRING LAMB FROM CANOE

75

CHEF AT HOST

INDIAN, JAPANESE AND THAI FOOD

Little India is located on Gerrard East between Hiawatha Road and Coxwell Avenue. Here you will find Madras Durbar, which offers ridiculously cheap and delicious southern vegetarian fare. Any chicken or meat that's spent time in the nearby Bar-Be-Que Hut's tandoor oven comes forth wonderfully tender with a gentle, smoky aroma enhanced by intriguing spices. At lunchtime, just follow your nose into any of the tiny storefronts for freshly made curries, rice and flatbreads. You can eat your fill for the same price you'd pay at a fast-food restaurant. In fact, many of these miniature restaurants are modeled on the cafeteria-style, display-case examples of western quick eateries. They even serve their meals on paper plates with plastic trays, but nearly everything is cooked fresh daily. Don't be shy about asking for mild dishes — most are, anyway. Fire-eaters can request extra chilies on the side. The Indian Rice Factory is on Dupont Street, a little out of the way, but its savoury variations of traditional curries and fragrant pilaus have attracted a loyal clientele for years. North Toronto's Cuisine of India (5222 Yonge St., 416 229-0377) does everything exceedingly well, including the city's finest tandoori chicken and seafood.

Sushi bars are plentiful in Toronto, and practically all of them serve impeccable fish and seafood, but your wallet will be lighter after eating these flown-in delicacies. Megumi on Church Street uses authentic Japanese herbs to garnish dishes that taste as delightful as they look, at a reasonable price too, while the room itself is soothingly quiet. Ema Tei, near Queen Street and University Avenue, and Edo on Eglinton Avenue West are highly regarded

dining rooms serving skillfully prepared full dinners to a sophisticated clientele. I've found the staff at both places to be exceedingly patient and helpful. Don't be put off by the appearance of Rikishi on Bloor Street near Ossington, about three kilometres west of Yonge. On closer inspection, everything is spotless, and the menu lists rarified vegetarian Buddhist temple offerings cooked with considerable care. This is another place where visitors can enjoy ordering small dishes of every description.

Serious sushiphiles should head straight for Hiro Sushi (171 King St. E., 416 304-0550) and put themselves in chef Hiro Yoshida's inspired hands.

Diners may find many of the new Thai places disappointing until they learn to avoid the ponderous, deep-fried appetizers and overly sweet curries loaded with chilies. The same Lao-Thai family owns Ban Vanipha (638 Dundas St. W., 416 340-0491) and Vanipha Lanna (863 St. Clair Ave. W., 416 654-8068). Both are splendidly authentic; you'll pay a little more at the latter for spiffier neighbourhood and décor. My current favourite is Young Thailand for a memorable salad of fresh, ripe pineapple with roasted cashews and carefully balanced spicing. There are three restaurants with the same name. This newest one's on John Street, just north of Queen. Spice Thai Café (250 Queen's Quay W., 416 598-0600), a short walk from the SkyDome extends kindly service in a quiet, intimate setting for first-timers and regulars alike.

SENATOR TORCH GRILL

GREEK, FRENCH AND ITALIAN FOOD

Toronto's Greektown, which extends along the Danforth from Broadview to just east of Pape Avenue is famous as far away as Athens. Once upon a time, diners were trotted straight into open kitchens in the back to point out their selections of roasted meat, potatoes and veggies afloat in ancient grease. Nowadays, most of the Hellenic fare here has lightened up considerably, without forfeiting its earthy appeal. Many of the little mom-and-pop establishments have given way to restaurants like the stylish Ouzeri, where ordinary braises and filo pies shine with cinnamon, mint and anise flavours. The lively décor and solid cooking at Christina's have made it a hot spot for some time now. Myth, serving tasty designer food in surreal surroundings, will cheer up sulky adolescents with pool tables and television, leaving the adults to dine in comparatively quiet surroundings. Endure the rambunctious crowds of beautiful

SAZIO'S

young people and the speedy waiters at Pan for inspired lamb loin with orange fig sauce and honeyed ricotta cheese for dessert. Sometimes, I find there's nothing more soul satisfying than a bountiful helping of moussaka (cinnamon-scented ground lamb with eggplant, potato and béchamel sauce) with rice and veggies for under ten dollars at Pappas Grill. Toronto's oh-so-serious French dining rooms disappeared way back. In their place, scores of genuinely interesting and less expensive little boîtes have sprung up all over town. Near High Park, Le Nouveau Parigo offers French icons like steak frites and escargots with a simple, gallic wine list to match. For the high-end cuisine, go to Pastis on Yonge Street and be sure to save room for the caramelized apple tart. On Bedford Road near Davenport Avenue, Le Paradis Brasserie-Bistro

accommodates throngs of young locals with budget-priced blackboard specials and friendly, French-speaking waiters. I can't omit two favourites — Provence (12 Amelia St., 416 924-9901) and Quartier (2112 Yonge St., 416 545-0505), each as different from the other as south is from north. Café Brussel (124 Danforth Ave., 416 465-7363), (okay, I'm cheating a bit. It's Belgian) specializes in mussels done a couple of dozen different ways, but everything I've tried here has been magnificent.

Toronto is still full of Italian bistretti and trattorie that dish out honourable home cooking, but these days most Italian restaurants look more like miniature galleries. College Street between Bathurst and Grace is lined with them. Standing out among these, Bar Italia rates a visit for its fabulous sandwiches or panini of cured meats, wild greens and fine olive oil on crusty buns. I've eaten great pastas at the College Street Bar, and a bit farther west at Grappa, although I prefer this last restaurant for its superb cornmeal-crusted baked sea bass. One of the favoured dinner spots in Little Italy is the charming, softly lit Giancarlo Trattoria, with one of the most romantic patios anywhere. A number of chefs have passed through it over the years, but the kitchen's always in top form. Centro, Zucca and Splendido, which are uptown, all guarantee splendid upmarket fare, extensive wine cellars and expert service. At Coppi, (3363 Yonge St., 416 484-4464), also uptown, *frutti di mare* or any of the seafood will fill you with awe; an intelligent, inexpensive wine list (approximately 20 different types by the glass) and housemade desserts are further cause for celebration. The candlelit stone cellar of Sotto Sotto, located on Avenue Road near Davenport, bewitches the diner with intoxicating aromas from the grill and wood-burning pizza oven. For the whole family, any link of the Il Fornello chain (there are several in central neighbourhoods) bakes heavenly pizza and serves an amazingly diverse clientele.

INDIAN RICE
FACTORY

FOUR-STAR DINING

Everyone wants to know about the sublime, four-star palaces where superstar chefs perform their nightly miracles. At Avalon on Adelaide Street West in the theatre district, Christopher McDonald creates brilliantly simple and elegant dishes out of everything from lamb shank to foie gras. His sweets are equally exquisite. At J.K. ROM, the beautiful dining room on the third floor of the Royal Ontario Museum, chef extraordinaire Jamie Kennedy practices his kitchen wizardry only at lunchtime. His signature heritage vegetables (all-but-forgotten strains of striped tomatoes, golden beets, etc.) taste as splendid as they look. Canoe, atop the Toronto-Dominion bank tower, is famous locally for its high-powered clientele, minimalist décor and the city's best view of the harbour. Diners with deep pockets and finely tuned palates turn up just for the innovative, Japanese-influenced cuisine and exquisite desserts. Bob Berman and Barbara Gordon team up their talents as well as their names at Boba on Avenue Road with spectacular results. Berman's unerring instincts for east-west flavour fusions draw sophisticated crowds, but I swoon over Gordon's enchanting homemade desserts. Then there are the comparative oldsters. Truffles at the Four Seasons Yorkville is a classic, and it's always reassuring to know that everything here, from seating to service, will be consistently first rate. North 44° on Yonge, Scaramouche near Avenue Road and St. Clair, Sen5es on Bloor and Rain on Mercer Street all boast gifted chefs, top-drawer service and lavish dining rooms where the whole evening, from breadbasket to cappuccino, feels magical. You can easily get out of these places for less than $100 for two, including tax and tip, if you order a single glass of wine each or, as many diners are doing these days, just go for a large bottle of mineral water.

THE ROOF AT THE
PARK HYATT

PRE-SHOW DINING

The theatre district that stretches along King, starting just west of University Avenue, is packed with eateries that specialize in quick, light, early dinners. Most are cheerful, friendly places with expert, fast service and fairly priced pre-show menus. Unfortunately, the quality of the kitchens can vary from heavenly to abysmal. I can vouch for La Fenice's pricey-but-worth-it Italian dishes, the lovely, romantic Fifth (225 Richmond St. W., 416 979-3000), where you can return for your dessert after the show at the Royal Alex, or Focaccia (17 Hayden St., 416 323-0719), practiced at getting everyone out in time for the New Yorker, just around the corner.

Yonge near Queen is the location of Toronto's second theatre district. Right behind Massey Hall and the Pantages Theatre is Torch Bistro (253 Victoria St., 416 364-7517) which is part of the Senator Restaurant. The cooking's just as good as ever; better yet, they haven't removed those romantic little booths with the velvet, pull-em-shut curtains. And upstairs they've still got the best jazz club in town. Queen West between University and Bathurst is the heart of the art scene. From patios and window seats, you can spend several enjoyable hours taking in the colours and flavours of bohemia. The Rivoli is an old-time, with enthusiastic staff, beautiful Asian-influenced food at bargain prices and a clientele of artists and rockers. For an even longer time, the Queen Mother has nourished poverty-stricken art students with generous portions of international snack foods — spring rolls, samosas and the

THE RIVOLI

like — at fair prices. Another great inexpensive restaurant

in the neighbourhood is Tiger Lily's, serving Chinese food, including plenty of vegetarian choices, with contemporary flair.

As long as Toronto keeps turning out gems like these, you may well want to follow your instincts and discover your own gastronomic treasures. *Buon appetito.*

SHOPPING

JOYCE GUNHOUSE AND JUDY CORNISH

Toronto's shopping matches that of any major international city, but what makes it special are the many outlets for Canadian products. Canadians are well-known for their clean, well-made designs in everything from children's wear to furniture.

THE EATON CENTRE

The Eaton Centre, located downtown on Yonge, and running from Queen Street to Dundas, is the most obvious place to shop in Toronto. The largest downtown shopping mall in North America offers a vast array of mid-priced to high-end stores on four levels and makes it an easy one-stop shopping area for the entire family. The lowest level of the mall features shops with moderately priced clothing, books, music and kitchenware. Here you will find chains such as HMV as well as some smaller stores and the Centre's food courts. The middle level features midpriced clothing stores Fairweather, Jacob and Esprit and gift stores such as Bowrings. The upper levels have a number of more expensive clothing and shoe stores for both men and women, including Jaeger, Harry Rosen, Braemar, Mirabelli, and Brown's; jewellery stores like the long-standing

WILLIAM ASHLEY'S

ON BLOOR STREET

Canadian company Birk's; and children's clothing and toy stores GapKids and the Disney Store.

BLOOR STREET

Bloor Street, between Yonge and Avenue Road (see also Bloor Street, p. 180), is the heart of Toronto's high-end shopping district. Fashion designers from around the world are represented — international names Chanel, Versace, Prada and Plaza Escada. Holt Renfrew, Canada's most fashionable department store, carries everything from international designers to Canada's own darling, Lida Baday. Baday's attention to detail, fit and quality has established her as an international and homegrown success. Holt's promotes other Canadian up-and-comers such as Joeffer Coac for Misura and Karen Palmer. While many of the shops on Bloor are expensive, not all price tags are in the thousands.

More moderately priced international clothing chains share the Bloor address such as Talbot's, Eddie Bauer, Benetton, and Club Monaco. For high quality menswear, try Harry Rosen's.

Bloor Street boasts top-notch beauty and health boutiques such as the Body Shop, MAC cosmetics and the Aveda boutique. This strip is also the place for shoes. There is Brown's in Holt Renfrew as well as Davids and Corbo. The famous Tiffany and Co. is just one store for jewellery, and Ashley's is excellent for fine china and crystal. The Roots flagship store is in a lovely new building beside The Pottery Barn and Williams-Sonoma. If you are not one for shopping, relax and read in either the Chapters book store near Avenue Road or Indigo just south of Bloor on Bay Street.

YORKVILLE

Slightly north of Bloor is another exclusive shopping area known as Yorkville. This area offers a mix of expensive restaurants and fashionable shops, featuring clothing, gifts, books and antiques. Here you will find the boutiques of Canadian designers Phillipe Dubuc, Marilyn Brooks, Linda Lundstrom, Jim Searle, and Nancy Moore for Motion Clothing Co. Delight in the finery and whimsy The Cashmere Shop, the National Ballet's Paper Things for stationery, the Toy Shop for kids, and Muti for hand-painted ceramic ware. Nearby

Hazelton Lanes provides indoor shopping with several chain stores and many exclusive boutiques. Among its shops are Aquascutum, Hugo Nicholson, and Petra Karthaus.

Travel north of Hazelton Lanes to discover a clutch of flower shops and antique stores. The little area north of Avenue Road and Davenport (known to Torontonians as "Av-Dav") includes several stores with visiting.

QUEEN STREET

For the young and hip who don't particularly like malls the lively Queen Street strip between McCaul Street and Spadina Avenue appeals(see also Queen Street West, p. 162). This strip is home to many unique stores, trendy restaurants, clothing, shoes, gifts, and home furnishings, ranging from high brow to retro cool. Start at Price Roman, the exclusive outlet for a collection of women's clothing. Further west you will hit the very hip Fluevog Shoe store. John Fluevog is an international success with his radically innovative shoe designs. Another highlight is Pam Chorley's Fashion Crimes and also across the street, her children's store, inspired by her daughter Jasmine, called Misdemeanours. Here one discovers little fantasies made out of velvet, lace and chiffon in adult and kiddie sizes.

For those willing to take a step beyond in young, urban fashion, there is Vice, inspired by the magazine of the same name, and Daily Fraiche, by Alex and Maria Michiot, a couple whose design team is based in Paris. Their clothes are innovative, clean-cut, and hip with a European flavor. On the other side of the street are two Get Out Side stores, where you will discover some of the funkiest shoes around at an affordable price and also clothing reminiscent of the styles worn by edgy Japanese youth. Nearby, B2, the younger version of Brown's, carries Prada-esque knock-offs for a fraction of the price. Then there are Caban and Urban Mode, two stores that offer hip home furnishings.

SILK CHIFFON SCARF (ABOVE) AND FRAMES FROM THE AGO GIFT SHOP

FURNISHINGS AT URBAN MODE

WEST QUEEN WEST

If you continue west along Queen, past Spadina, you will

encounter a bohemian neighborhood of independent shops. Among the tattoo parlors, textile outlets and coffee houses are high quality second-hand and designer clothing stores. No shortage of amazing furniture and home accessory stores exist here: Red Indian, Morba, and Quasi Modo are great for vintage furniture and collectibles, while other stores like Fluid Living and Style Garage mix contemporary with antique. Further west, you can visit Comrags, a boutique carrying the widest available selection from this Canadian clothing collection — everything from bathing suits to winter coats set in a whimsical setting.

This section of Queen Street is also home to independent music and record stores. New and used CDs and vinyl can be found at such outlets as Rotate This. Further along, the Japanese Paper Place carries various types of paper from origami to large hand-crafted pieces for creative souls who want to experiment. Then there is also the charming bath and beauty store, Iodine, staffed by its creator, Nurse Julie. Nurse Julie dresses in a red RN uniform and dispenses friendly advice on all your beauty concerns. Also check out the great Iodine bags made by Flertje.

THE BEACHES

The Beaches, in Toronto's east end, is also a hot shopping area. Beginning at Woodbine Avenue, the strip of Queen Street between Woodbine and Neville Park Boulevard has several popular chain stores mixed with children's clothing, toy book and gift shops. Here you will find Posh for women's clothing, Whatiff Kidsgear for kids' wear and Pier 1 for bright and appealing dinnerware, glassware, gifts and linens. This is an excellent area in which the family can spend a day shopping, eating and playing.

THE BEACHES, QUEEN STREET

ALONG YONGE STREET

Yonge Street from Eglinton Avenue to Lawrence Avenue is another upscale shopping area. Here, once again, are international clothing chains such as the Gap and Club Monaco, as well as Canadian stores such as Kaliyana,

Mendocino, and the Casual Way. There is also Sporting Life, a large emporium, featuring sports equipment, accessories and a wide range of clothing (both active and casual) for men, women and children. This strip also has stores like Future Shop, which sells computers and computer software, La Cache, which sells charming cotton clothing, and Restoration Hardware. If you are hungry, the delicious Dufflet Pastries shop is a gastronomic pleasure.

SHOPS AT QUEEN'S QUAY

COLLEGE STREET AND KENSINGTON MARKET

College Street between Palmerston and Grace has become a hot spot for Toronto's up-and-comers with its little pocket of independent stores. Modern clothing can be found at Girl Friday, Mink, Set Me Free, and Lilliput Hats, and music at Soundscapes. The young and hip hang out in Toronto's Kensington Market. Tucked between butcher shops, fish markets, cheese shops and spice stores are a handful of second-hand boutiques. Many of these carry new clothes from young designers. Dancing Days, Courage My Love and the Pineapple Room are the best for the ultimate find. For high quality men's clothing at discount prices, Tom's Place can't be beat.

QUEEN'S QUAY AND FRONT STREET

Queen's Quay and Harbourfront, near Toronto's waterfront, provide an urban oasis that offers great shopping in a park-like setting. In the Queen's Quay Terminal building, you will find a wide range of specialty shops like Dollina Dolls & Bears, The Canadian Naturalist, Art of Design, and Oh Yes! Toronto. Further west, at the foot of Spadina Avenue, is a permanent antique market and the site of summertime outdoor antique and flea markets.

The stretch of Front Street from Jarvis to Yonge is home to many of the city's live theatres as well as to diverse stores. High Tech carries advanced items for the cool and functional kitchen. Europe Bound outfits those who seek the great outdoors. Also on Front is Nicholas Hoare, a large and soothing bookstore, and Timbuktu, a large, colourful craft and clothing store. The St. Lawrence Market, a landmark since 1803, has an excellent farmer's market on Saturdays, and an antique market on Sundays. Local craftspeople also sell their goods here.

MODELS IN CLOTHES BY COMRAGS

KEY SHOPPING INFORMATION

Check the listings in this guide for addresses and telephone numbers.

Antiques and Collectibles

Stores that sell antiques and collectibles are scattered all over the city. There is a permanent antique market on Queen's Quay near Spadina. Some of the grander stores, such as R.A O'Neill Antiques and Stanley Wagman and Sons, are located in Yorkville. On Yonge near Summerhill Avenue, visit the Prince of Serendip and Perkins Antiques. Queen Street East has a pocket of more modest shops between Carlaw and Jones Avenues. Some other good stores to check out are Zig Zag and Eye Spy. Also try Red Indian and Quasi Modo.

Book Stores

If you like giant book stores, Chapters on Bloor Street, the World's Biggest Bookstore on Edward, or Indigo on Yonge north of Eglinton or on Bay south of Bloor are great. If you prefer smaller stores, try Nicholas Hoare on Front, Pages Books and Magazines on Queen West, or This Ain't the Rosedale Library on Church. For children's books, visit Mabel's Fables on Mount Pleasant Road.

Chain Stores

Here are some Canadian and International chains that you will find in Toronto: the Gap, GapKids, Banana Republic, Benetton, the Body Shop, the Bay, Club Monaco, Holt Renfrew and Talbots, Williams-Sonoma, and the Pottery Barn.

Canadian Clothing Designers

Discover what Canadian fashion has to offer: look for these labels: Comrags, Lida Baday, Ross Mayer, Wayne Clark, Loucas, Mimi Bizjak, Brian Bailey, Crystal Siemens, Misura, Olena Zylak, Linda Lundstrom, Marilyn Brooks and Motion Clothing Co. You will find them at Finishing Touches, Holt Renfrew, the Blue Angel, Sporting Life and Erietta's as well as in the designers' own boutiques.

Children's Stores

Great kids' clothes can be found at Roots, Club Monaco or GapKids. For toys, visit the Toy Shop in Yorkville.

FINE CHINA FROM ASHLEY

China and Crystal

For china and crystal, shop Ashley's on Bloor Street or Birks in the Eaton Centre.

Designer Boutiques

For Canadian labels, visit Price Roman, Psyche and Fashion Crimes on Queen West. Marilyn Brooks and James Yunker in Yorkville, Comrags and Lowon Pope on West Queen West.

International design labels include Holt Renfrew and Chanel boutiques, all on Bloor Street.

Gift Shops

Unique and unusual gifts reside at the shops in the Royal Ontario Museum and the Art Gallery of Ontario.

Home Furnishings

Shoppers will find a range of home furnishing stores from the Swedish giant Ikea to stores such as the Art Shoppe, Ridpath's Urban Mode, Du Verre, Hi Tech, Up Country, Constantine Antiques and Home Furnishings. Homefront, Morba and Pavilion offer unusual and one-of-a-kind home furnishings.

Jewellery

If money is no object, try Fabrice in Hazelton Lanes or Tiffany on Bloor Street. Birks has locations on Bloor and in the Eaton Centre. European Jewellery also has several locations throughout the city. Canadian designers include Karen Palmer and Richard Vermeulen.

Leather

Roots, Roger Edwards and Perfect Leather all feature leather clothing, shoes or handbags, as does Danier, which has several locations throughout the city.

Malls

If you are one of the stalwart people who like shopping at malls, try the Eaton Centre, Hazelton Lanes downtown, or Yorkdale, Square One, Sherway Gardens or Bayview Village in the suburbs.

Music

HMV or Canada's own Sam the Record Man are located around the city. Good bets on vinyl: Rotate This.

Men's Clothing

The best-known clothing store for men in the city is possibly Harry Rosen, with locations on Bloor Street and in the Eaton Centre. For very high-end menswear, try Rogo in the Exchange Tower. Tom's Place in Kensington Market features high quality men's business suits and casual clothing at discount prices. For casual wear, there are all the usual chains: the Gap, Banana Republic and Eddie Bauer. Canadian design menswear can be found at Hoax Couture and Boomer.

APPLIANCES FROM URBAN MODE

BLOOR STREET MERCHANDISE

Second-hand Clothing

Gently used and vintage clothing abounds at Preloved, Dancing Days, Courage My Love, the Pineapple Room, Circa Forty and Cabaret.

Shoe Stores

Toronto has all the usual shoe chains such as Brown's Nine West, Town Shoes, Pegabo and Aldo scattered throughout the city. It also has unique stores such as John Fluevog, Corbo, B2, Get Out Side and Roots.

SPORTS

DEREK CHEZZI

TORONTO MAPLE LEAFS (TOP)
THE AIR CANADA CENTRE (INSET)

Since the nineteenth century, national sports teams have called Toronto home. The players and venues hold a special place in the city's heart. It is home to 13-time Stanley Cup winners the Maple Leafs, two-time World Series champions the Blue Jays, The Argonauts, one of the country's oldest teams and up-and-coming teams like the Raptors (basketball) and Toronto Rock (lacrosse).

But Toronto does not rest on its laurels; the city is dedicated to bringing world-class sporting entertainment and amenities to fans. One of the more recent additions to the city's stable of sports complexes, which includes the historic Maple Leaf Gardens, is the Air Canada Centre (ACC). The home of the Toronto Maple Leafs, Toronto Raptors and Toronto Rock, the ACC is a comfortable venue boasting food, drink and merchandise outlets. You can find this all under one roof and only a short walk from Union Station, the rail transportation gateway to the city. More exciting sports developments are in the wings with proposals to develop the city's waterfront.

MAPLE LEAF
GARDENS

HOCKEY

You cannot visit Toronto without tripping over hockey culture, whether it's a visit to the historic Maple Leaf Gardens or the Hockey Hall of Fame, dinner at Wayne Gretzky's, or catching a game at the team's home the Air Canada Centre.

The Toronto Maple Leafs are an integral part of hockey history in North America. Toronto won its first Stanley Cup as the Maple Leafs in 1931, their first season in the then new Maple Leaf Gardens. Since then, the Leafs have made numerous playoff appearances and won the much-coveted Stanley Cup 12 more times. While the last time they held the prize was back in 1967, that does not prevent the city from cheering them on: nearly every game is sold out regardless of the team's standing. On February 20th, 1999, the Leafs played their first game at the well-designed Air Canada Centre (which they share with the Toronto Raptors & Toronto Rock); there is not a bad seat in the house. The Leafs' regular season runs from October to April. But buy your tickets early: demand for Toronto Maple Leaf tickets is huge and seats for home games are snatched up months in advance. Prices for tickets range from $35 to $170, with a seating capacity of 18,800. Call 416 815-5700 or visit www.mapleleafs.com for more information.

CARLOS DELGADO
OF THE BLUE JAYS

BASEBALL

Retractable roofs and comfortable seats have replaced the hard wooden benches of outdoor stadiums at modern-day major league baseball games, but the atmosphere is the same: a sunny day with a breeze coming in off Lake Ontario, radio in hand tuned to the game, the smell of sunblock, and the cup of a cold drink sweating in the summer heat.

The Jays have come a long way since their beginnings in 1976 when the American League voted to start up a franchise in Toronto. Since then, they've won five Eastern Division championships and were back-to-back World Series Champions (in 1992 and 1993). Sports buffs will remember that the Jays broke in their newly-built home, the SkyDome, with their first world series win. And while it's been nearly a decade since they've stepped up to the

playoff plate, in 1999 they made it all the way to the second-last round — enough excitement to whet the appetites of fans until the following spring.

The Jays' season runs from April to October. Single-game tickets cost between $7 and $49, including taxes and service charges for the 50,600 capacity stadium. Season tickets and box seats are also available. To purchase call 416 341-1234 or 1-888-654-6529, or online at www.bluejays.ca. For group tickets call 416 341-1122.

BASKETBALL

You must see a Raptors game if for no other reason than to watch Vince Carter strut his stuff. The man whom many have compared to Michael Jordan in ability came from nowhere to become the star of the Toronto Raptors and a darling of the NBA.

And the team isn't too bad either. The Raptors joined the National Basketball Association in 1995. In the ever-expanding world of spectator sports, this game gives you non-stop, on-the-court action. And it's hard to miss the troupe of Raptors dancers and the team's mascot who keep the crowds entertained between quarters.

To purchase tickets for the October to April regular season, call 416 366-3865 or TicketMaster at 416 870-8000 or visit www.nba.com/raptors. Prices range from $20 to $152 before service charges.

BLUE JAYS FAN

FOOTBALL

The Toronto Argonauts have been around since 1873, making them the oldest professional sports team in the city. They were formed from the Argonauts Rowing Club and were among the first teams to make up the Canadian Football League (CFL), which formed two years before its American rival the National Football League (NFL). More than one hundred years later, the Argos share their current home base, the SkyDome, with their ball club brothers the

TORONTO ARGONAUTS FANS

Blue Jays. While the stadium boasts such amenities as the SkyDome hotel and a private restaurant, a far cry from the wooden-splintered and freezing benches of Exhibition Stadium where the Grey Cup was once held, there is something for every budget at the Dome and the game is still very much the same. The differences between the NFL and the CFL are subtle — the Canadians play on a larger field allowing for more creative plays, and the three downs (instead of the NFL's four) propel the game at a quicker pace — but it offers the same intense and hard-hitting action.

The affordable ticket price makes football a favourite of the younger crowd. The season runs from July to November with a couple of pre-season games in June. Single game tickets can be purchased through the SkyDome box office. For season tickets call 416 341-5151 or go to www.argonauts.on.ca. Prices run from $14 to $48 for tickets.

LACROSSE

The city's most recent sports sensation has brought new life to a piece of Toronto history. The Toronto Rock, the city's first professional lacrosse team, began calling Maple Leaf Gardens home in 1998 after moving from their previous residence in nearby Hamilton. After a short stay at the Gardens, the Rock have made a new home at the Air Canada Centre. The league currently plays a 16-game schedule, and has grown to 13 teams in both Canada and the United States. The Toronto Rock have managed to win the league championship three times in their short history. The season runs from January to April. But while their popularity has gone through the roof, their ticket prices have not, ranging between $19 and $48 for a home game seat. Tickets can be purchased through TicketMaster at 416 872-5000 or in person at the Air Canada Centre box office. Group, box and season tickets can be bought through the Rock hotline at 416 596-3075.

MOLSON INDY CAR RACING

In what has become one of the most popular sport draws of the city, the Molson Indy is held in the west lakeshore area of the city for one weekend every July. From miles away, you can hear the roar of Formula One cars peeling around

WORLD CUP SOCCER FANS

TORONTO ROCK

MOLSON INDY

the Exhibition Place at speeds of up to 380 kph. The more than 160,000 fans fend off the summer sun with sunglasses and baseball caps to watch their favourite drivers wind their way past the CNE grounds in cars that weigh little more than 600 kg. But the spectacle around the race is just as much fun. Drivers are available for autographs, you can take a trip on a ride simulator and check out the exhibits at the consumer and trade show. The Molson Indy hits the streets in mid-July. Tickets can be ordered by calling 416 872-4639. For more information check out the website at www.molsonindy.ca.

OTHER SPORTS/PARTICIPATORY SPORTS

DON VALLEY GOLF COURSE

Toronto's world-class reputation for entertainment and sightseeing has also led many other sporting events to spring up in the city. Of increasing popularity among Torontonians is the annual International Dragon Boat

Festival held in June at Centre Island. Alternate Augusts, York University hosts the Women's Rogers AT&T Cup and the Men's Tennis Master Championship, held by Tennis Canada. The weekend event attracts many of the world's top-ranking players. If golf is your game, the Bell Canadian Open, the third-oldest national championship in the world, is held in the Toronto area every summer. The course, designed by Jack Nicklaus, is considered one of the finest in the world. Tennis and golf are about a 30-minute drive from the downtown core. The Rogers AT&T Cup, Men's Tennis Master Championship and Dragon Boat race are also accessible via public transportation.

Toronto also offers many opportunities for the activity-minded visitor. In winter, there are many ice skating rinks scattered throughout the city and numerous ski and snowboarding hills a short drive away. During the summer months you can get in some off-road cycling. There are also many good riding and hiking trails within the city limits. For golf enthusiasts, Toronto boasts many quality courses. Centre Island's paved paths make for some of the city's best inline skating. And the many public pools offer relief from the sticky summer heat.

See listings at back for more information on each of these.

PARKLANDS

If you have looked down on Toronto from the air or the CN Tower, you will have noticed how green it is. Tree-lined streets account for a large portion of this bird's-eye-view greenery, but the most significant contributors in terms of recreation, ecology and sheer acreage are the wooded ravines lining the city's major rivers, the lesser creeks and many tributaries that feed them; the string of islands just to the south of Toronto harbour and the long shore-based spit to the east of the islands; and the shore along Lake Ontario. This topography, sculpted by glaciers, storms and humans, has bequeathed to the city a unique inheritance.

The ravines, although precipitous in only a few places, were too steep to farm or build on and were prone to flash flooding. For these reasons they were left alone to a fortunate degree. Today, most of the ravines adjacent to Toronto's three rivers (the Humber, Don and Rouge) and three largest creeks (Etobicoke, Mimico and Highland) are parks — accounting for some 12 per cent of the whole city and covering over 8,000 hectares. Portions of these parks — some 5,000 hectares — are still wild and are home not only to squirrels, chipmunks, raccoons and skunks (all of which adapt readily to urban life), but also to groundhogs, opossums, porcupines, cottontail rabbits, red foxes, eastern coyotes and hundreds of birds and waterfowl. Paths, ideal for walking, jogging, biking or in-line skating, follow the course of the Humber and the Don,

TORONTO SKYSCRAPERS FROM ATOP THE DON VALLEY

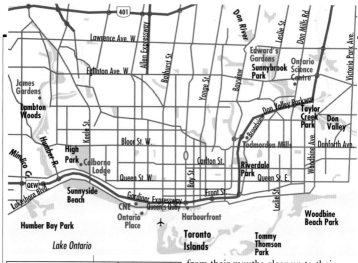

CENTREVILLE TRAIN AT TORONTO ISLANDS PARK

HUMBER VALLEY PARK

from their mouths clear up to their headwaters, branching out to follow many of their tributaries as well. The parks along these routes contain numerous additional recreational opportunities, from riding stables and golf courses to quiet formal gardens to a nineteenth-century town, a farm and a former brickworks. At access points to and throughout many of these parks, the city has erected signs informing visitors of the history of each area, of flora and fauna likely to be encountered, and of routes. Called "Discovery Walks," these self-guided tours link the city's ravines, parks, gardens, waterways and beaches to adjacent neighbourhoods. Brochures containing maps and detailed information about the flora, fauna and human heritage encountered on each walk are available at City Hall and all library branches.

The Toronto Islands create the sheltered Inner Harbour that was one of the key reasons the area was selected for settlement. Actually a collection of sand bars interrupted by lagoons and rivulets rather than truly separate entities, the group of islands originally was a peninsula; the narrow

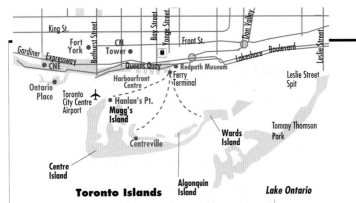

Toronto Islands

Lake Ontario

neck connecting it to the shore was destroyed by a series of storms in the 1850s, setting the islands permanently adrift. By the turn of the century, the islands had been enlarged with fill to three times their original size, and summer resorts, fancy homes and makeshift cottages covered much of them. They continue today to house an airport, a small community of permanent homes, an amusement park, several yacht clubs and a school. Nonetheless, with their fresh lake breezes and the silence that comes from the absence of traffic, they are wild enough to make you feel you have left the city far behind.

The Ontario shoreline has been dramatically altered since the area first was settled. Huge marshes have been drained and hundreds of acres of fill dumped to extend the city south of Front Street — in places by as much as half a kilometre. Roads and rails follow the line of the lake. Despite this, the 20-kilometre (13-mile) Martin Goodman Trail, which now runs the length of Toronto's waterfront, is but a small segment of an uninterrupted trail that stretches 325 kilometres (215 miles) from Stoney Creek, near Hamilton in the west, all the way to Trenton in the east. And the Leslie Street spit, built of construction debris to enlarge Toronto's harbour and help keep silt from filling it, has now become a significant habitat for shore and water birds, as well as an ideal spot for leisurely biking and in-line skating.

The demand of urbanites for parkland, in combination with three decades of increasing concern for the environment, is protecting and enhancing these green spaces. The lake, rivers and ravines are all far cleaner than they were only a generation ago, and various community groups are working to return them as much as possible to a state resembling that which settlers first cast eyes on 200 years ago.

TORONTO ISLANDS

One of the best things to do in Toronto on a warm summer day is take a ferry across the harbour to the islands. The ferry docks are located at Bay Street and Queen's Quay, behind the Westin Harbour Castle Hotel.

The boat ride is an absolute delight —

FERRY ARRIVING AT CENTRE ISLAND

SAILING IN TORONTO'S HARBOUR

a fast and inexpensive way to get away from it all ($5 round trip for adults, $3 for seniors and students 15-19 with ID, $2 for children under 15). The large, double-decked ferries leave every thirty or forty-five minutes for Centre Island. Smaller, single-deck ferries leave somewhat less frequently for Ward's Island and Hanlan's Point. The islands are connected by bridges, so except for the distance you will have to traverse to get from one to the others, it doesn't matter which ferry you take there or back. (Ferry departures vary depending on the season, day and time of day; call 416 392-8193 for schedules.)

When you arrive on Centre Island, a wide floral esplanade — the Avenue of the Islands, along which once were located all the commercial outlets of the long-gone resort community — leads you directly to Centreville, a modest summertime amusement park designed to resemble a nineteenth-century village with a petting zoo (Far Enough Farm). The facility is ideally suited to children from toddlerhood to about 10. It has some 24 rides, including bumper cars and boats, a railroad that tours the periphery of Centreville and a funicular that swings you out over an even larger area, a Ferris wheel, paddle boats, pony rides and a beautifully restored antique carousel that will appeal to all ages. There are playgrounds and fast-food outlets, although a picnic topped off with ice cream seems more in keeping with the atmosphere of the place. (Call 416 203-0405 for schedule and prices.) Nearby, you can rent canoes and bikes. (Note that bikes are not allowed on the larger ferries during certain times.)

IMPROMPTU PARADE ON CENTRE ISLAND

Ward's Island is the site of one of the islands' two remaining clusters of permanent homes; the other is on nearby Algonquin Island. A leisurely stroll around these communities is sure to lift your spirits: yes, it is possible even in the third millennium to live comfortably without stores or cars. Islanders bring everything

over from the mainland and truck it home on little wagons.
And as for the bright lights of the big city, the islanders
have the best view imaginable: they get to see them
twinkling across the harbour from the windows of their
modest, well-crafted homes.

A trip to Hanlan's Point will take you to the least
developed portion of the islands. And despite the proximity
of the Toronto City Centre Airport, it is not difficult, even
on the hottest summer days, to find a quiet spot along the
westerly beaches. At their southernmost point sits the
eighty-two-foot-high Gibraltar Point Lighthouse; built in
1808, it is the oldest structure on its original site in
Toronto, and looks quite handsome.

Spectacular views of the city
are to be had from many points
on the islands, and of course, on
the trip coming or going. Just to
the east of the mainland ferry
dock is one of the last of the
large industries still operating
along the shore, Redpath Sugar.
On its north-facing wall is a large
mural, The Hunter, by
internationally acclaimed
muralist Wyland, who has
painted almost 100 murals
throughout the world celebrating
marine life. This one is known as the Whaling Wall.
Redpath runs a small, free museum illustrating how the
stuff that feeds your sweet tooth is extracted from cane or
beets. (Open weekdays 9 a.m. to noon and 1-4 p.m).

HUMBER AND THE LAKESHORE

The Humber River was an important transportation route
for the area's native inhabitants, as it was for subsequent
explorers and missionaries. It was the route of choice to
reach Lake Simcoe, and from there the fur-rich northern
regions and waterways.

Although substantial building took place along its
shores in the succeeding centuries, the Humber again has
much of the
pastoral feel it
must have had in
earlier times,
thanks largely to
the destruction
wrought in 1954
by Hurricane
Hazel. Hazel
washed away
hundreds of homes
and killed eighty-
one people, doing
much of its
damage along the
Humber's lower
reaches; since
then, the shore has

THE HUMBER
VALLEY

SWAN IN HIGH PARK

HIGH PARK

been reforested and naturalized to prevent future flooding. Recreational opportunities along the Humber, in addition to biking and hiking, include a visit to Black Creek Pioneer Village, the Humber Valley Golf Course (416 392-2488), the Scarlett Woods Golf Course (416 392-2484) or nearby James Gardens (Edenbridge Drive at Royal York Road). The gardens of the former James estate are the height of Humber picturesque, featuring spring-fed ponds, rustic bridges and numerous imported plant specimens. Adjacent is Lambton Woods, site of a large wildflower preserve.

If you fly into Toronto and are headed downtown, ask your taxi driver to get off the Gardiner Expressway and take Lakeshore Boulevard and Queen's Quay instead. The Lakeshore starts just east of the Humber and, as the name implies, will take you along the shore of Lake Ontario, giving you a pleasing view and a grand sense of arrival.

Soon after switching to the Lakeshore, you will pass a series of buildings and sites that recall the days when the words Sunnyside (as this stretch is called) and amusement were synonymous in the minds of most Torontonians. First there are the remnants of the Sunnyside Bathing Pavilion, a truly palatial structure built in 1922 that provided change rooms for Lake Ontario bathers and a huge viewing area for watching regattas. Next, there is the still-operating Sunnyside Pool. When it opened in 1925, "Sunnyside Tank," as it was then called, was the largest outdoor pool in the world. Beside that was the enormous Sunnyside Amusement Park, which opened in the same year as the Bathing Pavilion and continued to serve as the city's main adventure playground until it was demolished in 1956. Finally there is the Boulevard Club. Although not the original building, the one you will catch a glimpse of was built in 1924; this club for lawn bowling, badminton, tennis, curling and other genteel sports has been at this location since 1905. As your taxi (or car or bike) heads east, you will weave between the Canadian National Exhibition (CNE) grounds to the north and Ontario Place to the south. After getting on to Queen's Quay, you will drive right by Harbourfront. For a dollar or two more, and an extra five minutes or so, you will

have bought yourself a pleasant — if brief — tour of Toronto's most unique lakeshore attractions.

HIGH PARK

In the west end of Toronto is High Park, one of the city's largest recreation areas. The 161 hectare park was the estate of architect and city surveyor John Howard, whose home, Colborne Lodge, sits on a height of land overlooking the lake. The lodge is now one of several heritage homes that have become city museums. Ecologically, the park is unique in being one of the few areas in Ontario to contain a savannah-type habitat treed with black oak. In addition to its several miles of bike and hiking trails, the park contains the full-service Grenadier Restaurant, several snack bars, a somewhat bedraggled small zoo, a large playground, numerous ponds and streams perfect for a bit of duck feeding, a motorized tram that permits you to see much of the park while comfortably seated, and a sculpture collection located mainly in the northeast quadrant. In the summer, there are band concerts on Sundays and walking tours on Sundays and Tuesdays (416 392-1748). As well, throughout the summer the Canadian Stage Company presents the Dream in High Park, its annual Shakespearean season opener, in a natural amphitheatre. Patrons bring blankets and picnic hampers (although drinks and sandwiches are available), and something or someone to lean against. The production is excellent; the setting, magical (416 367-1652 ext. 500 for schedules). You can reach High Park by subway (the stop is High Park) or by car (enter via Bloor Street just west of Keele Street). During the summer, the park's roadways are closed to cars on weekends.

VIEWS OF THE DON VALLEY

DON VALLEY AND THE SPIT

The Don was never a big powerful river, but it did once meander gently through its lower reaches and through a large marsh before draining into Lake Ontario at several points. The wetland gradually was filled in, ensuring that

Kingston Road would be passable year-round, and creating more land for industry. In the late 1800s, people got the idea that flooding could be prevented entirely and the Don made navigable clear up to Bloor Street (and hence suitable for more industry), if it were forced to flow between narrow concrete walls. Industry never did go much further north than Queen Street, flooding was reduced but not eliminated, and the Don River was made to look like a poor excuse for a canal. Today it enters Lake Ontario near only one of its original outlets, through

DON VALLEY FOLIAGE

something called the Keating Channel, which lies at the western end of the portlands, a large chunk of land for which myriad proposals have been made and shelved. As neighbourhoods grew to the north, many of the Don's tributaries were likewise forced between concrete walls. The concrete often encased them completely and they became part of the city's sewer system. The Don was further humbled by the construction of the Don Valley Parkway (the DVP) in the 1950s. Despite these questionable human endeavours, the Don Valley has remained a major refuge for flora and fauna and a rich source of recreational opportunities. Even better, over the past 15 years strong support for the environment has resulted in notable improvements to the Don. Thanks to community efforts, over 60,000 trees and shrubs have been planted in the valley. Large swaths of wildflowers and grasses are being carefully reseeded and a large marsh, just south of Bloor Street, was created to help cleanse the water and attract wildlife. You can walk, bike or in-line skate up the valley, or head directly to individual sites of interest. For

RIVERDALE FARM

information on tours or artwork call 416 392-1111 or 416 661-6000.

Three sites of particular note are rejuvenated remnants of nineteenth-century life. The most southerly (accessible from Winchester or Carlton Streets in Cabbagetown or from the south end of Riverdale Park, as well as directly from the valley via a footbridge) is the Riverdale Farm. From the 1890s to the 1970s, it was the site of Toronto's zoo. When the current Toronto Zoo opened, neighbours urged the city council to turn Riverdale Zoo into a farm. Almost by accident, it has become a very interesting little farm, for many of its animals and plants are rare examples of nineteenth-century strains that, were it not for the farm and a small but growing number of professional farmers across Ontario, might now be extinct. The farm is small, walkable in half an hour or so, but so pleasant with its meandering paths and ponds that it is easy to stay far longer. Proximity to the animals will delight youngsters, but be forewarned: this is not a petting zoo. In the spring, the wooded hillside abutting the farm comes alive with an amazing show of tulips, as the city's parks department has been sending all its used bulbs here for years. On the weekend after Labour Day, the farm hosts a festival serving

up flapjacks, fresh corn, cider and lots of activities for children. Craft exhibits, horticultural talks and other events take place throughout the year. (Call 416 392-6794 for details.) The farm is free and open every day of the year from 9 a.m. until 4 p.m. in the winter, 5 p.m. in spring and fall, and 6 p.m. in the summer.

Further north along the valley are two former industrial sites. The Brick Works, accessible from the Bayview Extension north of the Danforth, or the valley floor, was the last of Toronto's more than thirty brickyards to close. Now part of the park system, local gardening clubs have turned — or returned — its 16.5 hectares into a magical mixture of wetlands, marshes, meadows and forest. The former quarry face is internationally acclaimed by geologists for clearly displaying the successive waves of glaciation to affect much of North America.

SUNNYBROOK PARK

At Todmorden Mills and Art Centre, located near Pottery Road and Broadview Avenue, the industry represented is paper making. Here, long-gone grist and sawmills were replaced by the Eastwood-Skinner paper mill, a building said to have been continuously occupied longer than any other in Toronto. Also on the site are a rustic cottage built in 1797 and a mid-nineteenth-century house. Nearby, a wildflower preserve has been created. Although modest in scale, Todmorden offers a range of arts and craft activities (call 416 396-2819 for details). Accessible from the Don trail or from Pottery Road (off Broadview or Bayview).

East and north of Todmorden Mills is Taylor Creek Park, at the eastern end of which, near Victoria Park Avenue, is Dentonia Park Golf Course (416 392-2558). Further north, in the Central Don region, is another cluster of activity centres including Sunnybrook Park's top-quality sports fields, a Vita Parcours exercise trail, and near Eglinton Avenue and Leslie Street, the Central Don Stables. The stables feature two indoor arenas and some 15 kilometres (12 miles) of trails (call 416 444-4044). Also here, and easily reached from Sunnybrook Park, is Edwards Gardens. Like James Gardens, the site was once a family estate, in this case, that of the Milnes. It was purchased from them in the 1940s and donated to Toronto by Rupert Edwards. A pleasant place to walk, the garden has both formal components, including a large rose garden and an immense collection of rhododendrons, and natural areas, some of them with steep hills. The Civic Garden Centre located on the site at Lawrence Avenue and Leslie Streets is the headquarters for gardeners throughout the city. It has an excellent book-and-

AERIAL VIEW OF THE SPIT

gift shop, annual sales of plants, bulbs and seeds, and numerous lectures and tours (call 416 397-1340). At the extreme southerly end of Leslie Street (and not accessible by traveling along Leslie, which is interrupted for several kilometres) is the Leslie Street spit. Officially called Tommy Thompson Park, after the Toronto parks commissioner who became internationally famous for posting signs reading, "Please Walk on the Grass," the spit is entirely artificial. Since 1959, millions of tons of hard-packed clay, shale, construction debris and concrete have been deposited to create an irregularly shaped series of peninsulas that includes coves with names like Rubble Beach.

The original purpose of the spit, as noted above, was to create an outer harbour suitable for supertankers and to reduce silt build-up in the Inner Harbour. Incidentally, the spit created an amazing sanctuary for wildlife. More than 200 kinds of birds have been sighted; about 300 plant species have taken root, including an entire cottonwood forest; the ponds and marshes are home to a variety of turtles, toads, frogs and snakes; and more than forty species of fish are found in the surrounding waters. What becomes immediately evident here is the resilience of nature. Mere inches from roads on which trucks rumble with loads of rubble, dozens of types of wildflowers brazenly bloom. It might look a bit like a vacant lot were it not so large, so full of life and such an excellent vantage point from which to see the city. Do note, though, that it is windy even on a summer day and downright blustery the rest of the time.

LESLIE STREET SPIT

Also, there are few opportunities for shelter from the sun. No private cars are allowed on the spit, but a free shuttle van runs hourly along the full length of the spit from the TTC stop at the corner of Leslie and Commissioners Streets (call 416 661-6600 for schedule). Fill is dumped on weekdays, so the spit is open to the public only on weekends and holidays (from 9 a.m. to 6 p.m.)

RECREATION TRAILS

When Toronto was named North America's best cycling city by *Bicycle Magazine* in the mid-1990s, locals justifiably assumed it was based on the more than 125 kilometres of trails that wend their way through some 4,000 hectares of the city's parklands. In fact, the award acknowledged not only this extensive and highly popular resource, but also a slowly growing trend toward making cycling an acceptable alternative to using cars to get around town. Even before the award, the use of major streets for cycle commuting had risen by more than 50 per cent in the preceeding five-year period.

Since receiving the award, Toronto transportation officials have worked with cycling and in-line enthusiasts to expand the cycling network both on the city's streets and through its vast green areas. As a result, there are now more than 22 kilometres of dedicated bike lanes on city streets linking residential neighbourhoods to commercial districts, and providing access to residential trails.

SAFETY TIPS

Bicycles, rollerblades, pedestrians, cars, trucks and buses can be a lethal mixture. On-street bike lanes, also used by in-line skaters, help segregate traffic, but are no guarantee of safety. Only experienced urban cyclists should use most street routes for anything other than getting to and from off-street trails. To help you reach the access points to these trails, you are permitted to take bikes on all transit vehicles except during

BLADERS AND CYCLISTS ON THE BEACHES

103

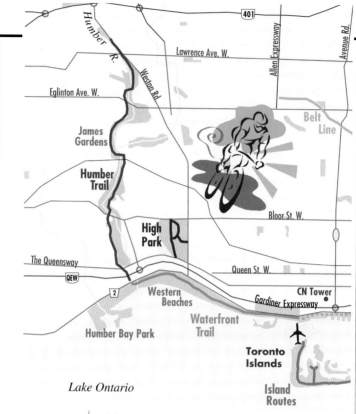

rush hours — 6:30 to 9 a.m.; 3:30 to 6:30 p.m.

The various off-street bike paths avoid traffic but still require attention to safety. Adhering to a few basic rules will ensure that your cycling, skating, jogging or hiking experience is a pleasant one. By law, bicycle helmets must be worn by anyone under 18 years of age. Also by law, you are required to have a bell on your bike. There is no law that says you have to use it, but warning others you are about to pass is a good idea. Skaters can use whistles to achieve the same goal. Remember that pedestrians always have the right-of-way. Whether on-street or off, signal your intentions. If you are riding at night, you must have a light on your bike. Finally, always lock your bike when leaving it unattended.

To protect the environment, off-trail mountain biking is permitted only in selected areas.

CYCLING ON THE WATERFRONT

ROUTES

Here are the most travelled off-road trails for cyclists, skaters, joggers and walkers in Toronto.

WATERFRONT TRAIL

The Toronto portion of the 325-kilometre route known as the Waterfront Trail, which extends from Stoney Creek near Hamilton in the west to Trenton in the east, consists of a dedicated off-street path stretching from the Humber River in the west to Victoria Park in the east. This 20-

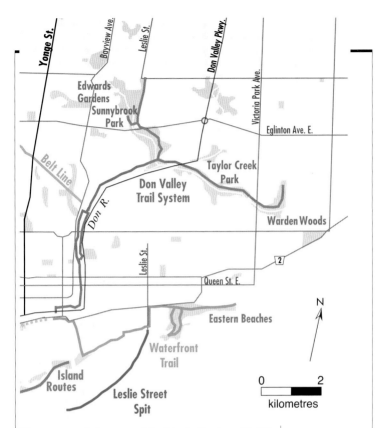

kilometre stretch, known as "The Martin Goodman Trail," is named after a former president of the *Toronto Star*.

If you pick up the trail from the foot of Yonge Street, you can take it eastward along Queen's Quay and south down Cherry Street through the Port Lands, over the shipping canal and still further east, along Toronto's outer harbour, past Ashbridge's Bay Park and through the eastern Beaches all the way to the R.C. Harris Filtration Plant. Turning north (left) at Cherry, will lead up the Don Valley (see below).

Turning south (right) at Leslie Street in the Port Lands, you will reach the Leslie Street Spit (also see below). Just past Ashbridge's Bay is the neighbourhood known as "the Beaches." Along this stretch, the path runs beside a lovely tree-shaded boardwalk, past numerous playgrounds, snack bars and washroom facilities, and is only a block from Queen Street East's fine restaurants and numerous shops. Further east, in the former City of Scarborough, the trail is entirely on city streets.

Following the trail westward from Yonge, also along Queen's Quay, will take you past the ferry docks (again, see below) and close to some of Toronto's major attractions — the CN Tower, SkyDome and Harbourfront. At Bathurst Street, you will be beside Little Norway Park, which commemorates the Norwegian aviators who trained at the nearby City Centre Airport during World War II. Next comes Coronation Park, named in memory of the crowning

of King George VI in May, 1937. You will be flanked by Exhibition Place to the north and Ontario Place to the south as you head on toward Marilyn Bell Park, named for the 16-year-old woman who, in 1954, was the first to swim across Lake Ontario. From there to the Humber River, the area is known as "the Western Beaches." Central to this area is Sunnyside Park, whose 1922 Bathing Pavilion remains intact. To the north at this point, and readily accessible, is High Park (see below). Just before you cross the graceful new suspension bridge spanning the Humber River, you'll pass the Lion Monument, a majestic limestone sculpture marking the 1939 visit to Canada of George VI. Construction of new apartments known as Humber Bay Shores provided an opportunity to develop new parkland. Of special interest are a new butterfly garden, a series of pond habitats used to filter storm water, Sheldon Lookout — a meditative park which contains large stones shipped from Muskoka — the restored mouth of Mimico Creek, and just a kilometre past the suspension bridge, a delightful new footbridge designed by Santiago Calatrara, architect of downtown BCE Place. The Waterfront Trail continues further into the former City of Etobicoke, sometimes as a dedicated off-street path, at times an on-street, but clearly marked route.

DON VALLEY

The Don River, with its tributaries, is ideal for cyclists, hikers, joggers and in-line skaters. The main route can be reached by taking the Martin Goodman Trail east along Queen's Quay and turning north at Cherry Street. In its lower reaches, the Don runs straight, having been converted from a meandering river to a canal over one hundred years ago. Here the path is narrow, heavily traveled, and subject to flooding after major summer downpours.

Just north of the Gerrard Street footbridge, however, the Don reverts to its winding ways, the path widens and the traffic lessens. To visit Riverdale Farm, climb the stairs at the footbridge. At Pottery Road, some five kilometres north of the start of the trail, you have a choice of routes and detours. To the east is Todmorden Mills, with its small museum and collection of nineteenth-buildings. To the west, along Pottery Road and then south on Bayview, is the Don Valley Brick Works. By following Bayview southward, you will reach the Rosedale Ravine turn-off. Here a 2-kilometre trail runs past St. James Cemetery and along a winding, well-treed stretch that has the feel of a 1920s picturesque parkway but is, in fact, only about 100 metres from busy Bloor Street, ending at Park Road, just north of Bloor and east of Yonge Street.

If you continue north along the Don from Pottery Road, the trail becomes hillier and brings you, after three kilometres, to E.T. Seton Park, named after the nineteenth-century naturalist and chronicler of the Don Valley. Here, at "the Forks of the Don," you again have a choice. Taking

the westerly Wilket Creek route will lead you to Edwards Gardens. Bikes are not permitted here, but the fine perennial, rose and wildflower gardens make for a delightful walk. The easterly Taylor Creek route is somewhat longer, eight kilometres, but gentler. It will take you through Taylor Creek Park, past the Dentonia Golf Course, which you must circumnavigate via a short off-trail route, and on through Warden Woods to Birchmount Road.

BELT LINE

This four-kilometre route is a favourite with joggers, but is well-suited to cyclists and walkers too. Situated along the short-lived (1892-94) interurban rail transit route built by John Moore, for whom the nearby Moore Park and Moore Park neighbourhoods are named, it runs from a few blocks north of the Eglinton West subway station (at the Allen Expressway) southeast to Merton Street and Yonge, just south of the Davisville station, and across the street from Mount Pleasant Cemetery. The cemetery, opened in 1873, is a treat for history buffs and horticulturalists, and ideal for a leisurely stroll. Virtually every tree that can survive Toronto's climate can be found here, as can the tombstones and mausoleums of many of the city's former foremost citizens. At least once each summer, the Royal Ontario Museum sponsors a well-guided tour through the cemetery. (Call 416 586-5513 for date and cost.)

ENTERING THE
BELT LINE

HUMBER VALLEY

Toronto's other major river, the Humber, provides a pleasant 13-kilometre ride or walk from the Lakeshore to Scarlett Mills Park, adjacent to the Scarlett Woods Golf Course, at Eglinton, or if you wish, an additional five kilometres or so all the way to Dixon Road. To reach the Humber from the lakeside Martin Goodman Trail, head north at Windermere Avenue, pass beneath the Gardiner Expressway, around the back of the Humber Treatment Plant and through South Humber Park. From here, a short, on-street jog up Stephen Drive is required before you rejoin the off-street path opposite the Humber Marshes.

The route travels in a gently winding northerly direction past the Old Mill (at Bloor Street) and on through Etienne Brûlé Park. In 1615 Brûlé became the first European to reach Lake Ontario. The route then passes through Home Smith Park and Lambton Woods to James Gardens, a former family estate with spring-fed pools and rare trees.

BEST BETS FOR FAMILIES

Here are three vehicle-free areas that are well-suited to people cycling, hiking, or skating with children.

LESLIE STREET SPIT

The Leslie Street Spit offers a 10-kilometre, there-and-back-again ride.

BEACHES CYCLISTS

It is a no-frills weekends-only experience; once you pass the ice cream truck and hot dog vendor usually parked at the entrance, there isn't a single amenity. What you get is a two-lane, flat, paved surface ideal for novice cyclists or skaters, as well as a fantastic view of the city, a plethora of birds and wildflowers and a fresh breeze.

THE TORONTO ISLANDS

By contrast, the Islands provide more amenities than you can shake a stick at. They are dotted with clean washrooms, drinking fountains and playgrounds. There is an amusement park, a formal garden, a small residential community, a few snack bars and even a restaurant, as well as a great view of the city, lots of grand old trees plus a fresh breeze. And you needn't even bring over a bike from the mainland; you can rent one — including bicycles built for two or large three-wheeled vehicles, at Toronto Island Bicycle Rentals (416 203-0009).

HIGH PARK

Much hillier than the spit or the islands, High Park offers a variety of activities. Among these are numerous off-path, bike- and blade-free trails on which to explore on foot one of the last remaining savannah oak forests in Ontario; Colborne Lodge, the original home of John Howard, an architect who came to Toronto in 1832 and became the city's official surveyor, who donated his 67-hectare estate, the core of the 137-hectare park, to the city; numerous snack bars and the Grenadier Restaurant; several duck ponds; a small tram that tours the park; a large collection of outdoor sculpture; and, in the summer, the "Dream Site" stage for Shakespeare(416 367-1652). The park's roads are off-limits to cars on summer weekends.

ORGANIZED ACTIVITIES AND SPECIAL EVENTS

A number of organizations offer guided tours of various neighbourhoods of historic or architectural interest as well as of parklands. Among these is the Parks Department of the City of Toronto (416 392-1111 or Access Toronto 416 338-0338), the Green Tourism Association (416 392-1288) and Heritage Toronto (416 338-0684). The Toronto Field Naturalists (416 593-2656) stick primarily to the wilds for informative hikes. Singles might want to check out A Stroll in the Park (416 484-9255). For do-it-yourselfers, there are "City Discovery Walks" of six of Toronto's most popular park areas. Brochures are available at city offices and libraries and on signage at entry points to the walks. In addition to maps, both signs and brochures show heritage sites, lost streams, natural features, flora and fauna likely to be encountered and nearby community points of interest. For cyclists, too, there are numerous opportunities to take part in guided tours; call the Toronto Cycling Committee for information (416 392-7592). Call Access Toronto to find out about a variety of cultural events hosted in the parks (416 338-0338.) Theatre fans will want to check out Shakespeare in the Rough in Withrow Park (416 536-0916 ext 2.)

ESPECIALLY FOR KIDS

Toronto is a great city for families with young children. There is lots to do, getting around is easy and the pervasive feeling of safety, cleanliness and comfort is a relief for parents. Almost all the attractions mentioned elsewhere make special provisions for young children. Many charge lower admission fees (if anything), and many, including the Royal Ontario Museum (ROM), the Art Gallery of Ontario (AGO), Harbourfront, the Toronto Zoo and the city's numerous historical sites, have activities geared to the younger set. Some of these special features are listed below. It is always wise to call ahead and find out what is happening on the day you intend to visit.

DINING OUT

With hundreds of restaurants to choose from catering to every imaginable taste and price range, eating with children in Toronto should be a snap. And so it was. Unfortunately, a wrinkle exists for the time being. Some years ago, a cowardly and heavily-lobbied city council reneged on a commitment to ban smoking in all eateries. In a move that defies logic, they decided that at least until 2004, any restaurant wishing to permit smoking would have to term itself a "bar." As a bar, it would have to meet Province of Ontario rules governing bars, which happen to forbid anyone under 19 from entering. Hundreds of restaurants were faced with the dilemma of whether to lose the business of families and non-smokers in general, or that of smokers — who often rack up big bar tabs. Some chose one set of customers, some the other, and there is no way to be sure — especially since some have changed back and forth — short of calling ahead.

RIVERDALE FARM

TREE KANGAROOS AT THE TORONTO ZOO

DINOSAUR
EXHIBITIONS IN THE
ROM

The Art Gallery of Ontario bends over backward to provide a fun introduction to gallery-going with its Family Sundays, which feature tours, animation stations, and various workshops. Also open during most regular gallery hours is the hands-on centre called Off the Wall!, an art-play area that is especially appealing to the under-eight set, with its dress-up area, and the opportunity for children to make their own slides, among other inventive activities (317 Dundas St. W., 416 979-6648).

Bata Shoe Museum: This boutique-sized museum's collection of shoes and costumes is very appealing to children with an interest in finery, and its sense of humour about its subject matter will appeal to adults. There are special hands-on activities for children on Saturdays (416 979-7799). Closed Monday, free the first Tuesday of every month.

CN TOWER

David Dunlap Observatory: Stargazers over seven can spend a Saturday evening (or a Friday in the summer) looking through one of Canada's largest telescopes if they are willing to make the trek north to Richmond Hill (Check www.astro.utoronto.ca for times or call 416 978-2016).

CN Tower: The CN Tower's glass floor, which lets you step out into space more than a thousand feet up in the air, is probably enough of a thrill for anyone, regardless of age. But the tower offers more, most of it geared to eight to fifteen-year-olds, with its ground-level MindWarp motion simulator, Q-Zar, a futuristic live-action game, LaserQuest and EcoDek, an aerial tour of Canada and interactive exhibits promoting green thinking (416 868-6937).

Children and Harbourfront go together better than a horse and carriage. In addition to the Kaleidoscope craft centre (2nd floor, York Quay), which for a dollar or two invites youngsters to make all manner of creative items, there are displays, shops, Cushion Concerts (about seven per year, Saturday mornings), special performances and the kiddie extravaganza, the Milk International Children's Festival, as well as playgrounds and skating (rentals available);(416 973-3000).

Ontario Place: Ontario Place was conceived with families in mind, so every age (except the curmudgeonly) is catered to. Of special interest for those with preschoolers is the highly innovative Children's Village play area and,

on hot days, the Waterplay area. The Children's Festival Stage (free) is a good place to wind down after visiting the more active spots. (416 314-9900, open mid-May through Labour Day, except the IMAX and Cinesphere, which operate year-round.)

Playdium: For gaming addicts, more than 260 interactive games, plus shows and an IMAX theatre (126 John St., 416 260-1400).

Royal Ontario Museum: Favourites with the younger set include the Bat Cave and the Dinosaur Gallery. Arms and Armour and the Reptile Gallery may be more specialized in their appeal. Children between six and 12 are welcome in the Discovery Centre on weekends (from 1 to 5 p.m.) and during holidays (during school days, the area generally is restricted for use by classes). The centre contains a hands-on exhibit that provides a sense of how

MUMMY IN THE ROM

museum staff study, work with and display specimens of all types. The ROM also offers special family programming that includes crafts, music, dance or storytelling. Free Fridays after 4:30 p.m. (416 586-8000).

Science Centre: For science nerds and nerd wannabes, the Science Centre is heaven. For everyone else, it's just plain fun. Preschoolers and early readers will enjoy the various demonstrations and many of the interactive exhibits, but will need a lot of parental guidance. If your children are older, you will want to pick a time and place to meet; the centre is huge, crowded and so packed with stuff, it's easy to get lost (416 696-3127). While there, you may also enjoy a film or two at the Science Centre's OMNIMAX, the three-dimensional version of IMAX (416 696-1000).

Toronto Police Museum and Discovery Centre:

ONTARIO SCIENCE CENTRE

WATERPLAY AT ONTARIO PLACE

Budding Sherlock and Shirley Holmeses will want to investigate this centre. Exhibits include historical items, such as old nightsticks, badges, guns and even a paddy wagon; a detailed display of forensic equipment, both new and old, including opportunities to see how fingerprints are identified and a crime video that tests your acumen as a witness (416 808-7020).

INFANTRY AND ARTILLERY AT FORT YORK

BACK TO THE PAST AND OUT IN THE COUNTRY:

Toronto has nearly a score of "living" or "hands-on" museums, most of them managed by the city's heritage department (416 338-3886). Call for information on tours and events — which almost always include special activities around Christmas, Easter, Victoria Day and Canada Day, as well as seasonal favourites like strawberry socials and harvest celebrations. Entry to the smaller sites is free or nominal, but even the larger ones are under $10. For a complete listing, see the index.

Children of all ages get a kick out of lending a hand at broom making, bread baking or any of the other many activities available at Black Creek Pioneer Village. Of special interest are the seasonal and Christmas festivities (1000 Murray Ross Pkwy., Jane St. and Steeles Ave., 416 736-1733).

If you prefer history in smaller doses, or closer to downtown, there are a number of sites that take less than the half day needed to see Black Creek. The oldest is Fort

BLACK CREEK PIONEER VILLAGE

ENOCH TURNER
SCHOOLHOUSE

York, where a garrison was established by the British in 1793. In summer, costumed interpreters give tours several times a day through the barracks, officers' quarters, and fortifications. The highlight for many visitors occurs on July 1 (Canada Day), and August 1 (Simcoe Day), when cannons boom, and mock soldiers are put through their paces (416 392-6907, adults $5, seniors and youths 13-18 $3.25, children 6-12 $3).

Two sites bracket the St. Lawrence district. Near the northwesterly corner, at Adelaide and George Streets, is Toronto's First Post Office. It has a small display of old philatelic material, is a working post office, and houses an excellent model of the surrounding neighbourhood, centre of the original Town of York (260 Adelaide St. E., 416 865-1833, free). At the easterly end of the district is the Enoch Turner Schoolhouse, Toronto's first public school. The classroom has been restored to closely resemble the 1849 original. Adjacent is the beautifully proportioned West Hall, originally used as a Sunday school but now a meeting room and favourite site for weddings, and Toronto's oldest surviving church, Little Trinity. Visits are free, but call to make sure someone can let you in (106 Trinity St., 416 862-0010).

The remaining downtown sites were originally private homes. All are fine examples of their architectural style and period, and provide visitors with lots of information about their occupant(s) and the times in which they lived. They are particularly attractive during the Christmas season, when the scent of pine boughs and hot cider laced with cinnamon wafts through their rooms. Mackenzie House was the home of William Lyon Mackenzie, a crusading journalist, Toronto's first mayor, and the leader of the 1837 Upper Canada Rebellion. It is a delightful townhouse that boasts a fully functional period printing press (82 Bond St., just east of Yonge St., south of Shuter St.). Colborne Lodge was the refined but relatively modest home of John Howard, the noted mid-nineteenth-century Toronto architect and engineer who donated much of the land that now makes up the south end of High Park, which, of course, is itself worth a visit. A large, rambling park in

Toronto Zoo

the west end, it has great terrain for hiking; fine playgrounds; a rather large and interesting collection of outdoor sculpture; the marvelous Dream in High Park setting for the annual summertime alfresco Shakespeare; a small tram that circumnavigates the park; and a little zoo. Spadina House, with its fifty rooms, is by far the grandest of these old houses and is as notable for its gardens as for its architecture (285 Spadina Rd.). As far as the wealth of the original occupants goes, the Grange ranks a close second (adjacent to and entered through the AGO).

It's hard to think of Casa Loma as a house — but it was a home. A storybook castle year-round, Casa Loma is especially enticing throughout December, when the place is fancifully done up for the season and chock full of entertainment in the form of puppets, music and plays, all of which are short and appealing to a broad age range (416 923-1171, $9 for adults; $5 for children, youth and seniors).

CASA LOMA (TOP) ZOO IN HIGH PARK (ABOVE)

Riverdale Farm sits at the edge of Cabbagetown and serves as a great bribe for kids who are leery of touring a nineteenth-century neighbourhood just for the fun of it, especially since it's open every day of the year and is free. The setting, at the edge of the Don Valley, is also a good jumping-off point for a more rural experience and is within walking distance of Todmorden Mills.

For budding botanists and avid gardeners, Edwards Gardens (416 392-8186) and the adjacent Civic Garden Centre in the Don Valley watershed offer respite from the city (777 Lawrence Ave. E., 416 397-1340), while the Allan Gardens, with its huge greenhouse, is ideal for a winter visit to the tropics (Carlton between Jarvis and Sherbourne Streets, at the edge of Cabbagetown, 416 392-7288).

EMILY CARR PAINTING AT THE AGO

Children will enjoy the ferry ride to the Toronto Islands and the amusement park, Centreville (open Victoria Day through Labour Day), may rate as one of the world's most relaxed. As well, there are numerous playgrounds nearby, bike, canoe, rowboat and paddle-boat rentals, two licensed restaurants, a good ice-cream parlour and all those ducks and geese. There are also a number of historic houses and museums located outside the downtown core. Most notable of these are Gibson House, in the former city of North York (416 395-7432), Montgomery's Inn in the former

Etobicoke (416 394-8113) and the Scarborough Historical Museum (416 431-3441).

PERFORMANCES, PERFORMING SPACES AND SPECIAL EVENTS

TSO Kids' Classics: One-hour thematic concerts preceded by a 20-minute introduction in the lobby — all specially designed to introduce young children to the joys of orchestral music — are presented on five or six Saturdays each year by the Toronto Symphony Orchestra at its regular home, Roy Thomson Hall. And, of course, there are numerous performances throughout the season that will appeal to children, especially around Christmas (60 Simcoe St., 416 872-4255).

Lorraine Kimsa Theatre for Young People (formerly Young People's Theatre): For over 30 years, the two stages at YPT's renovated industrial building have played to packed audiences of appreciative young people. Located in the St. Lawrence district, the theatre presents six or seven

THE NATIONAL BALLET'S *NUTCRACKER*

fine classic and original plays each year (165 Front St. E., 416 862-2222).

The National Ballet School: For aspiring dancers or anyone with a passion for ballet, nothing is more fascinating than a behind-the-scenes tour of dancers in the making. Tours are offered only rarely at the school itself (105 Maitland Street), but Open Houses at the Carsen Centre for the National Ballet of Canada (470 Queen's Quay West, 416 345-9686 x 17) are somewhat more frequent.

For performances by young people as well as for them, Toronto boasts several professional-calibre companies including: the Toronto Children's Chorus (416 932-8666); the Canadian Children's Opera Chorus (416 366-0467), which performs on its own and supplies young voices to the Canadian Opera Company when needed; and the Canadian Children's Dance Theatre (416 924-5657). Call for information on upcoming performances or check *Wholenote* for other groups and venues.

Canadian Broadcasting Centre (CBC): The CBC's headquarters is equipped with state-of-the-art sound and broadcast studios. Several times a year the corporation

NATIONAL BALLET
SCHOOL

hosts open houses at which you can meet broadcasting favourites and even take a turn at a mike. Various tours of the facility are offered on a daily basis, so call for details (416 205-8605). There is also a small museum for wandering down memory lane (open from 10 a.m. to 4 p.m.). Tickets for one of Canada's most popular TV shows, Royal Canadian Air Farce, are free but must be booked well in advance (250 Front St., across from the Metro Toronto Convention Centre, 416 205-5050). TV buffs may also be interested in the newly opened MZTV Museum (277 Queen St. W., 416 599-7339) that traces the development of broadcasting technology and programming through interactive displays. Tours by appointment or weekdays at noon, 2 and 4 p.m. Adults $6, students and seniors $4.

Two of Toronto's largest former vaudeville theatres, both of which now present mainstream plays, offer backstage tours. The Elgin and Winter Garden, the world's only functioning double-decker theatre, contains some of the most lavish and fantastical décor to be found anywhere and takes an hour and a half to tour (189 Yonge St., 416 314-2871, Thursdays at 5 p.m., Saturdays at 11 a.m., adults $7, children and seniors $6.).

Medieval Times Dinner and Tournament: You don't come here for the food; the jousting's the thing — fine equestrian skills, great costumes, beautiful beasts. Expect to spend a lot more than the basic $56.95 per adult and $38.95 per child for dinner, a beverage and the show, as kids beg for souvenirs (CNE near Dufferin Gate, 416 260-1234).

Milk International Children's Festival: This event is the largest of its kind anywhere; there are over 100 performances geared to kids, including film, music, dance, puppetry, theatre and even rope jumping. The fun happens over an eight-day period in late May at Harbourfront (416 973-4000, one-day pass around $8.50).

Kidsummer: Throughout July and August, Today's Parent magazine and a variety of other companies sponsor daily free or very low-cost events for children at sites throughout the city. Activities include concerts, behind-the-scene glimpses of productions, visits to factories and picnics. Some events require reservations. Listings appear in the summer issue of Today's Parent and are broadcast on several local media outlets (416 596-1991).

Santa Claus Parade: It's big, it's old (100 in 2004 — it predates the Macy's parade by a quarter century) and it ties up the whole city. So if you're here on the third Sunday in November, you might as well join the other 750,000 spectators. Check that weekend's papers for route information (416 599-9090, press #500).

THE LITERARY SCENE

Over the past three decades, Canada has built an international reputation for the high quality of its children's literature. The Osborne Collection at the Lillian H. Smith

Children's
Library
suggests one
reason for
this success:
an almost
100-year
tradition of
excellence in children's library programs that in turn
inspired donations of works, of which a fair number are on
display here. Also in the same building is the Merril
Collection of Science Fiction, Speculation and Fantasy,
named for Judith Merril, an outspoken supporter of such
writing and herself a prominent writer in the genre (239
College St., 416 393-7753), or browse at Bakka, Toronto's
oldest sci-fi bookstore (598 Yonge St., 416 963-9993).

Canada was also a pioneer in marketing children's
literature, having been home for more than a quarter of a
century to the beloved and influential Children's
Bookstore. The store is gone now, but others, such as
Mabel's Fables (662 Mt. Pleasant, 416 322-0438 and 2039
Bloor St. W., 416 233-9930) or The Constant Reader (111
Harbord St., 416 972-0661), which sells both new and used
works for children, compensate somewhat, offering
readings and meetings with favourite authors as well as
fine books. Animation and comic buffs will delight in
Animation Alley (365 Eglinton Ave. W., 416 482-5111),
Silver Snail Comics (367 Queen St. W., 416 593-0889) or
at 1,000,000 Comix (530 Yonge St., 416 934-1615) or
Hairy Tarantula (354 Yonge St., 416 596-8002). For
francophones of all ages, an array of works can be found at
Librarie Champlain (468 Queen St. E., 416 364-4345).

Tall and short tales can be heard year round on Friday
evenings at 8:30 p.m. at the church of St. George the
Martyr, adjacent to the Grange (behind the AGO), courtesy
of the Storytellers School of Toronto, which also sponsors
an annual festival of storytelling in late February (416 656-
2445).

Another literary highlight is Word on the Street, a book
fair held on Queen Street West on the last Sunday in
September. There are over 500 book and magazine sellers
and a raft of readings by kids' favourite authors. Check that
weekend's *Toronto Star* for details.

SPORTS AND RECREATION

Hockey Hall of
Fame: The late-
Baroque former
Bank of Montreal
building has been
well adapted to
its new use and
offers a glitzy
display of
Canada's most
popular sport (30
Yonge St., 416

SKYDOME

360-7765, adults $12, children 3-13 and seniors $7. Open daily 10-5, 9:30-6 Saturdays and 10:30-5:00 Sundays. Closed Christmas and New Year's).

Canada's Sports Hall of Fame: Located on the CNE grounds, this exhibit pays homage to Canadians' endeavours in some 50 different sports (416 260-6789, Monday-Friday 10 a.m.-4:30 p.m., free, except during the CNE).

SkyDome: Baseball fans will enjoy watching a Blue Jays game at the Dome. They will also enjoy getting the inside scoop on this wonder of technological wonders. Tours include a peek inside dugouts, dressing rooms, the media centre and the expensive private boxes, a film on how the facility was built and a look at the products of the archeological dig that preceded construction (416 341-2770, adults $9.50, $7 for youths and seniors, $6 children 3-16).

At the Air Canada Centre, Maple Leaf and Raptors fans can enjoy a game in their spiffy new home south of Union Station at 40 Bay Street. Call 815-5500 for tickets, although you may have to resort to scalpers for last-minute seats. If it's a tour you want at this self-styled "Theatre of Sport and Entertainment", you can catch one hourly between 10 a.m. and 4 p.m. so long as no sport or entertainment is underway (416 815-5982, adults $12, students and seniors $10, children $8).

Model railroad buffs can get a charge on the first Wednesday evening of every month or on the last three Sundays in February at the headquarters of the Model Railroad Club of Toronto (37 Hanna Ave., in the industrial area north and west of the CNE grounds, 416 536-8927).

Swimming in Lake Ontario is not for weaklings. The water stays cold right through the summer, and the beaches often are closed for even more unsavoury reasons. But if you want to brave it, the city runs a summer hotline (416 392-7161) for information on safe swimming areas. A better bet is to try one of the 78 free or low-cost large, clean outdoor public pools (416 392-7838 for locations and public swim schedules), or the 59 indoor pools open year-round (416 338-7665).

LEAFS IN ACTION

As you might expect, Toronto offers many opportunities for skating. Many parks have free outdoor rinks that are open from early December to early March (call 416 338-7465 or 416 392-1111 for hours and information on the few indoor arenas where public skating is available). At both Harbourfront and City Hall's Nathan Phillips Square you can rent skates — a big help for visitors who are unlikely to pack such unwieldy equipment. The former rink bills itself as the world's largest outdoor artificial facility, while the latter must be one of the most popular. (Additional recreational opportunities are to be found in the listings on page 209.)

ANNUAL EVENTS

ANNUAL EVENTS

With a Tim Horton's or other deep-fried pastry outlet on almost every corner, Toronto is sometimes referred to as the doughnut capital of the world. But it might better be called the festival capital. With a more ethnically diverse population than any other city, hardly a day passes without a public celebration of some sort, be it a street fair, a parade, a performance or a picnic. Add to this numerous neighbourhood festivals, international music, theatre, dance and literary or culinary events, and it's clear that staid old Toronto loves to party.

In addition, there are annual trade and specialty shows, usually held at the exhibition grounds, downtown at the Toronto Convention Centre, or near Pearson Airport at the International Centre, all of which have become major attractions for Torontonians and visitors alike. Many of them appeal to the entire family; these include the Boat, Auto, Dog, Cat, Bicycle, Hobby and Craft, Sportsmen's, Home and Garden Shows. Described here are just a few of the more colourful happenings that occur throughout the year; additional events are listed at the back of the guide, and in daily newspapers, *NOW* magazine, *eye weekly* and *Toronto Life*.

SCENE FROM CARIBANA

SCENE FROM THE NATIONAL BALLET'S *NUTCRACKER*

WINTER

The holiday season truly gets under way with the annual arrival of the National Ballet's *Nutcracker*. In 1995, this highly acclaimed work received a complete overhaul and remains

CANADA BLOOMS

a must-see.

A taste of Victorian or Edwardian Christmas is featured throughout the holiday season at all the city's historic homes (Colborne Lodge, Spadina House, the Grange, Mackenzie House and Casa Loma are some examples), where the décor and the scents of mulled cider and freshly baked goodies will envelope you and yours in good cheer (See listings under Museums for telephone numbers and locations).

In the early 1990s, Toronto joined the growing number of cities determined to make New Year's Eve an alcohol-free festive occasion, and began its own First Night celebrations. From about 7 p.m. on through the wee hours, a wide variety of entertainment catering to all ages and tastes is offered at about 16 downtown locations, all for the price of a single, inexpensive pass. As well, the city hosts a party at City Hall's Nathan Phillips Square with performers on stage from about 8 p.m. (For First Night information, call 416 362-3692; for all City Hall events, call Access Toronto 416 338-0338).

As winter grimly grinds along, people are wont to get a bit silly, hence the popular Molson Export Ice Canoe Race and Barrel Jumping Contest at Harbourfront in late January. Also at Harbourfront, throughout the last weekend in February, is the Toronto Storytelling Festival. (Call 416 973-3000 for all Harbourfront events.) If you're suffering from cabin fever, you may be ready to head for the hills by early March when maple sugaring is underway at all Toronto's conservation areas (416 661-6000).

SPRING

Whatever the calendar may say, Toronto's winter has traditionally ended in April with the opening of the Home Show at the Exhibition Place on the Exhibition grounds

SKATING AT NATHAN PHILLIPS SQUARE

(call 416 263-3000 for information on all shows at this venue). But now a more recent and wildly popular gardening show at the Convention Centre in mid-March — Canada Blooms — has become the harbinger of warmer weather (416 585-8000).

Another sure sign of spring in the city is Cabbagetown's Forsythia Festival, which offers a parade along Parliament Street and craft kiosks in adjacent Riverdale Park, for which organizers always guarantee the real thing will be in bloom (416 921-0857 for festival information). Home gardening in Toronto kicks off on Victoria Day weekend, and so does the Milk International Children's Festival down at Harbourfront. A single low-price pass permits entry to dozens of performances. The last weekend in May provides a real treat for native Torontonians and visitors alike when some 125 building owners invite the public to free tours of their historically and/or architecturally significant buildings at the appropriately named Doors Open Toronto (1-800-668-2746 or 416 325-5015).

Dragon Boat Festival

By June, festivals are in full bloom. There is the Toronto Worldwide Short Film Festival (call 416 445-1446, ext. 815), during which over 80 films are screened in five days in early June, and Hot Docs, Canada's international documentary festival (416 203-2155). In mid-June, there is North by Northeast (416 863-6963 for information or TicketMaster, 870-8000, for a pass, approximately $29), a three-day extravaganza featuring

up to 360 emerging rock bands playing at 24-clubs.

Also held in mid-June is one of the city's longest-running successes, Caravan. For $10 per person for a one-day pass or $20 for the ten-day period, you can purchase a "passport" to any of thirty or more pavilions featuring the cuisine, entertainment and crafts of the different countries represented in the city's cultural mosaic (416 977-0466).

A newer tradition is Bloom on the Beaches (416 365-7877), a leisurely literary experience held on and around June 16 that includes brunch, music, songs and readings. The event is a celebration of James Joyce's *Ulysses*. Its motto, naturally, is ReJoyce!

As the weather warms up, the waterfront plays an increasingly large role in festivities, of which the International Dragon Boat Festival at Centre Island in mid-

**FIREWORKS AT
ONTARIO PLACE**

June is one of the most colourful (416 598-8945). And then, to herald summer, on the last Saturday in June at Woodbine Racetrack there is the running of the Queen's Plate, the oldest stakes race in North America and the one at which people dress as though for Ascot. Royalty often makes an appearance — certainly on the track if not always in the stands (416 675-7223).

SUMMER

The air heats up considerably as the notes of the Downtown Jazz Festival waft from some 60 locations throughout the week following the summer solstice (416 928-2033). Free daytime concerts, including some especially for youngsters, and a farmer's market are a Wednesday fixture at Nathan Phillips Square, City Hall, from early June through September, where free evening concerts are also held on Fridays. Other summer-long specials include Kidsummer, a day-by-day schedule of free events for children, such as visits to factories and firehalls, craft-making opportunities, concerts and clowns (416 596-1991), and free indoor and outdoor films courtesy of the International Film Festival Group (416 967-7371 for times and locations).

Vying for fame and sparks of a different sort is the Pride Day Parade, held on the last Sunday in June to culminate Gay Pride Week. For colour and flair, it's hard to beat. Watch local newspapers for information, or call 416 927-7433. Canada Day, July 1st, provides an excuse for the year's largest outdoor public celebrations when almost every park in the city hosts performances and grand picnics. The largest of these is held at Exhibition Place, hosted by CHIN radio (416 531-9991). Theatregoers get a smorgasbord to choose from during The Fringe: Toronto's Theatre Festival (416 966-1062), held for 10 days in early July and featuring about 80 companies and 400 performances — none longer than an hour — playing mainly in the Annex area (near Bloor and Spadina). Other

**BICYCLE RACE
SPONSORED
BY CHIN**

standbys include the mid-July weekend Toronto Outdoor Art Exhibition at Nathan Phillips Square (416 408-2754).

On the noisier side, there is the Molson Indy on the third weekend in July, with its three solid days of car racing along the lakeshore and around the CNE grounds (416 263-3000). More acoustically pleasing is the largely open-air Beaches Jazz Festival in late July, at which more than 40 bands perform on the street and in area parks and clubs (416 698-2152).

The theatre fringe festival having proved so popular, there is now also a mid-August, 10-day Fringe Festival of Independent Dance Artists, featuring over 300 artists (416 410-4291). As well, in mid-August, Toronto's main alternative theatres host SummerWorks, a 10-day extravaganza with some 200 performances on four stages (416 410-1048).

SCENES FROM CARIBANA

Caribana, or the Toronto International Carnival as it is also called, the biggest, brightest, happiest festival by far, gets under way in early August. This midsummer Mardi Gras-type event includes over 30 competing bands, competitions for the King and Queen of the Bands, numerous performances throughout the city and a major arts festival on Olympic Island. Its pièce de résistance, the attraction that draws up to half a million people, is the parade held on the final Saturday of this two-week jump-up. Check for Toronto Carnival events at www.caribana.com.

After Caribana, the summer starts to wind down. The ever-popular Ex, which runs for the last two weeks in August and over Labour Day weekend, has signalled the start of a new school year for over a century. Along with its midway, amusement park rides and agricultural exhibits, there are dozens of performances daily and, on the Labour Day weekend, a stunning air show (416 263-3800).

FALL

The calendar says it's still summer, but the arrival of the Toronto International Film Festival, an important stop on the circuit that includes Cannes and New York, is a clear sign that fall is here. For 10 days, the city is filled with glitterati; there are gala parties nightly and all sorts of special shows — as well as, of course, more than 250 new films (416 968-3456).

The Canadian Open Golf Championship, held on the internationally famous and glitzy Glen Abbey course, the only Canadian stop on the Professional Golfers Association tour, closes the outdoor

WORD ON THE STREET

sporting season (1-800-571-6736), much as the Queen's Plate opens it. And then the literary season starts. On the last Sunday in September, Queen Street between Spadina and University Avenues is closed to traffic and opens as Word on the Street, a bookmart with stalls, readings and entertainment for all ages. See the *Toronto Star* the day before for a complete listing. Late September also sees Artsweek, an offering of performances, workshops and specialty tours covering the performing and painterly arts at various locations throughout the city (416 597-8223). Just as Artsweek winds up, the Made in Canada Festival of Canadian Music begins (416 593-7769, ext. 335 for information on this and other musical events).

Next on the calendar is another international biggie down at Harbourfront: the International Festival of Authors, with close to 100 public events (and thousands of private ones) and almost as many authors (416 973-4760). Harbourfront also offers weekly readings throughout the year.

Debate persists over whether winter begins with the early-November Royal Agricultural Winter Fair (416 263-3400), the mid-month Santa Claus Parade (416 249-7833) or the Cavalcade of Lights, held on the last Friday in November. The first is the highlight of the country-set's

year, with some of the finest showjumping and horsie events seen anywhere. All the other elements of a grand fair, the beribboned livestock and giant squashes, are also in attendance, as are the Four-H kids and a petting zoo.

Santa Claus started coming to town courtesy of the Eaton's department store just after the turn of the 20th century. The store has gone out of business, but the parade marches on. Finally, just days before *The Nutcracker* opens, the lights on the towering Christmas tree and around Nathan Phillips Square are switched on at 6:45 p.m. to the accompaniment of top-notch skaters in two free evening performances at the Cavalcade of Lights.

DAY TRIPS

BETTY ZYVATKAUSKAS

NIAGARA FALLS AND NIAGARA-ON-THE-LAKE

Without a doubt, Niagara Falls is the single most popular day trip for Toronto visitors. There are several bus tours available, or you can reach the falls in about two hours by car. For many decades, the thundering cataract was a honeymoon favourite, and that legacy still remains in many area motels boasting heart-shaped beds and whirlpool baths built for two. The tourism trade has brought with it a hefty dose of kitsch classics from wax-museum monsters to daredevil displays and amusement parks.

To enjoy the falls up close, nothing beats the "Maid of the Mist" boat rides. Since the mid-1800s, this tiny flotilla of tour boats has ferried passengers to the foot of the falls. Each boat takes several hundred raincoat-clad passengers on a 20-minute trip to pause at the foot of the magnificent Horseshoe Falls, where everyone gets a good soaking in the spray while listening to the commentary, which chronicles some of the daredevils who went over the falls in assorted contraptions.

The falls are only one highlight in this lovely area of scenic parkland. Head north from Niagara Falls on the Niagara Parkway, and you can enjoy one of the prettiest drives in North America. Don't miss the Niagara School of Horticulture's botanical gardens, the wonderful Niagara Parks Butterfly Conservatory and an outstanding arboretum.

The Niagara Parkway winds through some of Canada's most hospitable farmlands. Each spring, thousands of fruit trees bloom in the roadside orchards. Come summer,

HORSESHOE FALLS

NIAGARA APOTHECARY (ABOVE)
ARTILLERY PARK, FORT GEORGE (MIDDLE)
SHAW FESTIVAL (BOTTOM)

luscious peaches and cherries are sold at roadside fruit stands. Picnic venues abound, along with bicycle paths and hiking trails that explore the dramatic limestone cliffs of the Niagara Gorge. This is also wine country, and amid the vineyards are some wineries (including Reif Estate and Inniskillin) where visitors are invited to tour and taste.

The parkway ends at the historic town of Niagara-on-the-Lake, known for its gracious old homes and its theatre festival. Each summer, the popular Shaw Festival mounts critically acclaimed productions of the works of George Bernard Shaw and his contemporaries. Visitors looking for drama of a different sort can visit Fort George, the British garrison that was burned to the ground by

invading Americans during the War of 1812. Here, red-coated soldiers will tell you about nineteenth-century military discipline and the hardships of military life on the frontier.

Explorations of history continue on a walk through town. Among the self-consciously quaint "olde shoppes" that line the main street stands the Niagara Apothecary, a pharmacy whose interior has changed little since the store opened in 1819. Now operated as a museum, its shelves are stocked with an assortment of patent medicines, salves and potions.

NIAGARA-ON-THE-LAKE

WINERY TOURS

Some of Ontario's prettiest scenery can be found in the wine producing and fruit growing regions of the Niagara peninsula, a region known for great wines (many of which can be purchased only at the winery) and fine dining at winery restaurants. At last count, the region boasted nearly 40 wineries along the official Wine Route that starts in Grimsby and continues to Niagara Falls, with blue signs marking the way. Closest to Toronto is the wine-making area known as The Bench, part of the Niagara escarpment that parallels Lake Ontario, creating a microclimate for grape growing and some stunning vistas. Take a tour of the

vineyards at Vineland Estates, where an outdoor patio restaurant overlooks cliffs and acres of grapevines that slope south toward Lake Ontario. Cave Springs Cellars in the pretty village of Jordan welcomes visitors to their tasting bar. The adjoining On the Twenty restaurant is renowned for its pairings of food and local wines.

Wine Route road signs lead from The Bench to Niagara-on-the-Lake, where two major wineries have garnered kudos

FESTIVAL THEATRE AT STRATFORD

for both their wine and their very different styles. Jackson-Triggs' sleek, contemporary limestone building houses the latest in wine making technology and a chic Tasting Gallery where visitors sample a flight of three different wines with assorted cheeses on a vineyard patio. In contrast, Peller Estates resembles a European chateau with its peaked slate roofs and traditional architecture. Here cellar tours focus on the art of aging premium reds. An elegant restaurant where the six-course tasting menu changes weekly overlooks the vineyards. Many wineries feature special events (Hillebrand in Niagara-on-the-Lake is famed for its summer jazz series), but the biggest is the

STRATFORD

Niagara Grape and Wine Festival in September.

January brings icewine celebrations, as frozen grapes are harvested, then crushed while frozen to make Ontario's most famous and precious wine.

STRATFORD

Summer theatre abounds in southern Ontario. While Niagara-on-the-Lake has its Shaw Festival, Shakespeare finds his Ontario home in the magnificent Stratford Festival of Canada, just two hours west of Toronto in the town of Stratford, aptly situated on the Avon River. From its humble beginnings under a tent in 1952, the Stratford Festival has grown to encompass four excellent theatres at which both established actors (Peter Ustinov and Maggie

Smith, to name a couple) and brilliant up-and-comers are seen in many artfully staged productions. The Festival Theatre uses the Elizabethan theatres as its model, with a jutting stage that puts the action seemingly in the middle of the audience. The festival runs from early May through early November.

ST. JACOBS

Custom has it that a picnic on the grassy banks of the Avon River precedes attendance at either matinee or evening performances. Weather permitting, the setting is picture perfect. Willows overhang the river, where swans silently glide past the landscaped grounds of the Festival Theatre. In addition to the great performances onstage, visitors can enjoy a brilliant behind-the-scenes show on Sunday mornings, when there are backstage tours through the tunnels and technical spaces of the Festival Theatre.

Tours of the costume warehouse, which at 28,000 square feet is one of the largest in North America, reveal some of the magic of theatre props, from plastic armour to lifelike corpses.

WATERLOO COUNTY

To the east of Stratford lies the

ELORA MILL ON THE GRAND RIVER

lush farmland of Waterloo County, an area known for its German and Mennonite heritage. As you travel the rural backroads that connect towns with names such as New Hamburg, Baden and Heidelberg, it is not uncommon to find yourself sharing the road with the horse-drawn buggies favoured by Old Order Mennonites, who shun many modern conveniences with a view to preserving their traditional values. At St. Jacobs, you can learn more about their way of life at the Meeting Place, a museum run by

FARMERS' MARKET

both Old Order Mennonites and more liberal practitioners of the faith. The area is famed for traditions such as quilting, and in St. Jacobs you can still watch straw brooms being made by hand while a blacksmith practises contemporary artistry at the nearby forge. Waterloo County is known for its hearty German cooking, which

can be sampled at several country pubs such as the Heidelberg Inn, where a plate of pigtails cooked in brown sugar can be washed down with a fine pint of the house lager.

ELORA

Famed for its quaint stone architecture and its dramatic gorge, the town of Elora, about two hours northwest of Toronto, makes a delightful rural outing, especially during midsummer, when the town hosts a music festival with performances in such unusual and acoustically superb venues as the local quarry. Elora's dramatic 21-metre-deep gorge was carved by retreating glacial melt waters. Today the dark and fast-flowing waters of the Grand River are favoured by fans of fly fishing in pursuit of trout. Elora's riverside Mill Street boasts many attractively renovated stone buildings, including an old mill that has been turned into a country inn. The selection of gifts, crafts and jewellery make the street a favourite for shopping.

SHOPS ON MILL STREET IN ELORA

WINGS OF PARADISE

In Cambridge, Ontario, thousands of butterflies fly free in a tropical conservatory complete with lush plant life, waterfalls and gurgling streams. Iridescent blue morphos, bright orange Julia butterflies, yellow swallowtails, six-inch Atlas moths and black and red postmen are among up to 50 species that flit through the conservatory, looking for a free meal of rotting bananas and orange segments. In addition, the conservatory's lush vegetation —jasmine, lantana and passion vines — is chosen for both its beauty and nectar. Visitors who wear bright colours or sweetly scented perfume will find butterflies landing on them. On a winter day, this humid 930-foot conservatory feels like a tropical escape. In summer it is enhanced by four acres of outdoor gardens planted with nectar-rich flowers that attract wild butterflies. Monarch butterflies are tagged here

during their early September migration.

BRUCE TRAIL

When the need for a good, long hike sets in, many Torontonians head for the trail — the Bruce Trail, that is — a 770-kilometre hiking path that winds its way along the Niagara Escarpment from Queenston north to Tobermory. Roughly one hour northwest of Toronto, the trail passes through the Caledon Hills, where citified hikers can explore the scenery within easy reach of some fine country inns. At Caledon Hills, several clearly marked footpaths follow the Credit River and meander across cedar-covered hills, eventually connecting with the Bruce Trail. After working up an appetite on a vigorous country walk, hungry hikers head for the historic Cataract Inn for a satisfying lunch. Another fascinating spot along the Bruce Trail is the Crawford Lake Conservation Area near Milton, roughly 40 minutes west of Toronto via Highway 401. Here, great hiking trails meet a prehistoric Woodland Indian village, now

BRUCE TRAIL

meticulously reconstructed. Visitors walk into the smoky longhouses to see fur-covered sleeping benches and corn-grinding tools that would have been used more than 500 years ago. Many special programs allow visitors to participate in traditional native occupations, from making maple syrup in a hollowed log heated with rocks to celebrating the corn harvest. The hiking trails are wonderful, and one is even wheelchair accessible, with all-terrain wheelchairs on loan at the visitor centre.

SANDBANKS PROVINCIAL PARK

One of the world's most impressive fresh water sand dune systems lures beach-loving visitors 2.5 hours east of Toronto to Sandbanks Provincial Park. Situated in the lush farmlands of Prince Edward County, surrounded by Lake Ontario, this popular park is known for its towering sand dunes and exceptional beaches. Learn about dune ecology on the self-guided Cedar Sands nature trail, then swim at one park's two major sandy beaches or just relax in the

sun. The Outlet Beach offers easy access from the parking lot and the often-powerful Lake Ontario surf is popular with windsurfers and wave lovers. The West Lake sector (also known as Sandbanks Beach) is famous for its towering dunes that separate Lake Ontario and the warmer waters of West Lake. Nature lovers who walk along these dunes find solitude among marram grass, cottonwood poplars and wild grape vines.

PRESQU'ILE, TOTTENHAM AND KLEINBURG

Birds, beaches and butterflies make Presqu'ile Provincial Park a favourite of nature lovers. Located east of Toronto, Presqu'ile juts south into Lake Ontario. Almost an island, this peninsula is situated on a flyway that provides birds a place to rest and feed before and after crossing Lake

VISITORS AT CRAWFORD LAKE

LONGHOUSES, CRAWFORD LAKE

Ontario in their transcontinental journeys. Great rafts of migrating ducks and geese gather along the shore in early spring as they head north to their nesting grounds. By summer, the gulls and sandpipers are joined by beach-loving humans. Butterflies mark the end of summer as thousands of migrating monarchs travel south through the park.

SOUTH SIMCOE RAILWAY

For a family outing with universal appeal, the South Simcoe Railway offers a steam train ride to "nowhere." This 45-minute excursion departs from the village of Tottenham, just north of Toronto, with much huffing and puffing from Steam Locomotive 136, built in 1883 for the Canadian Pacific Railway. Today, Locomotive 136 is a star in its own right, seen on the popular children's television show *Shining Time Station*. Passengers ride in an assortment of old cars, including the last surviving 1926 model from the Toronto, Hamilton and Buffalo Railway. The eerie sound of the steam whistle drifts across farm fields as the train heads north, past a lazy creek where herons and turtles are sometimes sighted, to the town of Beeton, roughly eight kilometres north.

NIAGARA GRAPES

One of Canada's most impressive art galleries lies just a

few minutes to the northwest of Toronto, in the pretty village of Kleinburg. The McMichael Canadian Collection is home to a remarkable collection of works painted by the Group of Seven, among the first painters to depict the landscape in truly rugged Canadian style. That style is echoed in the dramatic stone and wood of the gallery's architecture. The gallery enjoys a setting as powerful as the art works it houses — hundreds of acres of Humber Valley forests all visible from the building's dramatic picture windows.

Roughly a 10-minute drive from McMichael is the Kortright Conservation Area, where you can enjoy more of that Humber Valley scenery as you walk the hiking trails or take part in one of the interpretive nature programs, many of which are geared to youngsters.

GAY TORONTO

SKY GILBERT

SAILORS AT WOODY'S

Toronto has one of the largest gay populations per capita of any city in North America. There is a thriving gay scene which offers many opportunities for socializing, entertainment and education. With a gay theatre, annual gay film festival and even two gay TV shows on Citytv and Rogers, Toronto is Canada's gay mecca. Tourists flock to the town partly because the people are so polite, if sometimes reserved, and partly because Toronto the Good is the most fun when it's being a little bit "bad."

FESTIVALS AND CULTURE

If you happen to be visiting Toronto at the end of June, Gay Pride Day is a must. It's one of the largest in North America, and takes place on the last Sunday of June every year. The town gets just about as nutty as Toronto can be as the colourful parade wends its way down the gay thoroughfare and up Toronto's main drag — Yonge Street. And Yonge Street is a real drag, on this day, with everything from "Bear" Floats to Dykes on Stilts. There are three entertainment stages and hundreds of booths selling the gamut of CDs to safer sex toys. Book early, because we

THE RAINBOW FLAG

"THE STEPS"

have visitors from all around the world who put Toronto first on the list of their North American Pride circuit. If you're visiting in late May, you might want to catch The Inside Out Lesbian and Gay Film and Video Festival, held in several of the main downtown cinemas. Toronto is experimental filmmaker Bruce LaBruce's hometown, as well as the stomping ground for John Greyson (Lilies), so the queer movie fare is bound to be stimulating. The festival shows gay and lesbian films from around the world and usually features some stunning premieres.

Staying on a cultural note, Buddies in Bad Times Theatre is also a must-visit. Toronto's Lesbian and Gay Theatre just celebrated its twentieth anniversary in its new 350-seat home at 12 Alexander Street. Favourites every year at Buddies include Rhubarb! — a festival of new works held in February which always features some challenging dyke and lesbian fare, Strange Sisters — a lesbian cabaret which happens two nights a year in fall and spring, and August's Fringe of Independent Dance (Ffida). Buddies' mainspace is a springboard for new Canadian playwrights and the smaller cabaret often features comedy (and a yearly queer comedy festival). The theatre also houses the trendiest mixed-yet-still-queer bar nights in Toronto. You'll find the youth crowd in their seventies duds grooving on the dyke Friday nights (men welcome!), and some of the prettiest trendoid boys in town dancing to Cher on retro Sissy Saturdays (women welcome!). Bar cover charge is a mere $3.

CHURCH AND WELLESLEY

CHURCH STREET
Culture of a slightly different kind is just around the corner. Church Street, between Bloor and Dundas, is Toronto's gay and lesbian village, comparable in every way to San Francisco's Castro Street. Most of the gay bars (and one lesbian one) and the bathhouses are located on, or very near, this vibrant street. Many of the businesses are gay owned, and all are gay positive. You'll find everything from gay tanning salons to gay video shops to gay veterinarians. It's a lively upscale street where gay and lesbian couples can feel comfortable walking hand in hand or even smooching.

If you want to get the lay of the land, so to speak, you might start at The Second Cup at the southwest corner of Church and Wellesley. Locals know it as "The Steps" because of the steps outside the coffee shop, which serve as impromptu seating. You can sit amid drag queens, hookers, leather guys and students from the local high school, sip cappuccinos and watch the human parade go by. If you want to have coffee with a preppier crowd, you might go across the street to Starbucks; the clientele there is usually white collar or collegiate.

If you want a little more than a coffee, there are tons of restaurants to serve you. The greasiest spoon is The Devon, just north of Wellesley, where the grilled cheese tastes like deep fried wonton. The Village Rainbow Restaurant (at the corner of Church and Maitland) is a greasy spoon with class, offering burgers and fries, and all day breakfasts in a sunny California environment with big windows and a patio on the street.

WILDE OSCAR'S

If it's summertime and patios are your style, try Wilde Oscar's, just across the street from Village Rainbow, which boasts a huge deck and the cutest waiters in town. Upstairs at Wilde Oscar's resembles a nineteenth-century male bordello decorated with Wilde memorabilia everywhere and lots of comfy couches for tired tourists. If you long for Italian food, try Trattoria Al Fiorno. And Byzantium and Babylon offer extensive martini menus with your meal. Byzantium, with its long bar and trendy surroundings, is famous as a holding pen for "A" gays (elegant post-white-collar attire only). These are not the only restaurants, or even the best, but might give you an idea of the variety you'll find on Church Street. If you want to eat off Church — but still in gay positive surroundings (it's always nice to sneak a kiss over dinner) — you might hit Living Well is the Best Revenge, on Yonge Street, or The Rivoli on Queen. College Street features a burgeoning queer (and arty) scene including Ciao Edie — a restaurant and bar just west of

THE VILLAGE RAINBOW

Bathurst — which is very gay, especially on Tuesday nights. Pimblett's Restaurant at Gerrard and Parliament provides full English meat and potato fare. Pictures of Queen Victoria and Edward VIII adorn the walls and transvestites often dine in the bar downstairs.

THE BAR SCENE

The bar scene on Church is varied and lively. The most popular by far is Woody's and its companion, Sailor (they have different names but are connected at the back). Sailor is Toronto's Cheers, featuring all the cutest boys and studliest men in beautiful surroundings: wood and brass with fireplaces, skylights, exposed brick and witty photos of all kinds of queens — including Elizabeth herself! On weekends the bar is packed. Thursday is "the Best Chest Contest", which always draws a crowd (competing out-of-towners are always welcome!). Sunday night is drag night on Church Street. You can start at The 501 — right at the corner of Church and Wellesley — at 6:30 p.m., and then move to Woody's and Crews later. Crews offers the raunchiest drag shows in town. Another popular place is The Barn, which used to be Toronto's only leather bar but now has graduated (on Wednesday and Friday nights) to the hip hop crowd — you'll find ravers bouncing there or playing pool almost any night.

For a visit to the real leather scene you must try The Toolbox at 508 Eastern Avenue, far from Church Street over the Don River and down by Lake Ontario. Not for the faint of heart, The Toolbox features a bear crowd who have "yellow hankie" parties, naked parties and a patio maze. (Note, there's no smoking in this bar except in the toilets, but that makes the toilets, well um, sort of social...).

For leather guys who are a little less adventurous, The Eagle on Church features very dirty

TOP: THE BLACK EAGLE

ENTRANCE TO WOODY'S

THE TOOLBOX

138

videos and a dark atmosphere. Sunday Night is Naked Night at The Eagle (at all times there is a dress code, no sandals or khaki pants — dark jeans and boots only). There's a friendly top to publicly whip your bum (if you ask him nicely), and a cute bootboy who just loves to spit and polish! Please note that most gay bars in Toronto welcome women, but women are especially welcome at Woody's, the Barn and The 501. Women are a little less welcome at leatherbars unless they're all leathered up. The barely post-teen rave boys hang out at Fly — a pretty three-floor disco on Gloucester Street, and The Guvernent down at the docks (both Saturdays only). For news about these boys, check out boostboys.com on the web. The rentboys hang out at Sneakers on Yonge Street at Alexander, the older men at Trax V (conveniently across the street) and the drag queens at The 501.

POPE JOAN

The bar choices for lesbians aren't quite as varied. Tango is right across from Woody's (next to Crews) and attracts a younger crowd than you'll find at Pope Joan at 547 Parliament Street, the longest-standing lesbian bar in town.

BEYOND BARS

The fun goes on late into the night after the bars close. For those with more on their mind than smooching and holding hands, Toronto offers six bathhouses. On or near Church Street, you'll find the Spa On Maitland and Toronto's Club Baths. The Spa is licensed and the Club Baths has a great little outdoor swimming pool which makes it feel like a resort in summer. Bears will enjoy the annual "Teddy Bear's Picnic" pool party every August. For women there is the annual Dyke Bathhouse night. The Cellar on Wellesley just east of Church draws a rougher and older crowd (their motto is "It's always dark"). If you're after

THE SPA ON MAITLAND

wild and raunchy times, check out the Barracks on Widmer Street, near Queen and Spadina. St. Mark's Spa attracts a young crowd, (almost right next to Trax V on Yonge). But the place where all the beauty boys display their gym bodies nightly is the Spa Excess at

SHOPS ALONG CHURCH

Jarvis and Carlton — a truly sexy bathhouse in the grand tradition, complete with a bar, glory holes, a pool table and a motorcycle.

Toronto has no true lesbian bathhouse yet. But dykes can pamper themselves at Good For Her at 181 Harbord Street, a store that "celebrates woman's sexuality." On Queen Street, Come As You Are provides a varied collection of dildoes and flavourful lubricants.

OTHER AMENITIES

If daytime fun is more your style, visit Glad Day Books on Yonge, or The Woman's Bookstore on Harbord. Both have a wide variety of queer titles and provide information about the gay and lesbian community. Queer shoppers won't want to miss Priape (men's fashions, leather, sex toys and magazines) on Church Street or Word on the Street (gay/lesbian t-shirts and trinkets) also on Church. For more detailed information about shops, services and organizations, pick

up *Xtra* magazine at The Second Cup. *Xtra* is a biweekly rag filled with political scuttlebut and gossip on local gay organizations. *FAB* is *Xtra*'s slick competition catering to a more middle-class (less political) crowd. Alternatively, have a look at the bulletin board at the 519 Church Street Community Centre — many community

519 CHURCH STREET COMMUNITY CENTRE

activities there are gay and lesbian.

No vacation would be complete without mention of where to get the best and latest safe-sex information. You can reach the Aids Committee of Toronto (ACT) at 416 340-2437. But Toronto is so cosmopolitan that it also is home to more radical organizations such as HEAL (Health, Education and Aids Liaison) at 416 406-4325.

Finally, there are lots of bed and breakfasts to make your stay comfortable, some right in the heart of the gay village, including the Cawthra Square Bed and Breakfast, 512 Jarvis Street and Catnaps. Church Street is surrounded by many major hotels, including Sutton Place and The Primrose. Toronto's charm is that it has all the advantages of a big city like New York, with all the safety and intimacy of a small town.

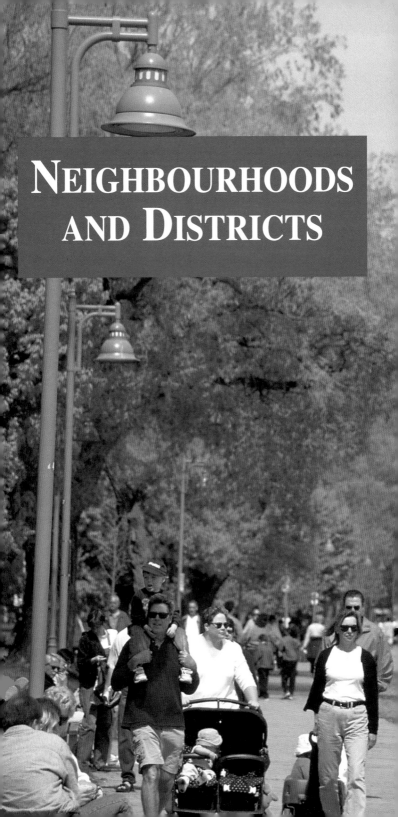

NEIGHBOURHOODS AND DISTRICTS

ST. LAWRENCE NEIGHBOURHOOD

OUTSIDE THE FARMERS' MARKET

The St. Lawrence neighbourhood, once the heart of Toronto's commercial district, offers lots to see and do. You will want to visit the bustling St. Lawrence Market to enjoy a tasty snack or lunch at one of the many stalls, stop by the Market Gallery or shop for crafts. You can stroll along Front Street, browsing for books, gifts, or clothing; or relax on the sunny patios of one of the many restaurants

on the Esplanade. For architecture buffs, the neighbourhood offers a cornucopia of interesting sights, from the fanciful nineteenth-century buildings on Front to the imposing St. James Cathedral on King Street.

THE HEART OF ST. LAWRENCE

The pulse of the district can best be taken at Front and Jarvis Streets, at the St. Lawrence Market. Located here are butchers, bakers, fishmongers and greengrocers who have served many of the same customers, virtually at the same location, for 50 years or more. As well as basic foodstuffs, there are stalls specializing in cheeses, pastas, rice, lentils, coffees, herbs, pies — even caviar! Prepared foods to take on a picnic or eat on the spot are also

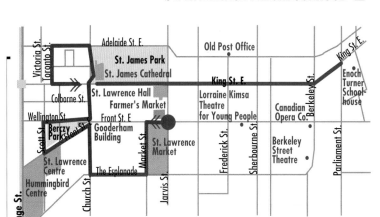

available, a favourite being sandwiches overflowing with what Americans call Canadian bacon and Canadians call peameal or back bacon. Although Saturday is its busiest day (you would have to arrive before 6 a.m. to find it less than jammed), the market is a busy spot on weekdays, too, especially as office workers hurry to do their shopping while grabbing a bite of lunch (except on Mondays, when the market is closed.) In addition to food, the market offers a sampling of crafts from many lands at the south end of the lower level.

The St. Lawrence Market sits like a large nesting goose atop an egg that actually is a remnant of the city's second

St. Lawrence Market

city hall, built in 1845. When in the late 1890s the seat of municipal government was moved, the city council decided to keep a portion of the old structure and build a market around it. The city hall's decorative stone and brick entrance is still

visible from outside, and when the market was renovated and enlarged in the 1970s, its classical rear façade was uncovered, becoming visible from inside. At that time, too, the former council chamber was renovated to serve as the Market Gallery. The gallery, which is free, is operated by the City of Toronto and houses well-curated exhibits of paintings, artefacts, photographs, maps and documents pertaining to various aspects of the city's past. To reach the gallery, enter via the Front Street entrance and take the elevator to the second floor.

OUTSIDE THE FARMERS' MARKET

Across the street from the Market is a gaily painted bunker-like building that houses a farmers' market every Saturday featuring fresh produce, Ontario-made cheeses and preserves, homemade pies and sausages, the best yogurt on this side of the ocean, and fragrant flowers and herbs. On Sundays, it houses a flea market.

INSIDE THE FARMERS' MARKET

APRÈS MARKET

If eating amidst hoards of shoppers isn't your style, exit from the St. Lawrence Market's lower level onto Market Street. Turn left, then right along Esplanade, long one of the most inappropriately named streets in Toronto. Even when it was named, the Esplanade was far from the graceful promenade promised by the railway barons in response to widespread complaints about the obstruction of the lake view by railway construction on the intervening landfill. Gradually, however, its name is becoming more apt. To the west, the former warehouses lining its north side have been renovated to accommodate numerous publishing houses and architecture and design firms on upper floors, while the ground floors are devoted almost exclusively to oversized bars and restaurants. The area's pioneer was the

local franchise of The Old Spaghetti Factory chain, while its neighbours include Scotland Yard, the very hot Esplanade Bier Markt serving 150 beers and staples like steak and frites from Belgium, and Finn McCool's Irish Pub. Around the corner on Church are The Keg Steakhouse, and Kobe, which serves Japan's famous Kobe beef.

AT THE FARMERS' MARKET

The next door up on Church Street is Le Papillon which specializes in crêpes; its oversized skylight permits many of the delights of eating outdoors, indoors. Along the south side of Front Street, between St. Lawrence Market and Scott Street, are a hodge-podge of shops including Nicholas Hoare, one of Toronto's most venerable book shops, a variety of clothing and shoe stores, the inevitable Starbucks café, a few restaurants of moderate calibre and a very Victorian bath, bedding and gift shop, Wonderful and Whites. At the corner of Market and Front Streets is a Liquor Control Board of Ontario (LCBO) wine and spirits shop. Its basement once housed the city's first pub.

A RARE COLLECTION OF NINETEENTH-CENTURY GEMS

The marvelous row of buildings housing these Front Street shops is best seen from across the street at Berczy Park.

SHOPS ALONG FRONT STREET

Like the buildings along the Esplanade, most were once warehouses; these, however, fronted on a prestigious commercial street. This difference is amply reflected in their fanciful façades. The one at 45–49 is particularly notable for being the last in the city made totally of cast iron.

Berczy Park, a lovely urban oasis, takes up the western half of the triangular block created by the intersection of Front Street, which once followed Lake Ontario's shoreline, with the north-south grid of the city. Seemingly tacked to the wall adjacent to the park is Derek

FRONT STREET SHOPS

Besant's humorous *trompe-l'oeil*; the Flat-Iron Mural uses as its canvas the neighbouring flat-iron-shaped Gooderham Building, built in 1892 and once the flagship of the distillery-owning Gooderhams. An instant success when it appeared in 1980, the mural has inspired the creative use of many an otherwise boring wall throughout the city. A very modest example lies across the street on Front at Church, helping the stuccoed wall of a newish box blend in with its elegant neighbours.

From Berczy Park, head east then north on Church Street. St. Michael's, seat of Toronto's Catholic archdiocese, Metropolitan United, the "Cathedral of Methodism," the First Lutheran Church, and St. George's Greek Orthodox Church (originally Holy Blossom Temple) are all on Church or neighbouring Bond Street. But the site at King Street on which now sits the Cathedral Church of St. James has always been the headquarters for Toronto's Anglican élite. It was built between 1849 and 1853, following the Great Fire of 1849 which devastated much of the downtown area, including the third wooden version of the church at that location. As a result of the fire, brick and stone supplanted wood throughout most of the area. The cathedral is a near-perfect reproduction of a fourteenth-century English gothic cathedral. Its 306-foot spire, the tallest in Canada, was for many years officially used to guide ships into the harbour. On

one of the headstones decorating the cathedral's front porch is a memorial to one John Ridout citing his consignment "to an early grave when a blight came..." The "blight" was a bullet fired by Samuel Peters Jarvis in Toronto's last duel, fought in 1817. Had he lived, Ridout might have met his relative, Thomas Ridout, one of the cathedral's architects. The lovely interior Tiffany window is dedicated to the Honourable William Jarvis — himself a relative of the other party in the fateful clash. In 1997, it became the only church of some 40 in North America with change-ringing bells to boast a "full ring" of 12 bells. On Sundays, they chime out patterns developed in the sixteenth-century. Monday evenings the bell ringers practice their pealing (call 416 364-7865 for times and tour information). On the remainder of the block is St. James Park, a charming garden tenderly restored to nineteenth-century horticultural dictates.

DEREK BESANT'S *FLAT-IRON MURAL* ON THE GOODERHAM BUILDING

CATHEDRAL CHURCH OF ST. JAMES

One block to the west is Toronto Street. From here it is possible to get a view of the last gasp, so to speak, of the St. Lawrence district's role as the commercial centre of Toronto. At the close of the century, George Gooderham, a prominent businessman, built the elegant, luxurious and thoroughly Edwardian King Edward Hotel in an effort to forestall the area's decline, which was a consequence of the city's westward and northward expansion. The hotel succeeded initially as a luxury establishment but failed utterly to stop the area's deterioration. Eventually, even the King Edward fell on hard times, but in the 1980s it was thoroughly modernized and restored to stand again as the epitome of a deluxe hotel of international stature. Along King to the

CATHEDRAL CHURCH OF ST. JAMES

KING EDWARD HOTEL

east, you will come to the fine French restaurant La Maquette sitting beside the Toronto Sculpture Garden. This unique space displays new work by Canadians in six-month runs all year. To the east, at Jarvis and King, stands St. Lawrence Hall. A graceful building, artfully endowed with a highly visible dome, a splendid display of carved stone, cast-iron balconies, as well as a lavish public hall, it fell on hard times after World War I but was lovingly restored and returned to its original purpose in 1967, Canada's centennial year. In its heyday — the second half of the nineteenth century — it was the centre of Toronto's social and cultural life. Soprano Jenny Lind sang here, Sir John A. Macdonald campaigned in its great hall, abolitionists spoke and P.T. Barnum presented Tom Thumb. St. Lawrence Hall also houses Biagio (155 King East), an Italian restaurant with a lovely patio.

A more leisurely pace is struck at two sites that bracket the St. Lawrence district. Near its northwest corner, at Adelaide and George Streets (260 Adelaide St. E.) is Toronto's First Post Office. This was actually Toronto's fourth post office, but it was officially deemed "the first" when Toronto incorporated as a city in 1834. It has a small display of old philatelic material and an excellent model of the original Town of York. It is also a working post office.

If you are convinced the 3 Rs ain't what they used to be, pay a visit to the Enoch Turner Schoolhouse, located at the easterly end of the district at 206 Trinity Street

10 TORONTO STREET

(862-0010). Built in 1848 beside Toronto's oldest surviving church, Little Trinity, the school was paid for by subscription from the wealthy congregants of St. James to serve the deserving children of poorer brethren who could not afford an education in the days before public education. It is notable not only for being the first public school in the province, but the first co-educational one, too. Its classroom has been restored to closely resemble the 1849 original.

KING STREET SHOPPING

From St. Lawrence Hall, stroll east along King. With so many of the area's older buildings having been converted to offices and studios for architects and other design professionals, it is not surprising that a significant number of the shops along the area's main shopping street cater to these industries. From the American 20th century classic Knoll (145) to modern Canadian Nienkamper (300), you'll find interior furnishings, lighting, framing, arts, crafts and antiques at shops like Up Country (212) and Italinteriors (359). Other fine shops include Vogue (175), which specializes in peculiar statuary; Arts on King (169), an emporium of useful and not-so-useful items for the home made by dozens of local craftspeople; and David E. Lake (237), with its fine old and rare books, maps and prints. By Parliament Street the stores begin to thin. Take a King streetcar westbound to return to your starting point.

ST. LAWRENCE HALL

THE WORKING PAST

If you are feeling industrious, hold off on the trip back and turn south on Parliament. Just before you reach the elevated Gardiner Expressway, you will spy a large limestone building. Constructed in 1859, this huge former gristmill and distillery sits in the midst of one of North America's largest collections of industrial buildings, some 45 of them. This 6-hectare site was until recently the headquarters of

FRONT STREET

LITTLE TRINITY CHURCH

the Gooderham and Worts distilling empire, which had its start in 1831, when James Worts, freshly arrived from Suffolk, England purchased the land and in partnership with his brother-in-law, William Gooderham, and set about building a mill. In short order, the two families became among the wealthiest in the city and their distillery the centre of Toronto's industrial district.

The area ceased long ago to be an industrial centre, and the last of the Gooderham & Worts buildings stopped serving its original function some dozen years back. While various dreamers and planners had a go at developing a future for the fine brick and stone buildings, they sat vacant. They were not unused, however, finding roles in at least 800 movies since 1990 — from "Don't Say a Word" with Michael Douglas, to "Bogus" with Whoopi Goldberg, to "Blues Brothers 2000" with Dan Aykroyd and a host of others. Meanwhile, new construction in the area began to attract a residential population. Now the fine old buildings – the old cannery, the main brewery and the former barrel

repair shop among them — are finding new roles as pioneers in the creation of a major new arts centre. The Sandra Ainsley Gallery and Jane Corkin Gallery, both well-known and highly respected in the Toronto art world, opened satellites of their original shops in the fall of 2002. Balzac, an excellent little coffee house, made its debut then as well. By the spring of 2003, more galleries, restaurants, craft shops, a live-and-work art centre and — appropriately enough — a brewery will all be up and running.

King Street East Shops

Enoch Turner Schoolhouse

FINANCIAL AND
THEATRE DISTRICT

CBC BROADCAST CENTRE

COMMERCE COURT

A bird's-eye view of Toronto at the close of the nineteenth-century would have revealed the spires of dozens upon dozens of churches poking high above the rest of the city — the spire of St. James Church was even used as a beacon to guide ships. By the 1920s, Toronto aspired more to progress than to godliness, and the skyline's spires had begun to give way to skyscrapers. This process continued through the booming 1960s, 1970s and 1980s, by the end of which the once prominent church spires and even the older skyscrapers were completely overshadowed by the sleek, mostly glass towers of banks.

Today, these towers appear at first to be the essence of Toronto's financial, business and civic core — the area bounded roughly by Yonge, Front, Dundas and John Streets. But despite the fact that Bay Street, the spine of downtown Toronto, is lined with the glass behemoths and, as the nation's financial centre, is frequently compared with New York's Wall Street, Toronto has maintained its vitality as a city precisely because this first impression is not entirely accurate. For it is also a fact that much of the older city remains, both in form and function. Despite being its commercial centre, Toronto's core continues to support a vast array of other activities.

Here lies its civic heart: the Old and New City Halls, and the provincial and municipal courts. Also playing a big role are theatres and concert halls: the Hummingbird, the

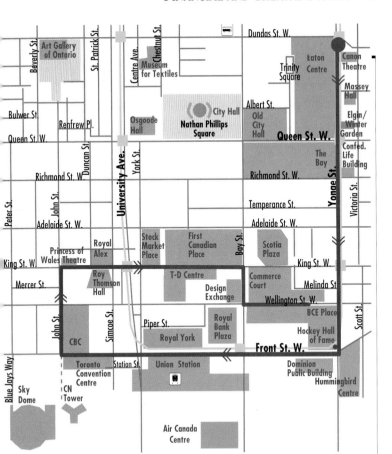

St. Lawrence Centre, the Royal Alex, the Princess of Wales, Roy Thomson Hall, Massey Hall, the Canon and the Elgin and Winter Garden Theatres. Sports are well represented by the SkyDome, the Hockey Hall of Fame and since February, 1999, the newest facility, the Air Canada Centre, which houses both the Raptors' basketball team and the hockey playing Maple Leafs. These leisure pursuits have spawned a slew of restaurants that cater to business people by day, and pre- and post-theatre goers and sports fans by night. Small but interesting art galleries in the core include the Toronto Dominion Gallery of Inuit Art and the Hudson Bay Company Gallery. All these activities, when combined with the miles of shops that line much of the underground PATH network, and the increasing number of office buildings that are being converted to residential lofts, make downtown Toronto lively day or night.

NEW CITY HALL

But as visible as the glass towers are from afar, they become difficult to differentiate up close. From the ground, many of the older buildings come into their own. They are generally interesting, built to the street, displaying the skill of stone and brick masons, of ironworkers. They often step back as they rise, ziggurat-like, with windows of varying sizes and columns and cornices that mimic those employed at street level added to the top floors. Originally designed to be visible from afar, many of these buildings were the biggest or tallest in their time: the Royal York Hotel was the largest hotel in the Commonwealth when it opened in 1927, and the old Canadian Imperial Bank of Commerce was the tallest building in the city for 35 years. Their interiors are not to be missed, especially their ground floors, which are filled with carved wood, wrought iron, cast brass, intricately laid marble, gilt-covered ceilings bedecked with chandeliers and a host of other fine details.

ABOVE: OLD CANADIAN IMPERIAL BANK OF COMMERCE BELOW: BANK OF NOVA SCOTIA, OLD & NEW

With the plethora of things to see and do, it is difficult to imagine "covering" the whole downtown in one attempt. There are bus and trolley tours that provide a good overview and can help you decide where to concentrate your energies. As well, a number of the major attractions, such as the SkyDome, the Canadian Broadcasting Corporation (CBC), City Hall, and many of the theatres, offer tours of their own facilities.

A CIRCLE OF PLAY AND DISPLAY

Yonge Street between Dundas and Queen is home to many of Toronto's best-known performance spaces, while several sites right on the Dundas-Yonge intersection are being redeveloped to house new theatres and cinemas. The Canon at 263 Yonge is across from the Eaton Centre and just south of the new facilities. Built originally as a vaudeville house in 1920, it was converted to a grand movie house when talkies supplanted live performances as the main form of

popular entertainment. When movie houses began to lose their appeal to television, it was converted again, this time to a six-plex. In 1988, it was restored and reopened as a legitimate theatre yet again, this time to house the wildly successful *Phantom of the Opera*.

South of the Canon, on Shuter just off Yonge, is Massey Hall, Toronto's Carnegie Hall–era concert hall. Noted industrialist and farm-machinery magnate Hart Massey built it as a gift to the city. Like its New York counterpart, it has marvelous acoustics. Unfortunately, its undersized

lobby always dulled the glamour of attending concerts, as it was too small to hold the audience during intermissions. Its appeal has been further reduced by numerous changes required to meet fire codes and it has become more like a variety theatre, with performers such as Gordon Lightfoot, Sharon, Lois and Bram, or the occasional rock star or country singer filling in for a night, but never building up a consistent repertory or audience.

The Elgin and the Winter Garden, the only double-decker theatres still operating in the world, are located to the south, at 189 Yonge. The larger 1,563-seat Elgin is decorated in Italian Renaissance-style plasterwork. It is quite magnificent, but it is the smaller, 991-seat Winter Garden above it that is truly amazing. Silk foliage hangs from plaster bowers, while thousands of tiny lights twinkle gaily in a completely fantastic pastoral setting. Built for vaudeville in 1913, the two theatres were easily converted to picture palaces, but the smaller upper theatre was closed for decades as no one was willing to invest the amount needed to meet fire codes for such a modest space. In the 1980s, however, the Ontario Heritage Foundation bought both theatres and restored them to their original glory. Productions such as *Cats*, *Joseph and the Amazing Technicolor Dreamcoat*, and performance troupes such as

Stomp have been playing to full houses ever since.

Restaurants and other nightspots are not so plentiful in this area as they are near the King Street theatres, but there are some exceptions. On Victoria Street are Terroni for rustic Italian fare, the Torch Bistro, a very good steakhouse, and

STAINED GLASS AT HOCKEY HALL OF FAME

HOCKEY HALL OF FAME AND TD CANADA TRUST TOWERS

upstairs from it the celebrated Top-of-the-Senator where jazz greats play nightly. On Yonge, the eclectic Superior features a smart sandblasted brick interior, and Baton Rouge, in the Eaton Centre's façade, serves some of Toronto's finest ribs.

On the southwest corner of Yonge at Queen is The Bay, the entrepreneurial descendant of Canada's oldest trading company (the Hudson's Bay Company), and one of the country's largest department store chains. Its wide bays, made possible with the introduction of steel frame construction in the late 19th century, proved perfect for displaying all the goods carried in the newly fashionable "departmental" stores of the day. Across Yonge, and slightly south is the striking Confederation Life building. When it was built in the 1890s, its towers were topped by sharply peaked roofs. Without the peaks, it now looks a bit more like a fortress. Either way, it was an eccentric choice for a staid insurance company.

Continuing south on Yonge, you will pass several fine low-rise buildings constructed just after the 1904 fire that wiped out much of this area, and, at number 67, the city's first skyscraper, a 15-storey structure built in 1905 by the New York firm of Carrere and Hastings for the now defunct Traders Bank of Canada. Just east of the corner at Adelaide, at number 10, is a posh little beaux-arts gem. Built in 1907 for the Birbeck Investment Company, it was restored in the 1980s by the Ontario Heritage Foundation, which is one of its tenants along with a number of other cultural organizations. The fine restoration job, including one of the few "personnel" elevators still operating in the city, has won the building numerous period movie roles.

Returning to Yonge, and still heading south, you will pass BCE Place (see below) before reaching the northwest corner of Yonge and Front. Here stands an ornately rococo former Bank of Montreal. From the sculpted characters hanging around outside, you will have guessed that this is the Hockey Hall of Fame. For over thirty years, the museum was located in a far smaller venue at the exhibition grounds. As part of the BCE. Place development, space was created for the museum in the renovated rococo Bank of Montreal building, an odd contrast with a sport that's sleek and fast. For hockey fans, it is a small paradise, containing everything from the original Stanley Cup to video displays of memorable plays. Gretzky groupies eager to see still more of his memorabilia will find it at his restaurant at 99 Blue Jays Way.

Just to the east, on the south side of Front, is the second cluster of Toronto's live theatres. First, there is The Hummingbird Centre for the Performing Arts. When it was

completed in 1960, this 3,200-seat house was the first large hall to have been built in the city since the turn of the century. It serves as home to the National Ballet and the Canadian Opera Company, as well as to visiting troupes representing various performing arts. The Hummingbird is well used and undoubtedly has a place in the hearts of many; it is here that the National Ballet performs its annual rite of Christmas, *The Nutcracker*, which was revamped in 1995, and that Mikhail Baryshnikov defected after a performance of the Bolshoi in June 1973. Some critics have come to find its fifties swooping style of architecture attractive, but none of these pluses quite make up for its mediocre sightlines and acoustics. To truly enjoy a performance, the most expensive seats are your best bet.

PORTICO UNION STATION

Just east of the Hummingbird is the St. Lawrence Centre for the Arts, which contains two theatres, the Jane Mallett and the Bluma Appel. A number of companies make the centre their home; chief among them the Canadian Stage Company, which was created in 1988 from the merger of the Toronto Free Theatre and CentreStage, both long-time players on Toronto's theatrical front. Also housed here is Opera in Concert and, under the same director, Toronto Operetta Theatre. Although brutishly bunker-like outside, the St. Lawrence boasts an interior that makes it equal to the arts it hosts.

Head west on Front Street, walking past the grand colonnaded Dominion Public Building to reach the next string of entertainment clusters that ring Toronto's financial district. Along the way, you will pass some significant representatives of this district, of which the first initially will catch your attention as a cheery glow emanating from the vicinity of the Bay and Front intersection. The source is the Royal Bank Plaza, the most eye-catching of the postwar generation of bank complexes. While the others are smooth, box-shaped structures, this one consists of two odd-shaped, almost triangular towers set at an angle to the street and sheathed in serrated curtain walls. To these glass walls were added some 2,600 ounces of gold, about $1.3-million worth at today's prices. The precious metal has proved to be more than worth its weight and a truly happy choice: it casts shimmering water-like reflections on nearby buildings, lighting up lower Bay Street on even the grayest of days and turning a fiery yellow at sunset.

GREAT HALL

The main beneficiary of the Royal Bank's golden glow is Union Station and its front plaza. Most visitors to Toronto today arrive by air, but in the days when virtually everyone came by train, ship or carriage,

ROYAL YORK HOTEL

this area served as the portal to the city. To welcome and impress all comers, a number of grand buildings were constructed in the 1920s. Union Station was chief among these. Opened in 1927 by the Prince of Wales, it is a colossal edifice stretching 750 feet along Front. It is also monumental in style with its awesome colonnade. Even more impressive is the great hall within. At 260 feet, it remains the largest "room" in Canada (not counting sports facilities), but nonetheless feels comfortable enough to calm even the most harried traveller. Train travel has diminished since its heyday, but because Union Station now functions as the terminal for Toronto's suburban commuter system as well as being a station on the subway system, it is even busier today than when it was built.

Also from the era of mail trains, but in a thoroughly deco rather than classical style, was the old postal station, south of Union Station on Bay. Gutted in 1997 to make way for the new home of the NHL Maple Leafs and the newly acquired NBA Raptors, major portions of its impressive carved façade remain visible. Inside the Air Canada Centre is a state-of-the-art sports facility that serves players and fans equally well. The seats are wide and comfy, the sightlines excellent.

On the north side of Front Street, across from Union Station and connected to it by the oldest of Toronto's underground passages is the Royal York Hotel, which also opened in 1927. It is one of the many fine château-style hotels built across Canada by the country's two main railroads, Canadian National (CN) and Canadian Pacific (CP). For years it was the largest hotel in the British Commonwealth and thanks to constant renovation and repair, it remains deservedly popular.

TORONTO CONVENTION CENTRE (BELOW) AIR CANADA CENTRE (BOTTOM)

Continue west on Front Street, across University Avenue. To your left (south) is the Toronto Convention Centre, most notable for its lack of an obvious front door. A huge facility — a major recent addition spans the railroad tracks still further south — it provides tonnes of space in which to host the ever-growing number of conventions held in the city. It is also the site for a number of trade and craft shows and specialty exhibitions.

Opposite the Convention Centre you will pass a silver cube wrapped in red bands that is the CBC Broadcast Centre. Probably no other building in Toronto has raised so much ire across the country. Canadians tend either to love or hate the CBC; few are neutral.

MAMMA MIA! AT THE ROYAL ALEX

Both the money spent on the centre and its design have been vigorously criticized. You might want to take a tour to see what the fuss is all about. Programs, both for radio and TV, are often taped in the main lobby for all to see and hear. Also on the ground floor are the CBC Museum and the Graham Spry Theatre, which programs CBC shows. Both are free. Best of all, there is the Glenn Gould Studio, in which a wide range of programs, from new music to chamber groups, is taped. Admission to this small, comfortable, and acoustically superb space is quite reasonable.

You are now at Front and John, within steps of two of the city's most popular tourist attractions: the SkyDome, home of the Toronto Blue Jays, and the CN Tower, the world's tallest free-standing structure. You are also on the edge of the city's third live-theatre district. Along King, Peter and John Streets primarily, but also on smaller streets such as Duncan, Mercer and Pearl, are many eateries catering to a wide variety of tastes to serve both the lunch and theatre crowds. The main performance spaces served by all these restaurants are Roy Thomson Hall, and the Royal Alex and the Princess of Wales Theatres.

ROYAL ALEXANDRA THEATRE

Roy Thomson Hall, on the south side of King at Simcoe, is home to the Toronto Symphony as well as to such classic groups as the Toronto Mendelssohn Choir. It was designed by West Coast Canadian architect Arthur Erickson and looks a bit like a glass volcano. By some unfathomable trick, it manages to look far smaller from outside than from within. After many complaints about the original acoustics, local architects KPMB with New York acousticians Artec rebuilt the interior in time for the fall 2002 season. Subsequent reviews of the sound have been raves. Across the street from Roy Thomson is the Royal Alexandra Theatre, a classic Edwardian jewel box. It is owned by Toronto businessman Ed Mirvish, who also purchased and restored the Old Vic in London. North America's premiere production of the long-running hit musical *Mamma Mia!* is currently showing with no end in sight. The Princess of Wales Theatre, located west along King at John Street, was built by son David Mirvish for Broadway extravaganzas and other large-scale productions. First there was *Miss Saigon*, helicopter and all, then came *Beauty and the Beast*

Commerce Court

and then *The Lion King*. Mirvish kept a tight rein on construction costs, but nonetheless managed to achieve a refined, lovely and extremely comfortable interior. Particularly noteworthy are the highly imaginative washrooms. In taking a gander at Toronto at play, you have skirted the city's financial core. Now it is time to plunge in.

THE MODERN BUSINESS DISTRICT

Head back east toward King and Bay crossing University Avenue. On this corner — or just off it, are the headquarters of four of Canada's largest banks (the fifth, the Royal Bank, was described earlier). Occupying much of the block on the northwest corner of King and Bay is First Canadian Place, headquarters of the Bank of Montreal, and its mate, the Exchange Tower, which houses Stock Market Place, an interactive exhibition space that explains the workings of the Toronto Stock Exchange. Appropriately, the consulting architect for these towers was

Sculpture at the TD Centre

the American Edward Durell Stone, for the whole of both buildings is clad in stone, white marble to be precise.

Across the street, on the northeast corner, is the reddish Scotia Plaza, the newer home of the Bank of Nova Scotia, and its more modest, older limestone home. The latter deco-style building was designed in the late 1920s by John Lyle, a noted Canadian architect of that period. At the southeast corner, is the Canadian Imperial Bank of Commerce's complex, the stainless-steel Commerce Court, designed by I.M. Pei, and the very solid, stone, old Bank of Commerce building. Inside Commerce Court is Jump, the supremely trendy (for the business-lunch set) and excellent restaurant featuring international fare.

On the southwest corner is the dark Toronto Dominion (TD) Centre, the first to raise its standard on Toronto's skyline. The architect engaged here was Mies van der Rohe, patriarch of the international modern movement. Mies designed two towers and the impenetrable-looking banking pavilion that stands right on the southwest corner.

BCE PLACE

Unfortunately, the TD seems to have been unwilling to leave well enough alone, and in the mid-1980s, added, to the south on Wellington Street, a fourth black tower, which makes a mockery of the careful placement of the first three buildings. Canoe, a fine restaurant with a Muskoka cottage-country theme, is on the 54th floor and offers a spectacular view to accompany the equally spectacular food.

TD's fifth and last tower squats menacingly on Bay Street atop the original hazy pink and beige Toronto Stock Exchange, the building that now houses the Design Exchange. The marriage is an odd one. Nonetheless, it did save the older building, which is an art-deco delight. The Design Exchange (or DX) is a non-profit organization devoted to good taste as expressed through commercial, industrial and architectural design. In addition to its excellent library, the DX hosts exhibits and lecture series on subjects ranging from interiors and urban design to furniture, clothing and gadgets (416 216-2160). It also contains a fine small shop.

While many of the financial district's modern buildings, such as the four banks, were set amidst wide open, windy plazas that landscapers have had to work hard at making

DESIGN EXCHANGE

more comfortable for mere pedestrians, the trend over the past decade has been to exchange these spaces for inviting, tall, well-lit interior plazas. BCE Place, at Bay and Wellington, is a case in point. Its block-long Galleria contains the façade of an older building that was demolished to make way for the project, shops with street-like fronts, and cafés that overflow into a wide and cheerful atrium. In fact, BCE Place has succeeded in attracting a number of good restaurants. Among them are Acqua, which offers Italian food in a water-theme setting; Masquerade Caffe and Bar, also Italian but more in the carnival than in the power-scene vein; and Marché, which is part of the city's Mövenpick stable and which has proved highly popular with lunch and theatre crowds for its eclectic marketplace atmosphere, food that's cooked before your eyes, and it's eye-popping desserts.

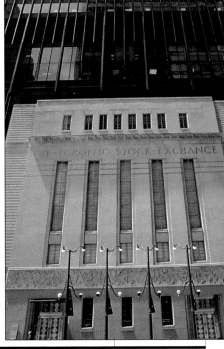

QUEEN STREET WEST

**THE HEART OF
QUEEN STREET
WEST**

Queen Street West is a slowly lengthening funky strip of shops, galleries, bistros and bars. Near the University of Toronto and the Ontario College of Art and Design and close to downtown, Queen West became the address of choice for many students, artists and other young people in the 1970s. They liked the neighbourhood shops catering to eastern Europeans, offering delicacies not found in

mainstream Toronto: homemade sausages, dumplings and desserts, pumpernickel and rye breads. Many of the stores and apartments were vacant, and the rents were low. By the late 1970s, the street had changed radically. New shops opened selling macramé, candles, off-beat clothes and old furniture passed off as antiques. Booksellers, chased from their digs on Gerrard Street by redevelopment, moved here. The street had long had a night life: country and western at the Horseshoe Tavern, jazz at the now defunct Bourbon Street Cafe, chatter and music wafting from the Portuguese Social Club, but now the street itself had become a major source of entertainment.

With the 1980s, the clothes became funkier; the music, raunchier. New clubs and theatres opened. The crafts became better crafted. New cafés, bistros and restaurants opened. The food became better; the booksellers, more numerous

— you could even find the Sunday *New York Times*. The Salvation Army Thrift Store became Le Château. The yuppies came; the New Agers came. Then Generation X came. The rents went up. Funk gave way to trendy, but the fun has stayed.

For the past decade, a wholesale conversion of the district's nearby manufacturing buildings to residential lofts has been underway. This, combined with the construction of buildings designed to look like manufacturing buildings converted to lofts, is pushing Queen Street's makeover further and further westward. A few years ago it reached Ossington,

STREET LIFE
(ABOVE)

where a former candy factory had been re-designed as home sweet home. It paused here for a while, as though baffled about how to get past the old Queen Street Mental Health Centre, a west end landmark so frequently referred to simply as "999 Queen" that its street address has been changed to 1001.

It overcame its hesitation, however, and now stretches so far west that it now connects to the district known as Parkdale, and in its westerly reaches is adopting the moniker "West Queen West." To be sure, there remain significant gaps in this westward march – areas where junk is genuinely junk and the luncheonettes genuinely grungy – but scattered amidst these remnants of the old Queen Street (which help keep rents down) – are a burgeoning number of galleries – almost 40 at last count! – and associated businesses catering to gallery-goers: restaurants, antique stores, art supply stores and so on.

FELICIAN SISTERS
CONVENT

FROM BARS TO CONVENTS

To begin your tour of the area, take the Queen streetcar as far west as you think you'll want to walk back, at least to the Ossington stop opposite The

DOWNWARD DOG YOGA SPA

Candy Factory (and next to the Chocolate Company Lofts). As you head back east, you will get a good taste within a couple of blocks of how Queen is changing: at least three clothing shops selling wares designed in-house (at 920, 880 and 878); some galleries and an artists' co-op (Artscape at 900, which has a refreshing little garden); a diner long-called "Swan", but only recently swanky (though still inexpensive), its first cousin, Oyster Boy, which specializes in oysters as its name implies, and Bar One, which offers excellent mid-priced Italian cuisine. As you continue eastward, you will soon pass the south entrance to Trinity Bellwoods Park, the site, from 1852 to 1925, of Bishop Strachan's Trinity College. Nearby shops of interest include Fleurtje (917), which sells bags designed in-house; Tin Taj (913), which is stacked to the rafters with hammered goods; and Japanese Paper Place (887), Ontario headquarters for origami practitioners.

The six or seven shortish blocks between the east side of Trinity Bellwoods and Bathurst Street, are chock full of additional interesting, one-of-a-kind shops of this sort – designers of furniture and clothes, galleries, dated or specialized wares, fancy used clothes, bars and restaurants. Among the

GRAFFITI

shops worth looking for are: World Art and Decor (803), notable for its high quality African and Caribbean art, crafts and music; Quasi Modo (789); which features Herman Miller's line of furniture for the home; Lululemon (734), home of wildly popular, lightweight Athletica clothing perfect for yoga and other meditative sports; Stephen Bulger Gallery (700), which specializes in photography; Comrags (654) the retail outlet for its

successful, mod outfits; authentic Canadian Indian arts and crafts at the Algonquians Sweet Grass Gallery (668), and authentic Himalayan arts and crafts right next door at the Tibet Shoppe; Romni Wools (658), a veritable knitters' heaven; and unusually beautiful southeast Asian crafts and furniture at Jalan (699). New and vintage clothing stores of varying quality and catering to a broad spectrum of special interests, also abound.

PETER PAN ON QUEEN STREET WEST

Highly-rated restaurants in this area — between Trinity on the west and Bathurst on the east — include Noce (783), long considered one of Toronto's top Italian spots; Cities (859), a bistro offering Mediterranean cuisine accompanied by microbrewery beer and jazz; Gypsy Co-op (817), which as a combination pool hall and beer parlour with good food thrown in has something of the area's old pioneering funk. There's a taste of the sweet back-to-the-land movement at Vienna Home Bakery (626), a delight for brunch with its thoroughly fresh, straightforward and simple offerings; of 90s elegance combined with excess (in the calorie department) at Dufflet Pastries (787); and of social conscience at the Raging Spoon (761), an inexpensive café operated by psychiatric survivors. Terroni (720), a traditional southern Italian trattoria has long been a neighbourhood fave. Little Tibet (712) is a newcomer to

CITYTV'S *SPEAKER'S CORNER*

the strip, but not to the city – it just moved here from Yorkville. But the standout in the area is the modest little Red Tea Box (696). Its meals are tasty and healthful, its ambience gentle and relaxing. It sells small quantities of lovely silk and lacquer items. And its desserts are positively exquisite works of art.

To the east, between Bathurst Street and Spadina Avenue, are numerous eateries of more than middling calibre, including Left Bank (567) and The Epicure Café. Arts and crafts also tend to move up the scale of quality the further east you go. In this stretch, too, is the best store in Toronto for ribbons and trim, Mokuba (575), and Abelard (519), an excellent second-hand bookstore. A few steps

north of Queen, at 25 Augusta, sits a large, impressive Victorian house. Originally a private home, it is now the Felician Sisters convent. On a different note, the club scene picks up its pace here with the Cameron (408), an old tavern that now sports enormous murals of Barbra Streisand and Pierre Trudeau, the Bovine Club (542) — formerly the Bovine Sex Club — and Savage Garden (550). Near Spadina, Chinatown meets the garment district, and fabric and notions stores abound. A more significant change in atmosphere arises from the change in scale as Queen suddenly widens east of Spadina. D'Arcy Boulton, Jr., who once owned the estate encompassing this area, hoped to influence the future width of Toronto's streets by laying out a wide avenue to front his property. Boulton also wanted to be able to see the lake from his house, the Grange. All that remains of his dream is the strip from Spadina to just past Soho Street. It is here that the Queen Street scene began in earnest. Now, however, although a number of shops and even more restaurants of note remain, the area increasingly is home to all the chain stores – especially for clothes – that you can find at a standard mall.

THE HAUTE OF THE ORIGINAL QUEEN STREET WEST

Eateries such as Le Sélect bistro (328); Peter Pan (373), originally Peter Pan Lunch; and the Queen Mother Café (208) are neighbourhood stalwarts, practically approaching middle age. Slightly younger is The Rivoli (332), Babur (273), which offers above-average Indian food, and the even younger Tiger Lily's (257), a noodle house owned by one of Toronto's best-known caterers and purveyors of fine foods. Also good is Ho Su Bistro (254) which features increasingly trendy Korean fare.

At Soho Street, just before Queen Street becomes narrow once again is the Black Bull Tavern, parts of which are thought to date from 1833, when Toronto was still

York, making it one of the oldest watering holes in the city. To the south, between Duncan and John Streets, is a stately office building clad in white terra cotta decorated with small casts symbolizing various aspects of publishing, reading and writing. Originally built for the Methodist Book and Publishing Company (later Ryerson Press), it is now the home of Citytv, whose mastermind, Moses Znaimer, introduced Toronto to blue movies back in the early 1970s. Also at Citytv, for one dollar, you can speak your mind on any subject to a TV camera and possibly catch yourself later on the station's program, Speaker's Corner. Znaimer has now opened his own museum – MZTV – lodged above the ChumCity store at 299. Here he has deposited his large collection of early and bizarre television sets and related ephemera. Tours are offered at noon, 2 and 4 p.m on weekdays or by appointment (416 591-7400). As if this were not enough, this stretch of Queen is also the centre of the annual, late-September Word on the Street festival, an immensely popular outdoor book fair that features readings, book bargains and activities for children.

At Simcoe Street, one short block west of University Avenue, there is a far greater change in atmosphere as the neighbourhood ends and the high-rise city looms before you. Connecting Queen West and the city, although completely anachronistic in relation to either, is the refurbished Campbell House, the Georgian home of Upper Canada's first chief justice, shifted from its original moorings next to Toronto's First Post Office (at George and Adelaide), and refurbished to serve as the home of the Law Society of Upper Canada, the trade union of Ontario's legal profession.

South of Queen along Richmond Street, from University westward, is a fairly new and thriving club scene. By day, many of the clubs serve lunch, and at dinner many attract the pre-theatre and pre-concert crowds, but it's late at night that they come into their own.

CAMPBELL HOUSE

CHINATOWN AND KENSINGTON MARKET

Chinatown, one of Toronto's most vibrant downtown neighbourhoods, radiates out from the intersection of Dundas and Spadina. Always crowded and bustling, the area offers great opportunities for dining and browsing. Some of the best Chinese and Vietnamese restaurants in the Western Hemisphere are located here. Enjoy hot and sour soup or barbecued duck before you visit the tiny shops selling everything from fresh produce to porcelain vases. Just to the north and west is Kensington Market, another entertaining destination for browsing. Here, you can enjoy a cup of espresso and a fresh croissant before shopping for a variety of goods. On the eastern edge of this area stands the Art Gallery of Ontario (AGO). Art aficionados will want to visit the gallery for its fine collection of Canadian work as well as its significant holding of sculpture by Henry Moore.

NEW YEAR'S IN CHINATOWN

CHINATOWN

If you did this tour with your eyes closed, Chinatown would be recognizable immediately through your sense of smell: the rich, pungent, moderately sweet scents of soy and sesame oil wafting through the air. With your eyes open, the source of the delightful aroma is made visible: dozens of shops festooned with glazed ducks, ribs and suckling pigs, a glimpse of butchers deftly carving portions for a seemingly endless stream of customers and an even greater number of cheerful, unpretentious restaurants, which are open until all hours and constantly full.

At night the streets are brightly lit — mostly in yellows and reds — setting off Toronto's old brick buildings in alternating warm and eerie hues. The pavement is jammed: singles, couples and family groups out for a stroll, shopping, chatting and hurrying to a favourite dining spot. Within the shops, often called "Trading Companies," masses of crisp green vegetables are piled high; the shelves are stocked with tins of abalone, turnips, bamboo shoots, water chestnuts and baby corn ears, as well as herbs and spices and dried foods ranging from jellyfish, squid and shrimp to mushrooms,

SHOPPING IN CHINATOWN

SHOPPING AND CHOPPING IN CHINATOWN

CHINATOWN AT NIGHT

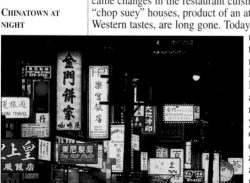

beans and lotus seeds. These stores also carry everything necessary for preparing and serving these exotic delights: woks and whisks, bamboo bowls for steaming rice, floral-patterned dishes, dragon-embellished platters and chopsticks of ivory, ebony, wood lacquered to an Imperial red, and even plastic. But your shopping will not be limited to food and kitchenware. Shops are also full to overflowing with items ranging from inexpensive fans, embroidered slippers, hand-carved animals and sandalwood boxes to pricey gifts such as silk dresses, jade and cloisonné jewellery and porcelain vases. The herbalists, with their natural cures for everything from stress and indigestion to baldness and infertility, are also worth a visit.

The Chinese community first grew up around Elizabeth Street, where new City Hall now stands, in the 1880s. It was a relatively poor community, eking out a living in service industries such as laundering and food. During the late 1950s and 1960s, its character and population began to change dramatically. It grew in size, scope and variety as a result of changes in immigration policy, substantial investment that flowed as a consequence of uncertainty about Hong Kong's future, the arrival of Vietnamese "boat people" (many of Chinese descent) and the demolition required to build the new City Hall, which forced the community westward. Today, although the Dundas-Spadina intersection (and surrounding blocks) remains the shopping, political and cultural hub for the thousands of Torontonians of Chinese descent, it is home to only a fraction of them.

With these changes in the Chinese community, in combination with the larger Toronto community's developing a more adventuresome and sophisticated palate, came changes in the restaurant cuisine. Most of the old "chop suey" houses, product of an attempt to cater to Western tastes, are long gone. Today's Chinese restaurants usually specialize in the dishes of one or more regions: Hunan, Beijing, Szechuan or Kwangtung (Canton) are among the areas represented. In recent years, fancy restaurants offering the haute cuisine of each of these areas have opened all around town. For the most part, Chinatown's restaurants continue to exemplify the flaky-

paint-and-Formica school of design, although many are excellent and inexpensive.

Favourites among Torontonians are numerous and include the New Sai Woo (130 Dundas near Elizabeth), one of the oldest and still popular, especially for banquets; also for seafood, Lee Garden (331 Spadina), Wah Sing (47 Baldwin), Xam Yu (339 Spadina) or Eating Garden (41 Baldwin); Chung King (428 Spadina) and Peter's Chung King (281 College at Spadina), both for their hot, zesty Szechuan or Singapore noodles; or Champion House (480 Dundas), known for its Peking duck; Lucky Dragon (418 Spadina) for dumplings or Swatow (309 Spadina), which also does a delicate eggplant with shrimps; Kowloon (5 Baldwin) for seafood or dim sum; or Happy Seven (358 Spadina) for mostly Cantonese.

Spadina Avenue, although mostly Chinese today — with a fair representation of Vietnamese — continues at its southern end to be the centre of Toronto's diminished rag, fur and needle trades. Early owners and workers in these sweatshops (for that is what they were and still are) usually were Jews who lived, worshipped and shopped along Spadina and in Kensington Market, which lies just to the west. In those days, Spadina was graced with two rows of trees on each side; it was a real avenue. Later, it became merely an inordinately wide street. Finally the street has been revamped: streetcars again trundle north and south heading all the way to Harbourfront, but still the new design does not quite achieve the treed splendour of the original.

ON SPADINA

SPADINA/QUEEN STREET DRAGON

EXILE TO KENSINGTON

BOISTEROUS KENSINGTON MARKET

If you walk west on Baldwin Street from Spadina, you will reach Kensington Market, a neighbourhood that was once almost exclusively Jewish but is now predominantly Portuguese, Latino and West Indian. Kensington's houses are small, often in disrepair and frequently painted chartreuse, aquamarine, forest green, orange, turquoise, lavender, mauve or blue, as well as the more traditional red or white. It has been said that the market looks like Kansas City

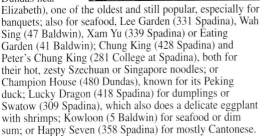

171

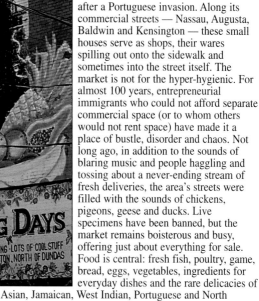

KENSINGTON MARKET

after a Portuguese invasion. Along its commercial streets — Nassau, Augusta, Baldwin and Kensington — these small houses serve as shops, their wares spilling out onto the sidewalk and sometimes into the street itself. The market is not for the hyper-hygienic. For almost 100 years, entrepreneurial immigrants who could not afford separate commercial space (or to whom others would not rent space) have made it a place of bustle, disorder and chaos. Not long ago, in addition to the sounds of blaring music and people haggling and tossing about a never-ending stream of fresh deliveries, the area's streets were filled with the sounds of chickens, pigeons, geese and ducks. Live specimens have been banned, but the market remains boisterous and busy, offering just about everything for sale. Food is central: fresh fish, poultry, game, bread, eggs, vegetables, ingredients for everyday dishes and the rare delicacies of Asian, Jamaican, West Indian, Portuguese and North African cuisine are all on hand. But shops are not restricted to selling food — far from it. You'll find dry goods and clothes, buckets and bicycles, furniture and bedding, electronics, paintings on velvet, tapestries in acrylic, everything including the kitchen sink — several, if you'd like.

Within Kensington Market, there are several places to eat, including the Boat (158 Augusta), a fairly expensive Portuguese restaurant, and Amadeu's (184 Augusta), also Portuguese and noted for its seafood and a delightful French boite, La Palette (256 Augusta).

If all this walking seems overwhelming but you really want a taste of the neighbourhood (in more ways than one), you could simply head back east on Baldwin Street. In its most easterly block, between St. George and McCaul Streets, two blocks north of the AGO, is an amazing collection of inexpensive to mid-priced restaurants, amazing not only because it is perhaps the only quiet, narrow, tree-lined side street in Toronto to have become home to so many eateries — 21 at last count — but because of the cultural variety they represent. Where else could you find five Chinese restaurants specializing in seafood (Baldwin Palace, Kowloon, Hua Sung, Wah Sing and Eating Garden), three eateries featuring delicacies of the Indian Subcontinent at Gateways of India, the Jodhpore club and Indian Choice, two in the subtle flavours of Japan (Fujiyama and Kon-nichi-wa are the best, the latter modeled in a modest way on London's wildly popular Wagamama chain), two offering a taste of France (Café LaGaffe and La Bodega, two of the earliest tenants on the street), as well as the Malaysian and Thai Mata Hari, the Mexican of Margaritas First Cantina and Tapas, the Korean Hana, as well as Italian fine dining at Porta Pane and

Italian desserts and coffees at John's, and an assortment of "international" spots such as Creations and Sensation Café as well?

Having run out of space, there are some more choices just around the corner on McCaul itself, including the lovely Cassis. For a sedate contrast to the modern eclecticism of immigrant capitalism, you can visit the Grange, located just south of the Art Gallery of Ontario. Built in 1817, the Grange was the very Anglo, Georgian home of D'Arcy Boulton, Jr., an early Toronto worthy. The oldest extant brick home in Toronto, the Grange housed the Art Gallery of Toronto (as the AGO was then called) from 1900 until 1918. As the gallery expanded, the gallery's curators and administrators used the Grange for office space. Following the 1960s expansion of the gallery, the house was fully restored. Admission to the home's interior is through the AGO only, but its front façade can be seen from the park directly south of the gallery. In the Boulton era, this was but a small portion of the Grange's private park, which stretched from Queen Street all the way to Bloor. Torontonians of the time were shocked at how far out of town Boulton's new residence was: for many years few roofs other than that of the Church of St. George the Martyr would have been visible from The Grange.

STREET LIFE IN KENSINGTON MARKET

Today the treed skyline has been replaced by apartments, offices and the CN Tower, but the church remains, although its tower burnt to the ground in the 1950s. It is now home to a chamber group, Baroque Music Beside the Grange, who perform using period instruments about twice a month, except in the summer (call 416 588-4301). The park remains, too. Still called Grange Park, it is now a city park rather than a private property and sits amidst an area that since the turn-of-the-century has been the centre of one of Toronto's biggest immigrant catchment areas.

QUEEN'S PARK AND THE UNIVERSITY OF TORONTO

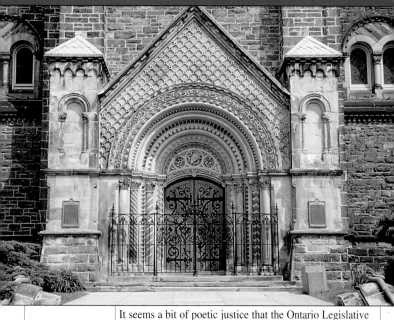

ROYAL ONTARIO MUSEUM

It seems a bit of poetic justice that the Ontario Legislative Assembly, the seat of the provincial government, which perches at the top of University Avenue, replaced a building that once served as a mental institution. In the early days, University Avenue was beautifully treed and stretched from this building clear to the lake. Today, the inmates have a view of one of the city's widest, virtually treeless streets, graced at its southern end mostly by standard-issue office buildings, many of them insurance companies, and at its northern end by a cluster of medically outstanding, but only occasionally distinguished-looking, hospitals — Mount Sinai, the Hospital for Sick Children, Toronto General and Princess Margaret. Queen's Park, the great green oval in which the legislature building is situated, is almost entirely surrounded by the St. George Campus of the University of Toronto (U of T), which consists of over 200 buildings spread out over 2.8 square kilometres (one square mile), making the university the largest landholder in Toronto (apart from various levels of government).

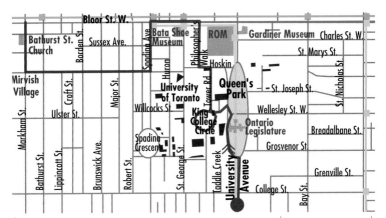

With over 55,000 students attending its 16 faculties and nine colleges, this university is also the largest in Canada.

On University Avenue just north of Queen's Park is the Royal Ontario Museum (ROM). Once part of the university, it is now independent, although still publicly owned. The university's influence is particularly strong in the residential and shopping areas to the west of the campus, from Spadina Avenue to at least Bathurst, between College and Bloor Streets. Many of the shops and restaurants along these main streets are bohemian, laid back and inexpensive. Nearby are a number of cultural icons, from the swank Bata Shoe Museum to the bargain basement, "world-famous" Honest Ed's department store. There is Toronto's deservedly world-famous Baroque ensemble, Tafelmusik, which plays in Trinity-St. Paul's United Church (427 Bloor Street West), as well as the Annex Street Theatre (730 Bathurst), and the Poor Alex Theatre (296 Brunswick), three of Toronto's numerous independent medium-sized and small houses.

THE ONTARIO PROVINCIAL LEGISLATURE AT QUEEN'S PARK

ONTARIO LEGISLATURE

The legislature building, best glimpsed from the south at about Dundas Street, is an isolated fortress surrounded by a moat of traffic. Like Toronto's Old City Hall, it caps a long vista, and was designed in the Richardsonian Romanesque style that was popular in the late nineteenth century not only for large public buildings, but also for the homes of the wealthy. Its designer was one Richard A. Waite, a British-born, Buffalo-based architect who was a poker-playing crony of several members of the provincial parliament (MPPs). Unsure of which of two detailed proposals submitted by local architects to pick for the construction of the building, the MPPs turned to their friend Waite. He modestly concluded that only he could undertake such an important commission, and offered his

UNIVERSITY COLLEGE

services for a mere $700,000, a figure about $150,000 more than the sum indicated by the locals. Local resentment notwithstanding, the offer of "the Buffalo individual" (as the press referred to him) was accepted. And for a mere $1.3-million, the "unspeakable" Waite provided them with their dream house.

Memories of the scandal were slow to fade, but there can be little doubt today that the legislators got their money's worth. The building is rich in detail, both inside and out; ornate carvings, trim, metalwork and windows grace it throughout. Its rooms and halls are both gracious and generous. It has the feel of a fine old men's club, which of course is what it largely has been. Those familiar primarily with modern surroundings of steel, marble, glass and stark white will fall comfortably into the building's embrace. When the House is sitting, all are welcome in the visitors' gallery.

Tours are available throughout the week during the summer months and on weekdays the rest of the year. Call 416 325-7500 for schedule information or take a self-guided walking tour. In its basement cafeteria, you can grab fairly good grub for exceptionally low prices. Better yet, if you know an MPP, you might be able to wangle an invitation to the fine restaurant.

CONVOCATION HALL

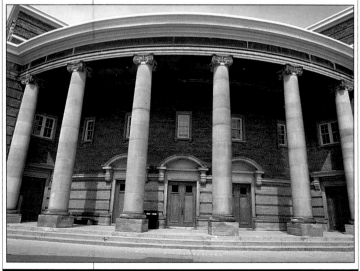

CONVOCATION HALL
INTERIOR

UNIVERSITY OF TORONTO

From Queen's Park and the nineteenth century, you can cross over to King's College Circle and step back a few more centuries into the gothic-looking parts of the University of Toronto. Since the 1850s, when University College was completed, the campus has been steadily changing with the addition of new colleges and faculties and the absorption of older ones such as St. Michael's.

The buildings that receive the most attention from modern visitors are University College, Hart House, Knox College, Trinity College and Chapel, and St. Michael's College, where Marshall McLuhan proclaimed, "the medium is the message."

Although of course not genuinely medieval, these structures strongly evoke their precursors (with modern plumbing), thereby providing the atmosphere of intellectual depth one expects of a serious university. Being among the older campus buildings, they also come replete with tales and myths. For example, the murder of stonemason Reznikov by his colleague and rival in love, the aptly named Diablos, is part of the lore of University College (UC). Also now at UC is the recently refurbished University Art Centre, while in neighbouring Hart House more art can be found at the Barnicke Gallery. Knox College, meanwhile, which so completely fits the image of the hallowed hall of higher learning, has become a movie star, winning feature roles in *The Paper Chase*, *Class of 44*, *Moonstruck*, *Dead Ringers* and Jell-O commercials.

Tours of the campus (offered three times a day throughout the summer) focus mainly on these Oxbridge-like Gothic and Neo-Classical buildings, such as Convocation Hall and the campus administrative centre, Simcoe Hall. The latter houses a complete model of the entire campus, which is good for an overview. Even if you are not taking a tour, you will want to poke around Hart House. This building was a gift to the university from the Massey Foundation and was named for Hart Massey, founder of the Varity Corporation farm-implement empire. It was designed as an undergraduate men's student centre, but now serves the entire community. It encircles a quadrangle used for outdoor summer concerts and contains a gym, a pool, lecture

MEMORIAL TOWER

ST. GEORGE STREET

rooms, assorted activities rooms (for music, billiards and so on), a chapel, a fine small theatre, the Barnicke Gallery and an excellent, moderately priced restaurant, the Gallery Grill, which is open to the public for lunch.

Finally, there are a host of wonderful modern buildings, such as Massey College, made famous by its long-time principal, author Robertson Davies; New College, which contains a quadrangle to rival those of the Victorians; Innis College, a comfortable, casual place that bespeaks a culture free from the grim formality of the older buildings; the well-designed, power-dressed Rotman School of Management; and the new, very odd looking campus residence imaginatively called Graduate House, with its crane-like superstructure overhanging Harbord Street.

To enable you to really savour the campus flavour, most of the residences offer accommodation from early May to late August. Unfortunately, there is no central booking system; each residence must be contacted separately. The numbers can be obtained from the campus housing service (416 978-8045). (For information about tours, call 416 978-5000.)

If a casual visit is more your style, you can head west from the north side of Queen's Park to Hart House Circle, south a bit to King's College Circle and west from there to take a northward stroll along the revamped St. George Street. For years, St. George sliced through the campus, an unfriendly river of traffic. In the mid-90s, however, a $1-million private gift from Judy Matthews was put to use creating a well-planted, narrower street with more space for bicycles and pedestrians. At the Robarts Library, with its grim concrete exterior and periscope-like tower which houses its rare books collection, turn west to wander along

ROBARTS LIBRARY

Harbord Street (see below), or east along Hoskin Avenue, and just before getting back to Queen's Park, turn north onto Philosopher's Walk, a pleasant path through a leafy vale that leads to the Royal Ontario Museum and to Bloor Street.

HONEST ED'S

BLOOR WEST, MIRVISH VILLAGE AND HARBORD STREET

Harbord Street itself is pretty nondescript, but between Spadina and Bathurst, there are at least half a dozen shops of note (and no less than five exceptional restaurants). Visit the Clay Design Studio/Gallery (at Brunswick), a potters' co-op; WonderWorks (79A) for New Age books, crystals, music, herbs, jewellery and other paraphernalia or Things Japanese (159), slightly farther west. In addition, you'll find specialty stores offering new and used books, several children's clothing stores and the beloved Harbord Bakery, whose bagels, challah, cookies and other goodies draw customers from across the city.

UNIVERSITY COLLEGE

If you continue walking west along Harbord, you will soon come to the stretch of Markham Street known as Mirvish Village. David and Ed Mirvish, the Canadian entrepreneurs who own Toronto's Royal Alexandra and Princess of Wales Theatres, also own these shops and restaurants. The buildings here have been tarted up a bit, making them almost too precious or quaint, but nonetheless this block houses numerous shops that are fun to poke through. Among these are David Mirvish Books (596), which offers a wide selection of art books, and Ballenford Books (600A), which specializes in architecture. You'll discover glassworks downstairs at Core (588). Comics are rampant at The Beguiling (601). Journey's End Antiques (612) offers a variety of estate antiques and, for dog lovers, the city's largest collection of French bulldogs! Of the restaurants, Southern Accent (595), Toronto's oldest Cajun spot, provides blackened everything (416 536-3211).

Bloor Street is of course one of Toronto's major thoroughfares, taking on the character of abutting residential communities as it wends its way through the city. Starting just west of Spadina is the university community, which has a wide selection of reasonably good, always comfortable, moderately priced dining spots.

YORKVILLE AND BLOOR STREET

An elegantly attired woman, her hair carefully tinted and styled in the latest mode, steps smartly up the street. Heads turn. But only momentarily. Attention soon is focused on a similarly in-vogue couple. He is tall, tanned and Ralph Lauren-ed; she is Chanel-ed to perfection. But even they can't hold the eyes of those who cruise by in Mercedes, Porsches and SUVs, or sashay along, the street their runway.

The place is Yorkville, centre of the Bloor Street-Annex axis. Fairly oozing with elegance and luxury, this area is the place to see and be seen. Bloor Street, often compared to Fifth Avenue or Michigan Avenue, is lined with shops of the first order: Tiffany, Davids, Cole Haan, Vuitton, Chanel, Hermes, Jaeger, Benetton and Giorgio, to name but a few. The Annex consists of blocks and blocks of comfortably large, thoroughly renovated, tastefully landscaped Victorian homes. Avenue Road, the boundary between the residential Annex and the commercial Yorkville, is home to international hotels, posh galleries and antique

TIFFANY ON BLOOR STREET

Roxborough St. W.
Chicora
Ramsden Park
Huron St.
Spadina Ave.
Davenport Rd.
Hillsboro
Bernard Ave.
Belmont St.
St. George St.
Tranby
Frichot
Admiral Rd.
Bedford Rd.
Berryman St.
Masonic Temple
ANNEX
Lowther Ave.
Avenue Rd.
Hazelton Ave.
Heliconian Club
Davenport Rd.
Yonge St.
Madison Ave.
Scollard
Church St.
Hazelton Lanes
Yorkville Ave.
Public Library
Pr. Arthur
Church of the Redeemer
Bellair
Fire Hall
Toronto Reference Library
Asquith
Cumberland St.
LM Treble Bldg
The Colonnade
Bloor St.

stores. Davenport Road, the northern boundary of the area, has become Toronto's main drag for interior designers to the carriage trade. And then there is Yorkville itself, with its narrow streets and hidden laneways stuffed with galleries (more than 25 at last count), boutiques and at least 15 restaurants worth a visit.

A LITTLE HISTORY

The area began life near what is today the busy Bloor-Yonge intersection. There, in the early 1800s, a far-sighted hotelier built the Red Lion Inn, the last stop on the main highway (Yonge Street) before a toll had to be paid to enter Toronto. The inn was a booming success. Residential development began in the mid-1830s, when Sheriff William Botsford Jarvis and brewer Joseph Bloor purchased land in the area and began laying out lots for what became the Village of Yorkville in 1853.

Built as a suburb of Toronto, Yorkville was home to professionals and the burgeoning middle classes: self-employed craftspeople, shopkeepers, clerks and the like. The air was good, the scene was rustic and starting in 1849 a horse-drawn omnibus ran between the Red Lion and the St. Lawrence Market on Front Street. In the 1870s, large lots were created west of Yorkville proper, specifically to attract the wealthy. Among those who built there was the Gooderham brewing family, whose 1890 Romanesque mansion at Bloor and St. George streets is now the fashionable York Club.

Yorkville became part of Toronto in 1883. The area to the west of it (roughly to Walmer Road) was annexed to the city in 1887 and to this day is called the Annex. Continually well-served by public transit and adjacent to the University of Toronto, Yorkville

CHURCH OF THE REDEEMER AT BLOOR AND AVENUE ROAD

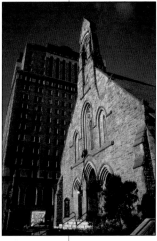

181

**TORONTO
REFERENCE LIBRARY**

maintained its upper class and upwardly mobile status to a large extent until the mid-twentieth century. Some of the larger homes were by then broken up into rooming houses, or served as shared accommodation for groups of students. But while there were scattered pockets of shabbiness, the area never became down and out.

In the 1960s, Yorkville became Toronto's hippie haven, filled with flower children, peaceniks and acid freaks, a drop-in centre for those who didn't trust anyone over 30. Although sometimes compared to Haight Ashbury, it really was more like the bohemian Greenwich Village, with a vibrant core of coffee-house folkies accompanying the tie-dyed T-shirts and recreational drugs. Here Joni Mitchell, Gordon Lightfoot, Ian and Sylvia Tyson and others got their start, and so did the Coffee Mill, which still serves an excellent cup of brew as well as tasty pastries and light snacks, albeit at a slightly different location.

Since those heady days, many of the area's buildings have undergone renovation, while others have been virtually reconstructed. There also has been a substantial amount of new construction. In Yorkville itself, this generally has taken the form of low-rise developments bearing the stamp of the former village's motifs of brick, back lanes, greenery, high art and oodles of sophisticated shops. Along Bloor Street and Avenue Road, there are new high-rise hotels and offices converted to luxury condos.

A YORKVILLE TOUR

Start your walk at the Bloor-Yonge intersection, taking a short two-block stroll north on Yonge before plunging into Yorkville. On Yonge, you'll find Thompson's Homeopathic Supplies (844), a pristine example of an old-type herbal apothecary that could be a museum were it not a shop; the Cookbook Store (850) and the Toronto Reference Library (789). The last, built in the early 1970s, has proved enormously popular with residents and tourists alike. With

its plant-filled atrium and sound-dampening waterfall, it lacks the austerity of reading rooms like the New York Public Library, La Bibliotheque Nationale or the London Museum, all of which immediately inform the visitor that Important Stuff Has Been Written Here, and instead is a welcoming, accessible kind of place.
At Yorkville Avenue, turn west and look at

HAZELTON LANES

two of the area's older civic institutions. The Fire Hall (22) was built in 1876, when Yorkville was still an independent village. The building deteriorated after annexation, and all but the tower was rebuilt in 1889. The entire building was refurbished in 1975, and Yorkville's official coat of arms, saved when the town hall was demolished, was placed over the doorway. Next door is the Yorkville branch of the Toronto Public Library (34), built in 1907. It was one of four Toronto libraries built with a 1903 endowment from American philanthropist Andrew Carnegie. It was restored and expanded in 1978. From here, continue west past Bay Street into the heart of Yorkville's shopping district, which stretches along Cumberland Street and Yorkville Avenue to Avenue Road, with significant bits on Scollard Street and north up Hazelton Avenue.

INSET: YORKVILLE FIRE HALL

As you stroll west along Yorkville, you will pass a wide variety of good restaurants and interesting shops. For Japanese food, try the very tiny Zerosun (69) or for Italian, Bellini (101). Further west, near Hazelton, pause to visit the Arctic Bear (125), which specializes in Inuit sculpture, prints and other native works.

If you turn north on Hazelton, you will come to a number of galleries that have made their mark on the Canadian art scene over the past two decades: Nancy Poole's Studio (16), Mira Godard (22) and Sable-Castelli (33), each of which

HELICONIAN CLUB

introduced Canadian artists of international calibre, as well as staged international shows of interest and importance. Two additional landmarks here are of note, each of which in turn served as the Olivet Congregational Church. The older, at 35 Hazelton, was built in 1876 and is one of only two surviving board and batten churches in Toronto. Since 1923, it has been owned by the Toronto Heliconian Club, a unique institution that was established in 1909 to bring together women engaged in the arts — writing, painting, music — and that flourishes to this day. The second

BLOOR STREET

YORKVILLE STREET SCENES

Olivet church was built in 1890 and is a classic example of Richardsonian architecture. The original interior was octagonal, with the pews radiating around the pulpit and organ chamber, putting every congregant directly under the preacher's eye. Since 1973, it has served commercial and office uses and is now home to three fine galleries.

When you've seen enough fine art, wander into Hazelton Lanes, a uniquely upscale shopping mall filled with boutiques offering fashions, specialty gifts, jewellery and one-of-a-kind furnishings. Around the corner from Hazelton, on Scollard Street, are still more galleries, two of which, Gallery One (121) and The Drabinsky Gallery (122), specialize in contemporary works. Retrace your steps to Yorkville to cut through Old York Lane to Cumberland. Here you will find the Guild Shop (118) for exquisite Canadian crafts. While you are here, be sure to have a look at the Village of Yorkville Park, which runs west from Bellair Street along Cumberland. The result of an international design competition, the park became the focus of much controversy, little of which has abated despite its having been the recipient of international awards. It is intended to provide a sense of the varying topography found in Ontario, ranging from an upland conifer garden to a wetland, to a birch grove, a wildflower

meadow and a massive granite outcrop moved here from northern Ontario and weighing 650 tonnes. It also features water falling from a steel frame that looks a bit like a harp that can play only one note, a stream and (at night) dramatic lighting.

A STROLL ON BLOOR STREET

From the Village of Yorkville Park, walk west to Avenue Road and then south to Bloor. On the northwest corner stands the Park Hyatt. Originally called Queen's Park Plaza Hotel, it was built between 1926 and 1929 as an apartment hotel. Atop it sits the Roof Restaurant, a romantic spot where the excellent view is sometimes matched by the food. Opposite, on the northeast corner, is the Church of the Redeemer, which redeemed itself by selling air rights to the rather ghastly Renaissance Centre that frames it. Here you can dine on Cal-Ital at Prego Della Piazza, literally in the bosom of the church.

THE PARK HYATT (MIDDLE)

HARRY ROSEN ON BLOOR (BOTTOM)

On the southeast corner sits a very distinguished example of neoclassical revival with a colossal portico, the L.M. Treble Building. Built as a donation from Lillian Massey Treble of the farm machinery family, the facility was intended "to educate young women in the scientific running of a household." Today, it has been renovated to serve as the flagship store for Club Monaco.

In addition to the Park Hyatt, the area's other hotels, the Intercontinental and the Four Seasons, provide several restaurants of note. Signatures, at the Intercontinental, offers global cuisine in an art-deco setting, while at the Four Seasons there are the stylish Studio Cafe, the French and highly rated Truffles and La Serre, a lounge that offers good lunches and brunches.

Head east along Bloor, and in addition to the aforementioned shops

CHAPTERS ON BLOOR

of international fame, you will find dozens of others such as the Gap, Banana Republic and Eddie Bauer. Recent additions include Roots — Canada's new flagship store— Williams-Sonoma, the related Pottery Barn Kids and a renovated Talbot's. Chapters, part of Canada's leading book chain, opened an outlet designed specifically to hold its 150,000 plus titles, and from its architecture section you get an excellent view of Yorkville Park. Holt Renfrew (50 Bloor St. W.), Canada's swankiest department store with fraternal ties to Niemann Marcus and Bergdorf Goodman, has its flagship store near Yonge.

Other Canadian favourites include William Ashley (55), Birk's (55), Stollery's (1) and Harry Rosen (82). In addition to the ever-present Body Shop (86), MAC (89) and Aveda (95) offer designer cosmetics. Specialty shops include the Irish Shop (150), with its lovely wools, Mont Blanc (151) for the fountain pen of your heart's desire and Amarynth (131) which sells Lalique and other fine, hand-blown glassware. If you are into the more traditional forms of smoking, there are several tobacconists in the area, but the most humorous, no doubt, is Groucho and Co. (150) on Bloor, near Avenue Road.

Also on Bloor is the Colonnade (131). Built in the early 1960s, it was the first large-scale project in Canada to combine residences, offices, retail outlets and a theatre. In fact, it was among the first in North America to do so, and it succeeds with an elegant design that provides a comfortable spot to stop and chat in the street while providing an excellent view of its many storefronts — to

THE COLONNADE

say nothing of the excellent views available from its large, well-designed apartments. Among the many favourite dining spots on or near Bloor are Scaccia for straightforward Sicilian fare at the ManuLife Centre (55 Bloor St. W.), Sultan's Tent for Moroccan atmosphere rather than ultrafine cuisine (1280 Bay), Pangea for well-prepared fresh foods in a friendly atmosphere (1221 Bay) or Host for an innovative northern Indian menu in a plush setting (14 Prince Arthur).

YONGE STREET

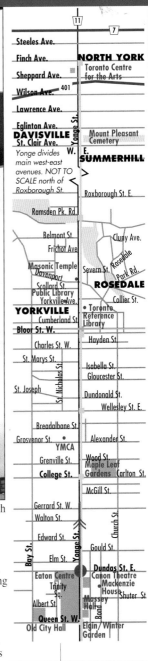

Steeles Ave.
Finch Ave.
NORTH YORK
Sheppard Ave.
Toronto Centre
for the Arts
Wilson Ave. 401
Lawrence Ave.
Eglinton Ave.
DAVISVILLE
Mount Pleasant
St. Clair Ave. W. E.
Cemetery
Yonge divides
main west-east
SUMMERHILL
avenues. NOT TO
SCALE north of
Roxborough St.
Roxborough St. E.
Ramsden Pk. Rd.
Belmont St.
Cluny Ave.
Frichot Ave.
Masonic Temple
Severn St.
Davenport
Scollard St.
ROSEDALE
Public Library
Yorkville Ave.
Collier St.
YORKVILLE
Toronto
Cumberland St.
Reference
Bloor St. W.
Library
Charles St. W.
Hayden St.
St. Marys St.
Isabella St.
Gloucester St.
St. Joseph
Dundonald St.
Wellesley St. E.
Breadalbane St.
Grosvenor St.
Alexander St.
YMCA
Grenville St.
Wood St.
Maple Leaf
College St.
Gardens Carlton St.
McGill St.
Gerrard St. W.
Walton St.
Edward St.
Gould St.
Elm St.
Dundas St. E.
Eaton Centre
Canon Theatre
Trinity
Mackenzie
Sq.
House
Shuter St.
Albert St.
Massey
Hall
Queen St. W.
Old City Hall
Elgin/Winter
Garden

Yonge is Toronto's legendary main north-south street, bisecting the city into east and west sides. Its first 53 kilometres (40 miles) were laid out in 1796, when the city itself was barely more than a figment of Lieutenant-Governor John Graves Simcoe's imagination. When Toronto's first subway line opened along Yonge in 1954 its continuing role as main street was ensured.

From its starting point at Queen's Quay, where Captain John Letnik presides over his floating seafood restaurant, through the city's financial district, alongside the Eaton Centre's

ship of commerce, past "the Strip," on to Bloor and northward past Davisville, Eglinton and other subway stops that once were village crossroads, the street offers entertainment ranging from soft-core porn to the international glamour of Broadway shows, and wares from discount electronics and fly-by-night footwear to the broad middle range of the Eaton Centre's hundreds of shops, to carriage trade antiquarians and clothiers.

The crowd and the attractions change from day to night, from year to year, from neighbourhood to neighbourhood, but Yonge always remains a safe street to walk and shop along. An amiable tackiness pervades much of the street's length while recent redevelopment shows signs of a rebirth. But no single activity — reputable or otherwise — has ever managed to gain ascendancy. Toronto's main drag is eclectic, safe and sometimes seedy, but always vibrant.

EATON CENTRE

Yonge Street south of Queen Street is discussed in the chapter Financial and Theatre District. This tour starts on foot at the Eaton Centre, which stretches all the way from Queen Street to Dundas Street, and continues north to Bloor. It is a manageable walk from Bloor as far north as St. Clair Avenue, but it is easier still to take the subway or bus to St. Clair and walk back to Bloor since it is all downhill. North of St. Clair, shops and restaurants start to get further apart, and you may wish to take a bus, subway, car or taxi to a destination and then walk around that area before moving on to the next one. Although there are a number of excellent restaurants between Lawrence Avenue and the North York City Centre, there is little else worth stopping for. The main attraction in what was, until amalgamation in 1998, the civic centre of North York, is the Toronto Centre for the Arts, adjacent to what was North York's city hall, public square (Mel Lastman Square), main library and art gallery. The Centre's larger theatre has hosted major productions such as *Showboat, Sunset Boulevard* and *Ragtime*, while a smaller space, the George Weston Recital Hall, a true gem of a hall, provides acoustics that enable it to attract the world's most distinguished soloists and chamber groups. The Museum of Contemporary Canadian Art, also housed within the Centre's walls, presents the cutting edge of today's art.

EATON CENTRE

From the 1880s until his death, a stern, teetotaling Timothy Eaton presided over the affairs of the street from the corner of Queen and Yonge. There, he and a Scot named Robert Simpson first established their competing dry goods stores. These men were to become the rulers of two of Canada's greatest department store dynasties and the self-styled

arbiters of the street's good taste. Not counting the Bay (now housed in Simpson's former flagship store), which can be reached by an enclosed walkway above Queen Street, the Eaton Centre is one-quarter mile long; its arched glass gallery 127 feet high. Its 300-plus shops are on three levels: food courts, "convenience" merchandise (drug stores, appliance repairs, records) and popularly priced fashions on the lowest; mid-priced clothing, jewellery and some specialty stores on the middle level; and on the most pleasant, uppermost level, higher-end fashion and accessories at stores such as Talbot's, Mirabelli and Banana Republic. Restaurants are scattered throughout. Although surpassed in size by the mammoth West Edmonton Mall, Eaton Centre remains the largest downtown shopping complex in North America, and since its construction in the late 1970s has almost always topped tourists' must-do list. A lot of Torontonians visit it regularly, too — over 42 million people a year in total.

MICHAEL SNOW'S *FLIGHT STOP* IN THE EATON CENTRE

The centre's new Yonge Street façade is an unloved postmodern mishmash meant to look like a line of separate buildings, enlivened by backlit billboard spaces. Its interior, however, with its fountains, fancy paving and soaring sky lit arch, was meant by architect Eb Zeidler to be reminiscent of Milan's airy Galleria, albeit with an exposed-duct-work industrial twist. The centre was accused of killing life on Yonge Street, so a new extension brought the walls out closer to the street, to allow for new stores and restaurants with access to the street at several points. While a few of the tackier areas along Yonge Street have changed little despite the centre, some of the best old buildings opposite the centre, in particular the Elgin, Winter Garden and Canon Theatres, along with the Ryrie Building, have all been restored to at least their former glory. In addition, many rundown buildings near Dundas were demolished to make way for the exciting new Dundas Square and a vast new entertainment and retail complex to come at the northeast corner.

Some thought that shopping in a mall would suburbanize or sterilize the downtown core. While there is no denying that the vast majority of the centre's retailers are chain stores, the sheer variety of goods, prices and people using the centre has ensured that urban vibrancy prevails. The vitality is augmented by artwork, most notably Michael Snow's flock of non-migrating geese; by some of the centre's surroundings, especially the sophisticated Trinity Square, which flanks the west side of the centre and which features a café, fountains, and a labyrinth for walking. Frequent performances occur, both scheduled (inside the mall, or at the new Dundas Square) and non-scheduled (at the corner of Dundas and Yonge). One block north of the centre (on Edward Street) is the similarly gargantuan World's Biggest Bookstore; it's actually not the largest in the world, but with about 100,000 titles, it comes close.

YONGE AT DUNDAS

DUNDAS TO BLOOR

Starting at Dundas and running north past Gerrard Street is the infamous "Strip." Here, there's no seeing the original buildings for all the layers of plastic, cardboard and neon signage covering even highly reputable stores such as Sam the Record Man.

Running west off Yonge two blocks north of Dundas is Elm Street. For some reason, it was the site of some of Toronto's earliest fine restaurants, a tradition that continues to this day with Barberian's (7), one of the city's first steak-houses; Oro (45); and Bangkok Garden, which has long offered Thai food in an elegant atmosphere.

From Gerrard north to College, there's a momentary interruption of the otherwise nineteenth-century character of the street. In the 1920s, it was thought that College Street soon would overtake Queen and King Streets as the centre of retailing. Construction of new buildings began on a vast scale, both along Yonge and eastward along Carlton Street. Kresge's, Toronto Hydro, Warner Brothers and most ambitious of all, what was to have been Eaton's flagship store, all bear the undeniable stamp of art-deco. The stock-market crash of 1929 interrupted plans for the area when less than a quarter of the Eaton's project, which was to have included a 40-storey office tower, had been completed. Nevertheless, Eaton's opened its grand store with an opulent deco interior. It closed, along with Eaton's original Queen Street store in 1977 when the first phase of the Eaton Centre opened. Much of the original deco interior still is visible, however, incorporated into the reworked College Park mall now within the walls. The legendary seventh-floor Eaton Auditorium, a concert hall and restaurant that has been closed for decades, is being restored and reopened in 2003 as an event space named The Carlu, after its French architect, Jacques Carlu.

Yonge serves as the boundary dividing the east side of Toronto from the west, and many of the smaller streets end at Yonge. The small, offset blocks created by all these dead ends have helped preserve Yonge Street's nineteenth-century scale along this stretch: it is difficult to assemble large blocks of land for megaprojects when there are so many little streets.

COLLEGE PARK IN FORMER EATON'S

This pattern also has created surprisingly quiet neighbourhood enclaves just around the corner from bustling Yonge Street, and nowhere is this more evident than between College and Bloor Streets.

TOWER OF FORMER FIRE HALL NO. 3

On Yonge itself, clear up to Bloor, except for a few government offices, you will find mainly shops offering fast food and its equivalent in clothing, cameras and electronics. The buildings here are less camouflaged than to the south, however, revealing more of the street's busy past. The tower jutting from the St. Charles is all that remains of Firehall No. 3, which was built in the 1870s. Around the corner on Grosvenor Street is the Metro YMCA, a sleek and muscular building appropriate for its purpose. On the other side of Yonge, at 26 Alexander Street, is another of Toronto's ever-popular early steakhouses, Carman's Club.

In the pleasantly sainted little area near Bloor (St. Nicholas and St. Mary's streets, St. Joseph Avenue) are two pleasant restaurants: Segovia, at 5 St. Nicholas offers a taste of Spain, and Le Matignon serves up French fare in a cozy setting at number 51. At Gloucester Street stands Gloucester Mews, originally the Masonic Hall, which was among the earliest renovation projects undertaken in Toronto. Just to the north at 675 is Postal Station F. It too was renovated early on, now serving as a Starbuck's, a McDonald's and a fitness club. Something about this stretch of Yonge seems always to have put it just on the edge of success without ever quite making it.

BLOOR TO ST. CLAIR

That feeling changes as soon as Yonge reaches Bloor. From there, north to Hogg's Hollow and with only the occasional break (for the Mount Pleasant Cemetery between Davisville and St. Clair, for instance), Yonge Street reflects the class and cachet of the neighbourhoods through which it runs. To its west lies Yorkville (see p. 180). To the east lies Rosedale, originally a wealthy suburb, and now one of Canada's wealthiest inner-city neighbourhoods. These are followed by such other areas as Moore Park, Lawrence Park and North Toronto, all comfortably upper-middle class.

Just past Yorkville's end at Davenport Road is the large Masonic Temple, which replaced the one at Gloucester Mews and was renovated in the mid-1900s to serve as a venue for concerts. It now is home to Open Mike with Mike Bullard, easily Canada's favourite late night talk show host (call 416 934-4737 for free tickets). Opposite is the original flagship Canadian Tire store (839), looking pretty modest by today's standards, despite having been spruced up recently. Here, too, are Ridpath's (906), for *Architectural Digest*-class furnishings, and Petit Pied and Bon Lieu (890) for kids shoes and clothes straight from the pages of Paris *Vogue*. Having passed these, you are already at the Rosedale subway stop, which seems more like the suburban

FORMER MASONIC TEMPLE

INDIGO ON YONGE

THE ROSEDALE DINER

ANTIQUES

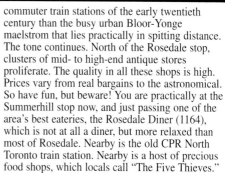

commuter train stations of the early twentieth century than the busy urban Bloor-Yonge maelstrom that lies practically in spitting distance. The tone continues. North of the Rosedale stop, clusters of mid- to high-end antique stores proliferate. The quality in all these shops is high. Prices vary from real bargains to the astronomical. So have fun, but beware! You are practically at the Summerhill stop now, and just passing one of the area's best eateries, the Rosedale Diner (1164), which is not at all a diner, but more relaxed than most of Rosedale. Nearby is the old CPR North Toronto train station. Nearby is a host of precious food shops, which locals call "The Five Thieves." Here, for a price, you can find such rarities as fresh gooseberries, red and black currents, figs, raspberries and blackberries year-round. There are bakeries and butchers and, opposite the thieves, two kitchen suppliers, Embros (1170) and Word of Mouth (1134), whose wares will enable all these delicacies to be properly prepared and presented. And if cooking isn't what you have in mind, but eating is, there are more restaurants still, before you reach St. Clair.

ST. CLAIR AND NORTH

Just north of St. Clair is Delisle, said to have one of the best wine cellars in the world, with food that almost matches.

It is a long hike from here up to Davisville, and despite the large number of high-rises right near that subway stop, it is the area to the north, just below and above Eglinton Avenue, that has become a nighttime hang-out for the well-heeled single and yuppie set. So much so that the intersection has become known as "Young and Eligible". Here you will find numerous small and mid-sized bars and pubs, and such draws as Indigo Books, Music and Cafe, and two large multi-theatre first-run cinemas, Canada Square and SilverCity. Just to the north is the old neighbourhood shopping district that has long served North Toronto, and is now a mecca for fine dining, mainly of a Cal-Ital nature, or some modest variation on that theme.

This area has a number of chain stores such as the Gap, Club Monaco and the Body Shop, but it also offers several stores that are unique. Perhaps the biggest draw (police are hired to direct traffic on busy weekends) is Sporting Life, which offers a wide selection of sports equipment and casual wear for the whole family. Also scattered along this stretch of Yonge is a large number of excellent children's clothing stores.

CABBAGETOWN

Cabbagetown most likely acquired its name in the late nineteenth century because Irish residents in the area often planted cabbages in their front gardens. Today, it is an affluent mid-town neighbourhood chockablock with almost every style of Victorian house imaginable. The area is worth a visit just for a look at its well-tended streets and gardens. But it has other attractions as well. On a fine day, you can picnic in Riverdale Park or take youngsters for a visit to the nearby Riverdale Farm. The quiet, well-treed St. James Cemetery, the charming St. James-the-Less Chapel, and the picturesque buildings of the Necropolis also offer interesting sights to explore. Finally, the Palm House at Allan Gardens, a

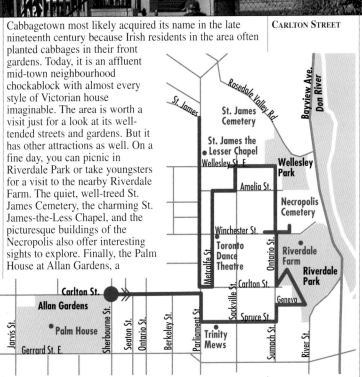

CARLTON STREET

glittering greenhouse on the edge of Cabbagetown, is worth a visit, especially if the day is grey, for its lush array of ferns, palms, and blooms.

A VICTORIAN NEIGHBOURHOOD

Start your tour at Sherbourne and Carlton at the edge of Cabbagetown. Set amidst a 13-acre park known as Allan Gardens, half of which was a gift from local politician George Allan, is a fanciful glass dome, the Palm House, connected to six small greenhouses. Contained within are an array of horticultural exhibits gleaned from the far-flung empire of Victorian times and beyond: a little swamp composed of Egyptian papyrus, Japanese sweet flag and Ontario pond weed, or a thick jungle with silver thatch palm from Trinidad, screw pine from Madagascar and poinsettias from Mexico. In short, a lovely glassed-in cabinet full of assorted collections and curiosities. Serious but extravagantly eclectic, this is a good place to get in the mood for a stroll through the rest of the neighbourhood.

TOP: ALLAN GARDENS
ABOVE: HOMES IN CABBAGETOWN

ALLAN GARDENS GREENHOUSE

THE HEART OF CABBAGETOWN

Head east on Carlton until you reach Parliament and then walk south to Spruce Street. The suggested walking route winds through the residential heart of Cabbagetown, providing a good sampling of the area's varied Victorian character. On the south side of Spruce Street just west of Sackville Street stands Trinity Mews, which incorporates the large, red-and-yellow brick, rehabilitated Trinity College Medical School, a remnant of the days when Toronto's General Hospital was located in the area. The former Ontario Medical College for Women stands a block south at 289 Sumach Street, now serving as a condo. East of Sackville on the north side are the Spruce Court Apartments, Toronto's first government-sponsored housing project, which was built in the Garden City fashion advocated by urban planners of the day and which is now a nonprofit co-op. Turn north on Sumach and head east along Geneva Street. For its entire length, this admittedly short

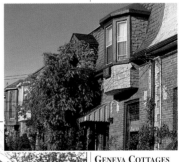

street is lined with totally intact working-class cottages in what is known as the "Alpha-style." You will now have reached Riverdale Park. The park spans the Don Valley, and this vantage offers a sweeping view of Riverdale, the community edging its eastern side.

Turn north alongside the park for a short walk to Riverdale Farm (p. 114), or head back to Sumach either by taking brick-paved Carlton Street or by cutting diagonally across the park. This portion of Riverdale Park (which has a wading pool, by the way) is the site of two high-quality craft fairs, one in spring and one in fall. At the corner of Winchester Street and Sumach is a sometime tea shop of ye olde variety where you may wish to pause for refreshments. Take a brief detour down to 156 Winchester, parts of which were built in 1830, making it one of the oldest homes in the area. It was originally the residence of Alderman Daniel Lamb, remembered today primarily as the founder of the Riverdale Zoo (now Farm). North of the park are the highly picturesque chapel, gate and gatehouse of the Necropolis Cemetery. This nonsectarian "city of the dead" is the final resting place of many of Toronto's early pioneers. Among them are the city's first mayor, William Lyon Mackenzie; Samuel Lount and Peter Matthews, both hanged for their

CARLTON STREET

GENEVA COTTAGES (ABOVE)

37 METCALFE STREET

RIVERDALE FARM

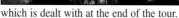

part in Mackenzie's 1837 rebellion; George Brown, a father of Confederation and the founder of the *Globe and Mail*; John Ross Robertson, founder of the rival *Toronto Telegram*; and Ned Hanlan, world-famous sculler. At the northern boundary of Cabbagetown is St. James Cemetery, which is dealt with at the end of the tour.

MODEST COTTAGES AND GRAND HOUSES

Continuing up Sumach and east on Amelia Street, along the edge of the Necropolis, will take you to Wellesley Park, which serves as the front yard for a number of homes. Walk north through the park, then turn west on Wellesley Street. Just past Sackville is a street sign for the Wellesley Cottages. Now a rarity, cheap housing of wood lath and stucco once was common. These cottages, all extensively and expensively renovated, retain their simple, almost rural look. Always a delight to visit, they are a special treat in mid-spring, when lilacs in their dooryards bloom. Zigzag your way south, taking in portions of Sackville, Amelia,

CHAPEL OF THE NECROPOLIS CEMETERY

Metcalfe, Winchester and Carlton Streets. At Winchester

NECROPOLIS CEMETARY GATE

and Metcalfe stands the Toronto Dance Theatre, originally a Romanesque church and one of the few nonresidential buildings in the area. Winchester was once a major thoroughfare, leading to a bridge across the Don River. Further down at 37 Metcalfe is another of the area's few really large homes, this one a rambling Italianate villa that once stood on substantial grounds but now is hemmed in tightly by its neighbours. And a real oddity, the only house like it in all Toronto, is the Shields house, at 377 Sackville. Originally a standard brick-and-frame structure, Shields decided to face it with stone. Additional atypically large homes are found along Carlton.

Once back on Parliament, head north. Opposite the high-rise enclave of Jamestown stand St. James Cemetery and St. James-the-Less Chapel. Suggestive of a thirteenth-century English parish church, the chapel is widely considered to be one of the most beautiful church buildings in Canada. Like the Necropolis, St. James is the resting place of many leading founders of Toronto and their families, among them the Gooderhams, Jarvises, Howlands and Mannings. Also of note here are the abundant funereal statuary and large mausoleums.

WELLESLEY COTTAGES

THE SHIELDS HOUSE (LEFT)
PROVENCE BISTRO (BELOW)

197

THE BEACHES

THE BEACH

The Beaches, just 20 minutes from downtown, is a distinctively relaxed community offering a range of recreational, entertainment, shopping and dining opportunities. About 100 years ago, a whole string of separate amusement parks and pleasure gardens stretched along the lake between Woodbine and Victoria Park Avenues. At that time, the area was a destination for city residents looking for a pleasant place to while away a

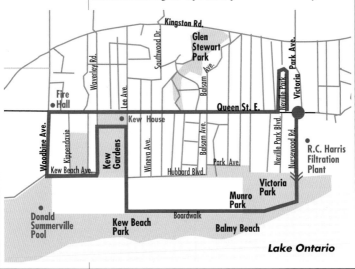

balmy Sunday. Each amusement park occupied a different site on the beach and often incorporated the word beach in its name. Hence, the origin of "the Beaches" or as some residents like to call the area, "the Beach."

Today, the neighbourhood still draws large numbers of visitors and offers a variety of enjoyable activities. Queen Street, the neighbourhood's spine, is lined with small boutiques and cafés, making it a favourite destination for shoppers. The beach that stretches along the area's southern edge is sandy and clean, the boardwalk that runs its length is well shaded, making a stroll comfortable on even the hottest days. There are sailboards for rent, numerous playgrounds, tennis courts and bowling greens. The residential areas between the lake and Queen Street (and north of Queen, as well) consist of tree-lined, shady streets with a variety of homes, some the winterized cottages of the summer resorts of long ago, many more that are substantial, often in the Arts and Crafts style.

R.C. HARRIS WATER FILTRATION PLANT

A DAY AT THE BEACH

Begin your tour by driving or taking the Queen streetcar to its eastern terminus at Neville Park Boulevard (the Neville "loop"). From there, walk up the hill, past Nursewood Road to the foot of Victoria Park Avenue and southward on the grounds of the city's water filtration plant for a fabulous view of the lake. To your east, you can see the Scarborough Bluffs, 350-foot-high deposits that consisted first of silt from when Lake Ontario was far larger than it is today, and then of boulders, clay and sand dragged back and forth by retreating and advancing glaciers. From 1879 to 1921, this was the site of Victoria Park, the most easterly of the amusement parks. In the 1930s, the city expropriated the park to build Public Works Commissioner Rowland Harris's dream of Byzantium, now called prosaically the R.C. Harris Water Filtration Plant. Looking like something only Cecil B. de Mille could concoct, it is one

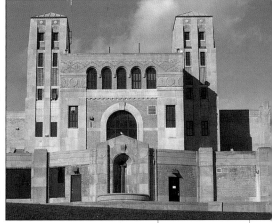

GAZEBO IN KEW GARDENS

of the last of the city's truly elegant works of public engineering, a palace to clean water for millions: floors of rose-coloured marble, brass fittings everywhere, tiles from Sienna, art-deco clocks — the works. The plant is frequently featured in films, ads and music videos, and – more importantly – played a prominent role in Michael Ondaatje's *In the Skin of a Lion*, which recently was selected as *the* book all Canadians should read. Tours were temporarily suspended in the wake of September 11th, but may resume. Check at 416 392-3566.

From here, wander down to the comfortably bouncy, well-shaded boardwalk, a favourite with Torontonians of all ages. Some remnants of the long gone amusement parks remain, but they are insufficient to give a sense of their scale or popularity. West of Victoria Park was Munro Amusement Park. Built by the street railway company, it was known as the "trolley park." Owing to a dispute between the railway company and the Munro family over rent, it only lasted four seasons. Still further west was Balmy Beach, the gift of a former mayor of the Town of East Toronto. It became the home of the Balmy Beach Canoe Club, whose favourite son, Roy Nurse, won three gold medals in the 1924 Paris Olympics. Part of the boathouse still stands, most of it used as a snack bar. Next came Scarboro Beach Amusement Park, the biggest of them all. It, too, was built by the street railway company and thrived from 1907 to 1925. Here, a Coney Island atmosphere prevailed.

And finally, there was — and still is — Kew Gardens, the brainchild of Joseph and Jane Williams, who, from the time they arrived to farm in the area in 1853, saved for the day when they could turn their 20-acre spread into a pleasure garden. In true British fashion, they opened Kew on Queen Victoria's sixtieth birthday. From 1879 until 1907, the Williams ran what today might be called a family camp. Jane and Joseph's son, also named Kew, built himself a fine house at 30 Lee Avenue and was left only with that house when the city expropriated Kew Gardens for parkland. The house is now used by the park's caretaker.

BEACHES BOARDWALK

Also still standing are the old Kew Beach Park Boat House and the recently restored Leuty Lifesaving Station. The lovely gazebo toward the northern end of Kew Gardens is used for free concerts throughout the summer, and is the focal point for Toronto's annual Beaches Jazz Festival, held in July.

KEW WILLIAMS HOUSE AT 30 LEE AVENUE

The boardwalk and adjacent bike path, the Martin Goodman Trail, continue westward across Woodbine Avenue to Ashbridge's Bay. Until the end of the twentieth century, Woodbine was the clearly defined western terminus of the neighbourhood — the area to the west being taken up by Woodbine (later called Greenwood) Racetrack. The track closed in the 1990s, however, a large community, somewhat arrogantly calling itself "the Beach" is being constructed on the site. A significant portion of the new development consists of parkland that will help green the lakefront and add to its recreational use. Although not yet complete, the new development is boosting commercial interest on Queen Street to the west of the Beaches in the area known as Leslieville.

HOUSES ALONG KEW BEACH

Between Kippendale Avenue and Woodbine stands the Donald Summerville Pool, an elephantine structure that overlooks the lake and actually houses three pools on its roof: a diving pool with about eight boards of varying heights, an Olympic-size lap pool and a smaller children's pool. There is only a modest charge for using the pools, and lockers are available. At Woodbine head north to Queen Street.

Were there no distractions, you could walk the length of Queen Street from Woodbine back to Neville in less than half an hour. The unique feel of the neighbourhood, that of a small town that caters to summer residents, makes this impossible. One of the clues to the area's sensibility is the number of stores employing puns in their names, from The Chopping Block (a butcher), to Soap Operas (a Laundromat) to The Grabbajabba (a coffee house.) In fact,

the number of coffee houses is remarkable. In addition to the many local one-off businesses, there are two Second Cups, Toronto's answer to Starbucks, of which there also are two. Sushi places abound, of which Aakane-Ya Japan (2214, reservations a must 416 699-0377) is by far the best. A reasonably-priced and tasty brunch is available from any of at least a dozen restaurants of which Sunset Grill (2006) and the Beacher Café (2162) are longstanding favourites. Italian restaurants are almost as numerous, the two best are to be found at either end of the area: Antoinette (2455 $^1/_2$, 416 698-1300) at the far east end, right next door to the fantastic Belgian Chocolate Shop, and somewhat west of the neighbourhood's traditional Woodbine boundary at Kingston Road, Gio Rana's Really, Really Nice Restaurant (1220, 416 469-5225). In between these are also numerous pubs, of which both Quigley's (2232, 416 699-9998) and Lion on the Beach (1958, 416 690-1984) offer music along with good brew and standard pub fare. Sprinkled throughout the neighbourhood is an

QUEEN STREET IN THE BEACHES

unusually large number of shops catering specifically to children: for haircuts (Little Tots Hair Shop), shoes (Children, Sneaky Kids) clothing (Jolly Tots) and furniture (Latitude for Living). There is even a Baskin and Robbins, although adults probably will prefer Licks (1960), a deservedly popular ice cream and hamburger emporium.

LITTLE ITALY, GREEKTOWN, INDIA BAZAAR AND THE KOREAN BUSINESS AREA

SHOPS IN LITTLE ITALY

Little Italy, Greektown, the India Bazaar, and now the "Korean Business Area" are four lively destinations, all only slightly off the beaten track. While you won't find the top tourist attractions in any of them, these neighbourhoods are nonetheless interesting places to explore, especially when you want to combine a good meal with a bit of browsing or shopping.

LITTLE ITALY

Little Italy, which is about 15 minutes west of Yonge Street on the College streetcar (506), stretches along College Street from just west of Bathurst almost to Ossington. Its heart, however, lies between Euclid and Shaw. Here the streetlights are festooned with lights in the shape of the boot of Italy, and the air is perfumed with garlic, basil, and a hint of espresso. Once the heart of Toronto's 415,000-plus Italian community, it is now the southernmost shopping and residential district of that community, which has moved north.

It never has been the Italy of the Via Venuto or the Pontevecchio, but rather the slightly provincial street of a nondescript Mediterranean city, a mélange of Italian with a dollop of Portuguese. Until very recently, stores like Rimini Family Clothing nudged Napoli Family Clothing, which jostled Firenze Clothing; these contained not the clothing of Milan's runways and *Vogue*, but the little black

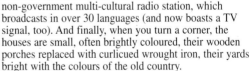

boots of working-class Europeans' children, the black garb of widows, the frilly dresses of young girls.

In just a few short years, this has largely changed. Gone or pushed further west are most of the old clothiers — replaced by a smattering of their Generation X counterparts — and many of the groceries that made the street bright with bell peppers, aubergines and oranges. Today the area seems devoted predominantly to ready-to-eat gastronomy, and increasingly is lined with restaurants, bars, bistros and clubs. While few are four-star eateries, most serve high-quality food in a comfortable setting at moderate to the low end of high prices ($90 to $160 for a complete dinner for two including a glass of wine each).

Although dining is the main object, there are a few shops worth a look. At 508 Bathurst, literally a few steps north of College, is Downeast a gift shop and gallery stocked entirely with the work – mostly folk art – of Atlantic and maritime Canadians. Lilliput Hats (462 College) is a custom millenary, Ewanika (490) carries custom clothes for professional women and Mink (550) custom jewellery ranging from subtle to delightfully gaudy. Peering into Motoretta (554), with its scooters "authentic and true" takes you straight to the Italy of "Three Coins in a Fountain." And while on the subject of water, have a look at Splish Splash (590), a combination convenience store, toy store and Laundromat. If words are your thing, you can browse for hours at the very fine, secondhand Balfour Books (601). Word lovers also will get a kick out of Fratelli Porco, an excellent, very Italian grocery and butcher, bountifully stocked with fresh and dried pastas great rounds of cheeses and — a special treat for Americans — prosciutto, which is owned by the aptly named "Pork Brothers." In evidence, too, are a smattering of old men's clubs, filled with smoke, talk and caffeine and the fabulous baked goods of the long popular Riviera Bakery (576). Also still here is CHIN, the world's first non-government multi-cultural radio station, which broadcasts in over 30 languages (and now boasts a TV signal, too). And finally, when you turn a corner, the houses are small, often brightly coloured, their wooden porches replaced with curlicued wrought iron, their yards bright with the colours of the old country.

BAKED GOODS AT THE RIVIERA

In the dining department it is hard to go radically wrong. For fairly traditional Italian fare in a comfy setting, there is Gamelle (468), Trattoria Giancarlo (around the corner at 41 Clinton) Grappa (797) and with the added advantage of being surprisingly inexpensive as well as excellent, Tavola Caldo (671). Also excellent, a bit more pricey and almost at Ossington is Café Societa (796). Less comfy and more limited is the delightful Café Diplomatico (594), which for more than 30 years has drawn customers from across the city to enjoy the great Italian tradition of mating espresso with a quick drink, a small bite, an Italian ice or other dessert. Pizza lovers will enjoy Giovanna

(637), which serves other robust fare as well, or for the thin-crust variety, John's Classic Pizza (591).

Another oldtimer, but completely revamped in a minimalist style to attract a younger crowd is Bar Italia (582). The more adventurous might try the Airport Lounge (492) – fusion cooking with a Japanese emphasis in a psychedelic setting. Weird but very good. In a similar vein, but with a more Italian slant and down-to-earth setting is Pony (488). Moving even further from Italian fare is the beautiful and ultra-chic Xacutti (503), where the Caribbean tastefully meets southeast Asia, and Brasserie Aix, which became *the* in place the moment it opened in 2001 even though its French fare does not always match its high price or reputation. Purely Caribbean and very cheap jerk can be had at Irie (808).

Portuguese favourites can be had Chiado (864), Sintra (588), which is a better deal at lunch, and further west at Piri-Piri Churrasqueira (928) or Cataplana (938). If your taste runs to the hotter aspects of Latin culture, you could try a Sunday evening tango lesson at Mania Bar and Lounge (722) or the 1:30 a.m. Saturday night drag show at El Convento Rico (750).

GREEKTOWN

Toronto's first Greek restaurant opened on Danforth Avenue in 1900. Along this street, and in the surrounding neighbourhood, immigrant Greeks settled in large numbers during the post–World War II era. Some of their early shops, the Athens Meat Market (which dates from 1951), Seven Stars Bakery and Hermes House of

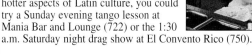

Bomboniere among them, continue to flourish. In the late 1960s and 1970s the souvlaki outlets and homey restaurants began to attract non-Greek Torontonians. It was exotic to stand over steam tables, point at unknown dishes and have them brought to your table. They were also cheap, cheap, cheap!

Today, the surrounding neighbourhood has changed, many of the Greeks having moved north and east; it is now a sort of off-beat yuppie enclave, filled with media types, editors, writers, musicians and artists (not your starving variety; these come with mortgages, kids and Volvos). But the Danforth, especially between Chester and Pape Avenues, remains exuberantly Greek. Since about 1988, it has seemed as though a new restaurant has opened every month. In the summer especially, the sidewalks are teeming with diners until all hours (the restaurants are open late and often are not crowded much before 9:30 p.m.), and whenever the weather is warm, doors and windows are flung open, the relaxed but always talkative customers adding to the festive street life.

For one weekend in early August, Taste of the Danforth, a festival of food, allows you to sample restauranteurs' wares before selecting the eatery at which you want to stop. Gone, though, are the steam tables with their admittedly overcooked and greasy offerings. It is evident, even in traditional dishes, these second- and third-generation Greeks have learned all the tricks of light cooking using fresh ingredients. And now that they're vying with each other for exotically designed spaces, the area has become a feast for the eye, as well as the ear and the palate. And if it no longer is cheap, cheap, cheap, most places still are relatively moderate in price ($55 to $75 for a complete meal for two, including wine).

On the long-established side, there is the casual Omonia (426), which has been serving lamb cooked on a spit and such familiar Greek specialties as calamari, tsasiki, moussaka and spanakopita since 1978, Pappas (440), a favourite with families, or the even older Astoria Shish Kebob House (390). Newer, more expensive and far fancier, but still traditional, are Myth (417), Nefeli (407) and Mezes (456). If you desire more innovative cuisine, there is the colourful little Pan on the Danforth (516), where standard dishes like lamb are inventively sauced or spiced. For partying there is Ouzeri (500A), which is a pioneer of the haute-moderne Greek cuisine having opened way back in 1990.

On the quieter side decoratively and acoustically, there is Avli (401) or Soda (425). For dessert, there is Demetre (400) or the cafeteria-like Iliada (550). Also, there are a number of very good non-Greek restaurants. Sher-E-Punjab, newly renovated in a sophisticated Indo-European manner, is justifiably considered one of Toronto's top Indian eateries. Mocha Mocha (489) is a neighbourhood favourite for lunch, as are the Auld Spot (347) for fine pub fare, Dora Keogh's (141), mainly for the many beers and Allen's (143), a New York–style bar with great burgers, beer, fries and desserts that sports one of Toronto's nicest outdoor patios at the rear.

As well, there are a growing number of shops of interest. Just east of Broadview is a pet emporium offering unusual treats for you to bring back to your stay-at-home furry friends and Another Story, a unique outlet for books for all ages on politics and social issues. Further east are Treasure Island for toys, Romancing the Home, Alchemy, Blue Moon, Lily Lee, Robin Kay, and a growing number of others for both imported and locally designed clothing, jewellery and items for the home. There are two outlets that provide household necessities for the environmentally conscious. The more clothing-oriented of these is housed in Carrot Common, a mini-mall that also has a health-food supermarket, a Japanese restaurant and a number of the many kids' clothing shops along the Danforth.

Starting in 1996, Greektown became a destination for tour buses done up as fake trolleys. The neighbourhood is also easy to reach via the Bloor subway line, at Broadview, Chester and Pape subway stops.

INDIA BAZAAR

The commercial heart of Toronto's much smaller East Indian community is located in the east end, along Gerrard Street East near Hiawatha Road, about 20-25 minutes east of Yonge on the College streetcar (506). Here, the street is permeated with the pungent scent of incense and an array of spices. The area comes alive during India's major festivals: for Muslims, the end of Ramadan (Id Ul-Ftir) in late winter or early spring; for Hindus, the celebration of spring (Holi) and of lights (Diwali) just before the winter solstice. On summer weekends, street vendors sell spicy roasted corn, fresh off the grill. If you enjoy Indian cooking but can't find black mustard seeds, dried tamarind or black cardamom pods, bring a shopping list to any of the host of grocery stores! Or stop into

Nucreation Fashions, Maharani Fashions, or one of the many other outlets selling truly beautiful silks and saris, "Punjabi suits and fancy Duppatas."

While the very best of Indian cuisine is elsewhere, nowhere else in the city offers so much variety, so strong a sense of India's varied regions and cultures. In addition, in this area you will find meals that ranges from very good to excellent at extremely modest prices ($20 to $30 for complete dinners for two, including a glass of wine or, more appropriately, a beer) in what might be charitably be described as modest settings. Best among these are Bar-Be-Que Hut (1455), which specializes in tandoor and grilled meat dishes and on weekend evenings provides musical entertainment; Madras Durbar (1435), with its savoury, southern, "pure vegetarian" fare, such as masala dosai, a huge, crêpe-like affair made from a blend of lentil and white rice flour, filled to bursting with turmeric-covered potato (Do not confuse this with the similarly named restaurant at 1386); and the newer Udupi Palace (1460), another vegetarian spot, that is also excellent and offers a wider selection. Surprisingly, the latter is a chain, with outlets in far flung Indian centres like Sunnyvale and Livermore, California. For meat-eaters, there is Lahore Tikka near Highfield, which in terms of décor, price and service seems the Indian equivalent of

SCENES FROM THE
KOREAN BUSINESS
DISTRICT

a fast-food, drive-in, but is nothing like it in terms of taste. Try such northern delicacies as samosas and meat kebabs or superb tikkas on a variety of breads.

KOREAN BUSINESS AREA

The name is not a sexy one, but certainly is apt. Although only five short blocks between Palmerston Boulevard and Christie Street, virtually every floor of every building along this strip of Bloor Street contains Korean businesses – everything from banks and pharmacies to hairdressers and photographers – some 25 of which are restaurants, tea houses or bars. Unless you speak Korean, however, the only really interesting shop is the Korean Central Market (675), a sort of low budget department store filled to overflowing with household items, many not carried in your typical hardware or kitchen store.

At the "higher" ($60 for dinner, including a drink), fancier end of the dining scale are Sejong (658), Korea House (666) and Korean Village Han Kuk Kwan (628). All offer traditional Korean dishes, which are often built around stews or soups that use or are accompanied by kimchi – a variety of vegetables that are pickled or fermented using red peppers, garlic, green onion, radishes and other spicy seasonings. Bar-be-que is another Korean staple, although in some restaurants, you will find that this meat, too, has been stewed rather than grilled. Korean food can be very, very hot; if you are not accustomed to extreme spiciness, be sure to ask about the

temperature when ordering. On the "low" end – as low as $4 for a main dish! – there is Um Ji Bun Sik (615), Seoul Restaurant (621), Happy House (623), Monay House (665), Bak Chong Dong Soon To Fu (691). At all of these, most of the dishes are do-it-yourself. That is, the ingredients are placed in a pan at your table, and you are in charge of cooking and serving. All these spots are very crowded at supper, which seems to be a bit earlier than in many other cultures. Of these spots, the best is Joon's Korean Cuisine (605). Although priced similarly and offering roughly the same menu, Joon's cafeteria style decor is somehow warmer, friendlier, better thought out and, yes, cleaner. For dessert try the walnut cakes at Hodo Kwaja (656) or Walnut Cake and Coffee (680). These are little walnut-shaped pastries stuffed with a variety of nut or bean pastes — walnut being the most common.

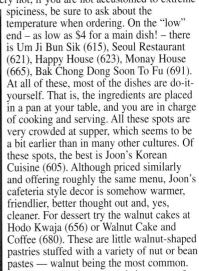
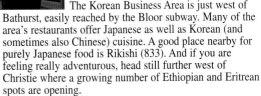

The Korean Business Area is just west of Bathurst, easily reached by the Bloor subway. Many of the area's restaurants offer Japanese as well as Korean (and sometimes also Chinese) cuisine. A good place nearby for purely Japanese food is Rikishi (833). And if you are feeling really adventurous, head still further west of Christie where a growing number of Ethiopian and Eritrean spots are opening.

Contents

GETTING THERE

Set on the northwestern shore of Lake Ontario, and located farther south than Minnesota and much of Michigan, Metropolitan Toronto is one of the most accessible cities in North America by highway, air, rail and water.

BY AIR

- Lester B. Pearson International Airport: Located in the northwestern corner of Metro Toronto, the airport is accessible from highways 401, 427 and 409. Trillium Terminal (Terminal 3) serves Air France, Air Transat, American Airlines, British Airways, BWIA International, Canjet, Cathay Pacific Airways, Cubana, Delta, EL AL, Jetsgo, KLM, Korean Airlines, Northwest, Olympic, Pem-Air, QANTAS, Royal Airlines, TWA, US Air and others. For information call 416 776-5100. Terminal 2 serves Air Canada (domestic and U.S. flights), Tango, United Airlines, Westjet, and others. Terminal 1 serves Air Canada (international flights), Air Ontario, Alitalia, All Nippon Airways, American Trans Air, and others. Some thirty-five major airlines offer regularly scheduled flights. For information on Terminals 1 and 2 call 416 247-7678.
- Toronto City Centre Airport: Located on the western tip of a series of islands in Toronto Harbour, this island airport handles scheduled, private and corporate flights. The airport serves Air Ontario. For information call 416 203-6942.

BY ROAD

Whether approaching Toronto by car or by bus, the traveller will reach Toronto by one of several major routes paralleling the shore of Lake Ontario. Highways 401 and 2, and the Queen Elizabeth Way, enter Toronto from the west. Highways 401 and 2 also enter Toronto from the east. Hwy. 400 runs from the north and connects with Hwy. 401. Major bus routes converge in Toronto. Out-of-town buses arrive and depart from the Toronto Coach Terminal, located at 610 Bay St. Service to points all over Ontario and Canada is frequent and fast. National and regional bus lines serve Metro Toronto. Call 416 393-7911 for bus company fares and schedules.

BY RAIL

Toronto is served by the VIA Rail Canada System, the network that provides all rail service throughout Canada (with connections to the Amtrak system through Niagara Falls, New York). Union Station is located on Front Street, between Bay and University (across the street from the Royal York Hotel). The station is right on Toronto's subway line, and is within walking distance of SkyDome, the CN Tower, the financial district and many downtown hotels, shops and restaurants. Call 1-800-361-1235 or 416 366-8411.

TRAVEL ESSENTIALS

MONEY

Currency can be exchanged at any Toronto bank at the prevailing rate. If you use a small local branch, it's best to call ahead to confirm their capacity to exchange, on the spot, any currency other than American funds. There are currency exchange booths at the airport, and at many of Ontario's Travel Information Centres near the U.S./Canada border. Ontario Travel Information Centres can exchange Canadian dollars for most major international currencies, and vice versa. If you wish to exchange a large amount, or to exchange a less common currency, telephone ahead to ensure the centre can serve you. Units of currency are similar to those of the United States, excepting the Canadian one-dollar (loonie) and two-dollar (toonie) coins.

Most major North American credit cards and traveller's cheques are welcome in Toronto, including American Express, Carte Blanche, Diners Club, EnRoute, MasterCard and Visa. Many stores and services will accept U.S. currency, but the exchange rate they offer may vary greatly. Since there are no laws enforcing foreign currency rates of exchange, we strongly recommend that you convert to Canadian funds before you make your purchases.

American visitors may also use bank or credit cards to make cash withdrawals from automated teller machines that are tied into international networks such as Cirrus and Plus. Before you leave home, check with your bank to find out what range of banking services its cards will allow you to use.

PASSPORTS
American visitors may be asked to verify their citizenship with a document such as a passport, or a birth or baptismal certificate. Naturalized U.S. citizens should carry a naturalization certificate. Permanent U.S. residents who are not citizens are advised to bring their Alien Registration Receipt Card. Citizens of all other countries, except Greenland and residents of St.-Pierre et Miquelon, must bring a valid passport. Some may be required to obtain a visitor's visa. For details, please consult the Canadian embassy or consulate serving your home country.

CUSTOMS
Arriving
As a nonresident of Canada, you may bring in any reasonable amount of personal effects and food, and a full tank of gas. Special restrictions or quotas apply to certain specialty goods, and especially to plant-, agricultural- and animal-related materials. All items must be declared to Customs upon arrival and may include up to 200 cigarettes, 50 cigars, 200 grams of manufactured tobacco, and 200 tobacco sticks. Visitors are also permitted 1.14 litres (40 oz) of liquor, 1.5 litres (50 oz) of wine, or 8.5 litres (24 x 12-oz cans or bottles) of beer.

You may bring in gifts for Canadian residents duty-free, up to a value of $60.00 (Canadian) each, provided they do not consist of alcohol, tobacco, or advertising material. For more detailed information, please see the federal Customs (Revenue Canada) website (www.rc.gc.ca), the Customs information booklet "I DECLARE," or contact Revenue Canada, Customs/Border Services Office,

#303, 6725 Airport Rd., PO Box 6000, Mississauga ON L4V 1V2, 905 676-2853. In Toronto, call 416 973-8022 (weekdays) or 416 676-3643 (weekdays and holidays).

Departing
For detailed customs rules for entering or re-entering the United States, please contact a U.S. Customs office before you visit Toronto. Copies of the U.S. Customs information brochure "Know Before You Go" are available from U.S. Customs offices or by mail. You can also call the U.S. Customs office in Toronto at 905 676-2606. Travellers from other countries should also check on customs regulations before leaving home.

TAXES
Goods and Services Tax (GST)
The federal Goods and Services Tax is 7%. This is a value-added consumption tax that applies to most goods, purchased gifts, food/beverages and services, including most hotel and motel accommodation.
Provincial Sales Tax (PST)
The Ontario provincial sales tax is 8% on any goods you buy, but not on services or accommodation.
Room Tax
A 5% provincial tax (in place of PST) is added to most tourist accommodation charges, as well as the 7% GST.
Food Service
In restaurants, 7% GST and 8% PST will be added to the food portion of your final bill, as well as a 10% provincial tax on alcoholic beverages (in addition to the 7% GST).

GUIDES AND INFORMATION SERVICES
Toronto offers docking facilities and complete services for boaters. For information on harbour facilities, call the Toronto Harbour Commission at 416 863-2000.

- Transport Canada Airport Information: Located in Terminals 1 and 2 of Pearson. Multilingual information available on the airport, flights and tourist attractions. Call 905 676-3506.
- The City of Toronto: Toronto City

Hall, 100 Queen Street W., Toronto ON M5H 2N2; call Access Toronto at 416 338-0338.

- Tourism Toronto: Queen's Quay Terminal at Harbourfront, Ste. 590, 207 Queens Quay W., Toronto ON M5J 1A7; 416 203-500, 1-800-363-1990; www.tourism-toronto.com
- Visitor Information Ontario: For comprehensive travel information about the Province of Ontario (including Toronto), visit the Ontario Ministry of Tourism's Travel Centre in The Eaton Centre; or call 1-800-ONTARIO (English), 1-800-268-3736 (French). In Toronto, call: 416 314-0944 (English), 416 314-0956 (French).

GETTING ACQUAINTED

TIME ZONE
Toronto falls within the Eastern Standard Time Zone.

CLIMATE
Here are average Toronto temperatures, highs and lows; fluctuations from the norm are common:

Jan.	30.1 °F to 18.1° F 4.1°C to -7.7°C
Feb.	31.5°F to 18.9°F -4.3°C to -7.3°C
March	39.5°F to 26.7°F 2.2°C to 2.9°C
April	53.4°F to 37.8°F 11.9°C to 3.2°C
May	64.3°F to 47.2°F 17.9°C to 8.4°C
June	75.6°F to 57.4°F 24.2°C to 14.1°C
July	80.3°F to 62.3°F 26.8°C to 16.1°C
August	78.7°F to 61.2°F 25.9°C to 16.2°C
Sept.	70.8°F to 54.2°F 21.6°C to 12.3°C
October	59.6°F to 44.8°F 15.3°C to 7.1°C
Nov.	46.1°F to 35.3°F 7.8°C to 1.8°C
Dec.	34.2°F to 23.4°F 1.2°C to -4.8°C

Average annual rainfall: 27.25_/68.9 cm.
Average annual snowfall: 53.2_/135 cm.
Average temperatures are +7.4°C (45.3°F) in spring, +20.7°C (69.3°F) in summer, +10.8°C (51.4°F) in autumn, and -3.3°C (26.1°F) in winter.

GETTING AROUND

TRAVELLING IN TORONTO
Metro Toronto is laid out in a grid pattern of major north-south and east-west arteries. Streets not on the grid follow natural features such as ravines and escarpments. The following expressways provide access to the city from the major highways: the Don Valley Parkway, the Gardiner Expressway, and the Allen Expressway. If you're a member of any recognized auto club affiliates (AAA, CAA, etc.), the CAA Toronto at 461 Yonge St., 416 221-4300, will provide all club services. Head Office 905 771-3111.

Public Transportation
Toronto's clean, safe and efficient public-transit is operated by the TTC (Toronto Transit Commission), and consists of over 4,000 kilometres of subway, bus, RT and streetcar routes. Many of the principal downtown bus and streetcar routes, including those which run along Queen, College, St. Clair and Eglinton, operate 24 hours a day. Night bus service is also available along Yonge and Bloor streets and Danforth Avenue. Exact fares are required and day passes are available. For information on subway, streetcar and bus routes, schedules and fares, call Customer Information at 416 393-4636 (7 am-10 pm).

GO Transit
Regular GO Bus and Train service to Oshawa, Hamilton, Georgetown, Brampton, Milton, Newmarket, Richmond Hill, as well as limited service to Barrie, Guelph, Sutton and Uxbridge. Call 416 869-3200 for more information.

Ferry Boats to the Toronto Islands are operated by the City of Toronto Parks and Recreation Dept., Island and Ferry division. They leave from the foot of Bay street on a regular basis. Call 416 392-8193 for schedules and rates.

By Car

A valid driver's license from any country is good in Ontario for three months. Evidence of a car's registration is required (a car-rental contract will also serve). If you are driving into Ontario or importing a vehicle, bring with you its registration documents, and either a Canadian Non-Resident Motor Vehicle Liability Insurance Card (obtained from your insurance agent), or else the insurance policy itself. If you're driving a rented car, bring a copy of the rental contract. Speed limits are measured in kilometres per hour and vary depending on the type of road, with 400-level controlled-access highways having the highest limit. Speed limits on most highways are 80 to 90 kph, and 100 kph on freeways. On city streets the normal speed is 50 kph unless otherwise posted. Seat belt use by passengers and drivers is mandatory in Toronto. One kilometre equals about 5/8 of a mile. To convert from kilometres to miles, multiply kilometres by 0.6. To convert from miles to kilometres, multiply miles by 1.6. Metric measurements are used for motor fuel. 1 litre equals about one-quarter of an American gallon, or about one-fifth of an Imperial gallon. A litre of gasoline costs between 70 and 80 cents a litre at time of publishing.

Car Rentals

Avis, 1-800-TRY-AVIS, downtown: 416 777-AVIS, www.avis.com; Discount Car Rentals, Yonge and Bloor, Charles Promenade, 730 Yonge Street: 416 921-1212; Dollar Rent-a-Car, downtown: 416 979-5678, airport: 905 676-1300; National Car Rental, 1-800-227-7368, www.nationcar.com; Thrifty Car Rental, Royal York Hotel: 416 947-1385; Consult the Yellow Pages for more agencies.

TOURS

- Scheduled sightseeing of Toronto and Niagara Falls. 184 Front St. E., #601; 416 594-3310.
- A Taste of the World — Neighbourhood. Unearth off-beat nooks and crannies of Toronto's ethnic neighbourhoods: Chinatown, Kensington Market, etc. 416 923-6813.
- All About Toronto. Step-on guide service, very professional, yet fun and exciting. 27 Clovercrest Rd., 416 495-8687.
- CU Tours Incorporated. Daily tours year-round of Niagara Falls. 610 Bawes Rd., #14, Concord ON L4J 4A4.; 905-660-6255 or 1-800-792-8877.
- Civitas Cultural Resource City Walk. Entertaining tours of historic areas of the places, people and events of Toronto. May 1 to end of October. 44 Walmer Rd., #305; 416 966-1550.
- East Toronto and Beach Area Tours. Historical and contemporary tours including Greektown and East India Village. 147 Lee Ave.; 416 691-5229.
- Haunted Toronto. Ghost walks throughout Toronto. 416 487-9017.
- Helicopter Company. Offers a bird's-eye view of Toronto. 416 203-3280.
- Lost World Tours. Their eco-friendly, personable approach gives you a unique view of Toronto. Here's your chance to visit the out-of-the-way places that other tourists never get to see! Your tour will be customized to your interests. Contact ottoreid@hotmail.com 416-947-0778 or 1-800-567-9753. www.lwt.ca
- National Helicopters Inc. Spectacular sightseeing rides featuring the Toronto Islands, CN Tower, SkyDome and Casa Loma. Operates May to September; 11339 Albion-Vaughan Rd., Kleinburg ON; 905-893-2727 or 1-888-361-1100
- Summer Walking Tours. The Heritage Toronto summer walking tour series offers a wide variety of walks exploring many areas and topics of Toronto. For more details call 416 338-3886 or visit www.heritagetoronto.org
- Tripmate Travel and Tour Guide Company. Experienced multilingual guides highlight the beauty, history and culture of Toronto and Niagara. 222 Spadina Ave.; 416 599-8892.

- Toronto Footsteps. Become a Torontonian for a day; smaller groups and families welcome. 416 483-5483.
- Unique Views. Dynamic, interactive and interesting tours of Toronto. 171 Parkside Drive, Unit 1; 416 531-7770.

BOAT AND YACHT TOURS

- Empress of Canada. Toronto's luxury yacht cruises around the Toronto Islands. 260 Queen's Quay W., #1408; 416 260-8901, Fax: 416 260-5547, www.spectranet.com/Empress.
- Great Lakes Schooner Company. See Toronto's skyline from the open deck of a tall ship. April to Oct. 249 Queens Quay W., #111; 416 260-6355, Fax: 416 260-6377, www.greatlakesschooner.com
- Jubilee Queen Cruises. Tour Toronto's harbour aboard a luxury 120-foot river showboat. April to Oct. 207 Queens Quay W., 416 203-7245, Fax: 416 203-7177.
- Klancy's Yacht Charters Incorporated. Cruise Lake Ontario aboard the Klancy II, one-hundred-passenger custom-designed yacht. 1001 - 480 Queen's Quay W.; 416 866-8489, www.klancycharters.com
- Mariposa Cruise Line Limited. One-hour narrated harbour tours, private charters, lunch cruises and dinner cruises. 207 Queen's Quay W., #415; 416 203-0178, www.mariposacruises.com
- Miss Toronto Yacht Charters and Tours. Unique seventy-foot Florida-style yacht suitable for all occasions. 264 Queens Quay W., #506; 416 861-0437. www.chartermisstoronto.com
- Nautical Adventures. Two unique ships for corporate functions, receptions, parties, special events, and public cruises. 1 Yonge Street, #104; 416 364-3244, Fax: 416 364-6889. www.nauticaladventure.com
- Toronto Harbour Tours. An entertaining, one-hour, fully narrated cruise of the Toronto Harbour. April to November. 145 Queen's Quay W.; 416 203-6994.

ACCOMMODATION

Tourism Toronto operates a central reservation service representing 123 member properties throughout the Greater Metropolitan Toronto Area. Contact them at Queen's Quay Terminal at Harbourfront Centre, P.O. Box 126, 207 Queens Quay West, Toronto ON M5J 1A7; 416 203-2500, 1-800-363-1990 (North America), Fax: 416 203-6753. The services of the Travellers Aid Society include providing tourist information, maps and suggestions on what to see and do in Toronto, and acting as a link between stranded travellers and social services agencies. Contact them at Room B23, Union Station, Toronto ON M5J 1E6; 416 366-7788, Fax: 416 366-0829. Approximate prices are indicated, based on the average cost, at time of publishing, for two persons staying in a double room (excluding taxes): $ = $50-$90; $$ = $90-$180; $$$ = $180-$300; $$$$=above $300. If you're travelling at the last minute or looking for hotel savings during the off-season, try using the services of the Diner's Club Hotel Savings Hotline at 1-800-567-8850. The service does not require that you be a Diner's Club user. It offers a range of hotel options at good rates for same-day accommodation. However, during busy periods you can't rely on this service to have any inventory of rooms. The service does not help if you're booking in advance, though it can give you an idea of how low a specific hotel will go when it is not too busy.

For the locations of downtown and midtown hotels, see the map on page 8.

HOTELS: AIRPORT

- Days Hotel and Conference Centre, 6257 Airport Rd., Mississauga ON L4V 1E4; 905 678-1400, 1-800-329-7466, 1-800-387-6891 (ON, QC), Fax: 905 678-9130. Indoor pool and health club. Airport shuttle service. $$
- Delta Toronto Airport Hotel, 801 Dixon Rd., Etobicoke ON M9W 1J5; 416 675-6100, 1-800-668-1444, Fax: 416 675-4022, deltanet@deltahotels.com, www.deltahotels.com. Eighteen-

hole golf course. Continuous airport shuttle. Swimming pool and spa/fitness centre. $$
- Holiday Inn Select Toronto Airport, 970 Dixon Rd., Etobicoke ON M9W 1J9; 416 675-7611, 1-800-465-4329, Fax: 416 675-9162, 10441.2323@compuserve.com. Complimentary airport shuttle service. Indoor/outdoor pools, sauna and whirlpool. $$
- Holiday Inn Express Toronto - North York, 30 Norfinch Drive, North York ON M3N 1X1; 416 665-3500, Fax: 416 665-0807. Complimentary continental breakfast. $
- International Plaza Hotel and Conference Centre, 655 Dixon Rd., Toronto ON M9W 1J4; 416 244-1711, 1-800-668-3656 (Canada and USA), Fax: 416 244-9584. Indoor waterslide park, nightclub, swimming pool/fitness centre. $$
- Regal Constellation Hotel, 900 Dixon Rd., Etobicoke ON M9W 1J7; 416 675-1500, (Res) 1-800-268-4838, Fax: 416 675-1737. rsvn@regalconstellation.com Secretarial, business and audio services. Swimming pool and spa/fitness centre. $$
- Sheraton Gateway Hotel, Terminal 3, Departure Level, PO Box 3000, Mississauga ON L5P 1C4; 905 672-7000, Fax: 905 672-7100, shelly_clark@sheraton.com. Attached to Terminal 3 of Pearson International Airport; saunas and a restaurant. $$-$$$
- Toronto Airport Marriott Hotel, 901 Dixon Rd., Rexdale ON M9W 1J5; 416 674-9400, 1-800-905-2811, Fax: 416 674-8292. Volleyball and basketball court on property, golf and tennis nearby. Swimming pool and spa/fitness centre. Secretarial services and business centre. $$
- Travelodge Toronto Airport, 925 Dixon Rd., Etobicoke ON M9W 1J8; 416 674-2222, 1-800-387-3933, Fax: 416 674-5757. Swimming pool, health club and sauna. $$
- The Wyndham Bristol Place Hotel, 950 Dixon Rd., Toronto ON M9W 5N4; 416 675-9444, 1-800-996-3426, Fax: 416 675-4426, bristolplc@wyndham.com. Five-star property with business centre and Women Travellers business

select rooms. Swimming pool and spa/fitness centre. $$$

HOTELS: DOWNTOWN
See the map on page 8 for the map references.

- Best Western Primrose Hotel - Toronto-Downtown, 111 Carlton St., Toronto ON M5B 2G3; 416 977-8000, 1-800-268-8082, Fax: 416 977-4874. Saunas/exercise room and an outdoor swimming pool. $$. **Map 10**
- Bond Place Hotel, 65 Dundas St. E., Toronto ON M5B 2G8; 416 362-6061, 1-800-268-9390, Fax: 416 360-6406. Walking distance to all top tourist attractions. $$. **Map 16**
- Cambridge Suites Hotel, 15 Richmond St. E., Toronto ON M5C 1N2; 416 368-1990, 1-800-463-1990, Fax: 416 601-3751, reservations@tor.cambridgesuites.com. Complimentary continental breakfast, spa/fitness centre. $$$. **Map 19**
- Crowne Plaza Toronto Centre, 225 Front St. W., Toronto ON M5V 2X3; 416 597-1400, 1-800-227-6963 (Canada), Fax: 416 597-8128, reservations@crowneplazatoronto.com. Swimming pool and spa/fitness centre. $$. **Map 28**
- Days Inn Toronto Downtown, 30 Carlton St., Toronto ON M5B 2E9; 416 977-6655, 1-800-329-7466, Fax: 416 977-0502. Heated indoor pool, sauna and fitness centre. $-$$. **Map 9**
- Delta Chelsea Inn, 33 Gerrard St. W., Toronto ON M5G 1Z4; 416 595-1975, 1-800-243-5732, Fax: 416 585-4375, www. deltahotels.com, reservations@deltachelsea.com. Swimming pool and spa/fitness centre; business centre. $$. **Map 12**
- Travelodge Toronto, 621 King St. W., Toronto ON M5V 1M5; 416 504-7441, Fax: 416 504-4722. Free continental breakfast, morning and evening coffee, tea, and donuts. $. **Map 23**
- Grand Hotel and Suites Toronto, 225 Jarvis St., Toronto ON M5B 2C1; 416 863-9000, 1-800-324-7263, Fax: 416 863-1100, www.grandhoteltoronto.com, kblack@grandhoteltoronto.com.

Spa/fitness centre. $$. **Map 22**

- Hilton Toronto, 145 Richmond St. W., Toronto ON M5H 2L2; 416 869-3456, 1-800-267-2281, Fax: 416 869-3187, www.hilton.com, info_toronto@hilton.com. Heated indoor/outdoor pool with health club. $$$. **Map 18**

- Holiday Inn on King, 370 King St. W., Toronto ON M5V 1J9; 416 599-4000, 1-800-465- 4329, Reservation Fax: 416 599-4785, www.hiok.com, info@hiok.com. Swimming pool and spa/fitness centre. $$. **Map 21**

- Hotel Le Germain Toronto, 30 Mercer St., Toronto On M5V 1H3, 416 345-9500, 1-866-345-9501; Fax: 416 345-9501 reservations@germaintoronto.com, www.germaintoronto.com. New boutique hotel is a small, luxurious cross between a bed and breakfast and a large luxury hotel. In the entertainment district. $$$-$$$$. **Map 36**

- Hotel Victoria, 56 Yonge St., Toronto ON M5E 1G5; 416 363-1666, Fax: 416 363-7327, reception@hotelvictoria.on.ca. A small historic property located in the heart of Toronto's theatre and financial district. $. **Map 26**

- Le Royal Meridien King Edward Hotel, 37 King St. E., Toronto ON M5C 1E9; 416 863-9700, 1-800-543-4300, Fax: 416 367-5515, www.lemeridien-hotels.com. An elegant hotel, renowned for its Edwardian splendour. Spa/fitness centre; business centre. $$$. **Map 24**

- Madison Manor Boutique Hotel, 20 Madison Avenue, Toronto ON M5R 2S1 416 922-5579, 1-877-561-7048, Fax: 416 963-4325, info@madisonavenuepub.com, www.madisonavenuepub.com/madisonmanor/. Four floors in a Victoria manor; no elevator. Non-smoking. Complimentary continental breakfast. $$-$$$. **Map 33**

- Marriott Eaton Centre, 525 Bay St., Toronto ON M5G 2L2; 416 597-9200, 1-800-905-0667, Fax: 416 597-9211, www.marriott.com. Swimming pool and spa/fitness centre; business centre. $$. **Map 15**

- Metropolitan Hotel, 108 Chestnut St., Toronto ON M5G 1R3; 416 977-5000, 1-800-668-6600, Fax: 416 977-6351. Swimming pool and spa/fitness centre. $$. **Map 13**

- Novotel Toronto Centre, 45 The Esplanade, Toronto ON M5E 1W2; 416 367-8900, 1-800-668-6835, Fax: 416 360-8285, tcenmail@aol.com. Swimming pool and spa/fitness centre. $$. **Map 29**

- Quality Hotel Downtown, 111 Lombard St., Toronto ON M5C 2T9; 416 367-5555, 1-800-228-5151, Fax: 416 367-3470. $-$$. **Map 20**

- Ramada Hotel and Suites Downtown, 300 Jarvis St., Toronto ON M5B 2C5; 416 977-4823, 1-800-567-2233 (Canada and U.S.A.), Fax: 416 977-4830, ramada@ntecom.ca. Indoor swimming pool and spa/fitness centre. $$-$$$. **Map 11**

- Radisson Plaza Hotel Admiral, 249 Queens Quay W., Toronto ON M5J 2N5; 416 203-3333, 1-800-333-3333, Fax: 416 203-3100. Business centre; swimming pool. $$. **Map 32**

- Renaissance Toronto Hotel at SkyDome, 1 Blue Jays Way, Toronto ON M5V 1J4; 416 341-7100, 1-800-237-1512, Fax: 416 341-5091. One quarter of the rooms have floor-to-ceiling windows which offer an exclusive view of the stadium. Business centre; swimming pool and spa/fitness centre. $$. **Map 30**

- Royal York Hotel, 100 Front St. W., Toronto ON M5J 1E3; 416 368-2511, 1-800-441-1414, Fax: 416 860-5008, reserve@ryh.mhs.compuserve.com. Business centre; swimming pool and spa/fitness centre. $$-$$$. **Map 27**

- Sheraton Centre Toronto Hotel and Towers, 123 Queen St. W., Toronto ON M5H 2M9; 416 361-1000, 1-800-325-3535, Fax: 416 947-4874, www.sheratoncentretoronto.com, reservations@sheratoncentretoronto.com. Olympic-sized pool, sauna, hot tub, sundeck, spa/fitness centre and children's playroom. $$$. **Map 17**

- The SoHo Metropolitan Boutique Hotel. 318 Wellington St. W., Toronto ON M5V 3T3, 416 542-1472, Fax: 1-801-315-7442. New luxury boutique hotel in the entertainment district with all the amenities. $$$-$$$$ **Map 37**

- Strathcona Hotel, 60 York St., Toronto ON M5J 1S8; 416 363-3321, 1-800-268-8304, Fax: 416 363-4679, strathcona@sprint.ca. $-$$. **Map 25**
- Toronto Colony Hotel Downtown City Hall, 89 Chestnut St., Toronto ON M5G 1R1; 416 977-0707, 1-800-387-8687, Fax: 416 585-3157, torres@attmail.com. Business centre; health club, two pools. $$. **Map 14**
- The Town Inn Suites, 620 Church Street, Toronto ON M4Y 2G2, 416 964-3311, 1-800-311-5045, Fax: 416 924-9466, www.towninn.com/ Apartment suites with kitchen facilities.
- Westin Harbour Castle, 1 Harbour Sq., Toronto ON M5J 1A6; 416 869-1600, 1-800-228-3000, Fax: 416 361-7448, www.westin.com, harca@westin.com. Swimming pool and spa/fitness centre. $$-$$$. **Map 31**
- The Windsor Arms, 18 St. Thomas St., Toronto ON M5S 3E7; 416 971-9666, Fax: 416 921-9121, Windsor@slh.com. Small, centrally-located luxury hotel with spa and 24-hour butler service. Small pets allowed. $$$$. **Map 34**

HOTELS: MIDTOWN
See the map on page 8 for map references.

- Comfort Hotel Downtown, 15 Charles St. E., Toronto ON M4Y 1S1, 416 924-1222, 1-800-228-5150, Fax: 416 927-1369, comfort@nhgi.com. $. **Map 7**
- Four Seasons Hotel, 21 Avenue Rd., Toronto ON M5R 2G1; 416 964-0411, 1-800-268-6282, Fax: 416 964-2301. Toronto's only CAA/AAA Five Diamond hotel. Swimming pool and spa/fitness centre. $$$. **Map 2**
- Hotel Inter-Continental Toronto, 220 Bloor St. W., Toronto ON M5S 1T8; 416 960-5200, 1-800-267-0010, Fax: 416 960-8269, www.toronto.interconti.com, rsvnstaff@interconti.com Swimming pool and spa/fitness centre. $$$. **Map 4**
- Park Hyatt Toronto, 4 Avenue Rd., Toronto ON M5R 2E8; 416 925-1234, 1-800-233-1234, Fax: 416

924-4933. Spa/fitness centre. $$$. **Map 3**

- Quality Hotel by Journey's End, 280 Bloor St. W., Toronto ON M5S 3B9; 416 968-0010, 1-800-228-5151, Fax: 416 968-7765. $$. **Map 6**
- Sutton Place Hotel, 955 Bay St., Toronto ON M5S 2A2; 416 924-9221, 1-800-268-3790, Fax: (416) 924-1778, www.suttonplace.com, res@tor.suttonplace.com. Indoor swimming pool and spa/fitness centre. $$$. **Map 8**
- Toronto Marriott Bloor-Yorkville Hotel, 90 Bloor St. E., Toronto ON M4W 1A7; 416 961-8000, Fax: 416 961-4635. www.marriott.com. Spa/fitness centre. $$-$$$. **Map 5**
- Howard Johnson Inn Yorkville, 89 Avenue Rd., Toronto ON M2R 2G3; 416 964-1220, 1-800-446-4656, Fax: 416 964-8692. $-$$. **Map 1**

BED AND BREAKFASTS
Toronto has over 200 bed and breakfast establishments, operating either independently or grouped together in association, several of which are listed below in our introductory selection. You may also want to visit www.bbcanada.com, under Toronto, to view a select list of b and bs online.

- Abodes of Choice Bed and Breakfast Association of Toronto, 102 Burnside Dr., Toronto ON. Co-op group of homes in desirable neighbourhoods with affiliates across Canada. Various locations. $
- Alcina's Bed and Breakfast, 16 Alcina Avenue, Toronto ON M6G 2E8; 416 656-6400, alcinas@idirect.com. Centrally located Victorian home. $
- Allenby Bed and Breakfast, 223 Strathmore Boulevard, Toronto ON M4J 4P4; 416 461-7095. AAA approved renovated house, centrally located. Shared baths. $
- Annex House, 147 Madison Ave., Toronto ON M5R 2S6; Tel/Fax: 416 920-3922. $
- Beaches Bed and Breakfast, 174 Waverly Rd., Toronto ON M4L 3T3; 416 699-0818, Fax: 416 699-2246. Close to the lake, streetcars, parks, shops and cafes. $
- Beaconsfield Bed and Breakfast, 38 Beaconsfield Ave., Toronto ON

M6J 3H9; Tel/Fax: 416 535-3338, beacon@idirect.com. Brochure available. $
- Bed and Breakfast Guest Houses - Association of Downtown Toronto, P.O. Box 190, Station B, Toronto ON M5T 2W1; 416 410-3938, Fax: 416 483-8822. bnbtoronto@globalserve.net, www.bnbinfo.com Toronto's largest selection of fully inspected Victorian homes in downtown Toronto. Non-smoking. $
- Bed and Breakfast Homes of Toronto, P.O. Box 46093, College Post Office, 444 Yonge St., Toronto ON M5B 2L8; 416 363-6362. Thirty welcoming homes, all near transit. Call or write for a free brochure and then contact chosen host directly. $
- Beverley Place, 235 Beverley St., Toronto ON M5T 1Z4; 416 977-0077. Fax: 416 599-2242. Awarded Government of Canada Tourism Ambassador Certificate. $
- Feathers Bed and Breakfast, 132 Wells St., Toronto ON M5R 1P4; 416 534-2388. An artistic Victorian home in a great downtown location; five-minute walk to subway, a choice of European-style cafes, live theatre and antique shops. Close to ROM, Casa Loma, Yorkville, and U of T. $
- French Connection Bed and Breakfast, 102 Burnside Drive, Toronto ON M6G 2M8; 416 537-7741 (Res.), 1-800-313-3993, Fax: 416 537-0747. Freshly baked European-style breakfast. $-$$
- Homewood Inn, 65 Homewood Ave., Toronto ON M4Y 2K1; 416 920-7944, Fax: 416 920-4091. All rooms with colour TV and fridge; some with kitchens. $
- Jarvis House (A Bed and Breakfast in Downtown Toronto), 344 Jarvis Street, Toronto ON M4Y 2G6; 416 975-3838, Fax: 416 975-9808, www.jarvishouse.com Central downtown Toronto. Private bathrooms. $
- Palmerston Inn Bed and Breakfast, 322 Palmerston Blvd., Toronto ON M6G 2N6; 416 920-7842, 964-2566, Fax: 416 960-9529. Non-smoking only. $-$$
- Philomena and Dave Bed and Breakfast, Bloor Street and Spadina Avenue, Toronto; 416 962-2786,

Fax: 416 964-8837, valladp@echo_on.net. Reservations required. $
- Robin's Nest Bed and Breakfast, 13 Binscarth Rd., Toronto ON M4W 1Y2; 416 926-9464, Fax: 416 926-3730, robinsnestbandb@toronto.com Private bathrooms. $-$$
- Toronto Bed and Breakfast Inc., Box 269, 253 College St., Toronto ON M5T 1R5; 1-877-922-6522, beds@torontobandb.com, www.torontobandb.com. Eighteen homes in the registry. $
- Vanderkooy Bed and Breakfast, 53 Walker Ave., Toronto ON M4V 1G3; 416 925-8765, Fax: 416 925-8557. Relax and enjoy the pond in the garden with resident cats, Blue and Quila. $

HOSTELS AND COLLEGE RESIDENCES

Almost all of the residences listed below are available in summer only, but they provide a safe, economical alternative to hotels. Make sure you book in advance.
- Hospitality York, York University, 4700 Keele St., North York ON M3J 1P3; 416 736-5020, Fax: 416 736-5648. Swimming pool and spa/fitness centre. May to September. $
- Hostelling International Toronto, 76 Church St., Toronto ON M5G 1J6; 416 971-4440, 1-800-668-4487, Fax: 416 971-4088. Central location. Rooms have vanity ensuite and air conditioning. Kitchen and laundry. $
- Massey College-University of Toronto, 4 Devonshire Place, Toronto ON M5S 2E1; 416 978-2892, Fax: 416 978-1759, pat.kennedy@utoronto.ca Downtown Toronto. May to August. $
- Neill-Wycik College-Hotel, 96 Gerrard St. E., Toronto ON M5B 1G7; 416 977-2320, 1-800-268-4358, Fax: 416 977-2809. Shared kitchens and washrooms. Sauna. May to August. $
- The Residence, 90 Gerrard St. W., 22nd floor, Toronto ON M5G 1J6; 416 340-3750, Fax: 416 340-3923, wycik@inforamp.com. Central downtown location. Shared kitchen, bathroom and laundry facilities. $

- Ryerson Polytechnic University, 160 Mutual St., Toronto ON M5B 2K3; 416 979-5296, Fax: 416 979-5212, cloganb@acs.ryerson.ca Mid-May to August. $
- University of Toronto at Scarborough, 1265 Military Trail, Scarborough ON M1C 1A4; 416 287-7369, Fax: 416 287-7323 jmartin@scar.utoronto.ca, www.scar.utoronto.ca/. East Metro location. Mid-May to August. $
- University of Toronto-St. George Campus, 45 Willcocks St., Toronto ON M5S 1C7; 416 978-8735, 1-888-834-7778, Fax: 416 978-1081, conference.services@utoronto.ca. Central location. Rooms with ensuite bathrooms. Mid-May to August. Swimming pool and spa/fitness centre. $
- Victoria University, 140 Charles St. W., Toronto ON M5S 1K9; 416 585-4524, Fax: 416 585-4530, www.vicu.utoronto.ca. May to August. $-$$
- Y.W.C.A. Woodlawn Residence, 80 Woodlawn Ave. E., Toronto ON M4T 1C1; 416 923-8454, Fax: 416 923-1950, ywcagen@ywcator.org. Women's residence, centrally located. Rates include breakfast. $

TOP ATTRACTIONS

Toronto is replete with attractions. Here we have chosen to provide a selective listing of many of the points of interest. Check local newspapers, *Toronto Life* magazine, *eye weekly*, *Now* magazine, www.torontotourism.com and www.toronto.com for more information.

- Allan Gardens. Huge greenhouses. Carlton and Sherbourne Sts.; 416 392-7288.
- Black Creek Pioneer Village. A recreated nineteenth-century village. Open year-round. 1000 Murray Ross Pkwy., Downsview ON M3J 2P3; 416 736-1733.
- Campbell House. Toronto's only Georgian historic house. Restored 1822 residence of Sir William Campbell. Open year-round. 160 Queen St. W.; Toronto, ON M5H 3H3; 416 597-0227, www.advsoc.on.ca
- Canadian National Exhibition, Exhibition Place, Lakeshore Blvd., between Strachan and Dufferin; 416 393-6000 or 416 263-3800.
- Canadian Broadcasting Centre (CBC). See behind the scenes at a world-class radio and television production facility. Open year-round weekdays. 250 Front St. W., room 3C409, P.O. Box 500, Station A, Toronto ON M5W 1E6; 416 205-3147.
- Casa Loma. Toronto's majestic castle estate. Open year-round. 1 Austin Terrace, Toronto ON M5R 1X8; 416 923-1171.
- Centreville Amusement Park. A turn-of-the-century theme amusement park located on the Toronto Islands, a short ferry ride away. Open Victoria Day to Labour Day and weekends only in September. Toronto Islands, 84 Advance Rd., Toronto ON M8Z 2T7; 416 203-1113.
- CN Tower Limited. The world's tallest free-standing structure. Open year-round. 301 Front St. W., Toronto ON M5V 2T6; 416 360-8500 or 416 868-6937.
- David Dunlap Observatory. Site of the largest optical telescope in Canada. 123 Hillsview Dr., Richmond Hill; 416 978-2016, www.ddo.astro.utoronto.ca
- Enoch Turner Schoolhouse. Toronto's first school; call ahead to book a visit. 106 Trinity St.; 416 863-0010.
- Fantasy Fair. This indoor amusement park features a Victorian town with eight rides, games, restaurants and a children's play area. Woodbine Shopping Centre, 500 Rexdale Blvd.; 416 674-5437.
- First Post Office. 260 Adelaide St. E., 865-1833. Free admission.
- Gibson House. Restored 1851 farmhouse of rebel, politician and surveyor, David Gibson, his wife Eliza and their family. Open year-round. Special weekend events. 5172 Yonge St.; 416 395-7432.
- Grange Historic House. The oldest brick house in Toronto built in the 1830s. Open year-round. 317 Dundas St. W. at the Art Gallery of Ontario, Toronto ON M5T 1G4; 416 979-6648, www.ago.on.ca
- Harbourfront Centre. Year-round centre features cultural and

recreational activities. 235 Queens Quay W., Toronto, ON M5J 2G8; 416 973-3000, www.culturenet.ca/harbour

- Heritage Toronto. Visit one of five historic sites: Colborne Lodge, home of John George Howard (at High Park), 416 392-6916; Fort York, the nineteenth-century fort that recreates the drama of the war of 1812 (off Fleet St., east of Strachan), 416 392-6907; Mackenzie House, home of William Lyon MacKenzie, Toronto's first mayor (82 Bond St.), 416 392-6915; and Spadina House, a magnificent 1866 estate with fine art and elegant furnishings (285 Spadina Rd), 416 392-6910. Contact **Toronto Convention & Visitors Association,** P.O. Box 126, 207 Queens Quay West Toronto ON M5J 1A7; 416 203-2600, fax: 416 203-2600, toronto@torcvb.com
- Kortright Centre for Conservation. Canada's largest nature centre. Open year-round. 9550 Pine Valley Dr., Woodbridge ON L4L 1A6; 905-832-2289.
- Lillian H. Smith Children's Library. Houses the Osborne Collection of Early Children's Books. 239 College St.; 416 393-7753.
- Medieval Times Dinner and Tournament. Re-enactment of an eleventh-century medieval banquet. CNE near Dufferin Gate, Exhibition Place, Toronto, ON M6K 3C3; 416 260-1234.
- Ontario Place. Unique entertainment complex on Toronto's waterfront. Open mid-May to Labour Day. 955 Lake Shore Blvd. W., Toronto, ON M6K 3B9; 416 314-9900 or 416 314-9811, www.ontarioplace.com
- Ontario Science Centre. Over 800 interactive exhibits emphasizing fun with science. Open year-round. 770 Don Mills Rd., Don Mills ON M3C 1T3; 416 429-4100 or 416 696-1000, www.osc.on.ca
- Paramount Canada's Wonderland. Canada's 300-acre premier theme park. Open weekends in May and fall, daily late-May through Labour Day. 9580 Jane St. (400 North to Rutherford Rd. Exit), Vaughan ON L6A 1S6; 905-832-7000, www.canadaswonderland.com

- Queen's Quay Terminal: A specialty retail centre with unique shopping and dining on Toronto's waterfront. 207 Queens Quay W.
- Riverdale Farm, 201 Winchester St.; Daily 9-5; 416 392-6794.
- Toronto Police Museum and Discovery Centre. Exciting new museum with interactive displays featuring police and crime memorabilia. Exhibits include vehicles, weapons and infamous criminal cases. 40 College St.; 416 808-7020.
- Toronto Zoo. World-class zoological park featuring over four thousand animals. Open year-round. 361A Old Finch Ave., Hwy. 401 and Meadowvale Rd., Scarborough, ON M1B 5K7; 416 392-5900, www.torontozoo.com
- Waterfront Regeneration Trust. The Trust coordinates the 325-kilometre Waterfront Trail that stretches along the shore of Lake Ontario. 207 Queens Quay W.; 510, Toronto ON M5J 1A7; 416 943-8080.
- Wild Water Kingdom. Canada's largest outdoor water park. Open June through Labour Day (waterpark), April to October (mini-golf). 7855 Finch Ave. W., Brampton ON L6T 3Y7; 905 794-0565, www.wildwaterkingdom.com

MUSEUMS

- Bata Shoe Museum, 327 Bloor St. W.; Tues., Wed., Fri. and Sat. 10-5, Thurs. 10-8, Sun. 12-5; 416 979-7799, www.batashoemuseum.ca
- CBC Museum, 250 Front St. W.; Mon. to Fri. 9-5, Sat. 12-4; 416 205-5574, www.cbc.ca/museum
- City of Toronto Archives and Research Hall, 255 Spadina Rd.; Mon. to Fri. 9-4:30, Sat. 10-4:30, 416 397-5000, archives@city.toronto.on.ca, www.city.toronto.on.ca/archives
- Gardiner Museum of Ceramic Art, 111 Queen's Park; Mon., Wed., Fri. 10-6, Tues. and Thurs. 10-8, Sat. 10-5; 416 586-8080, Fax: 416 586-8085, www.gardinermuseum.on.ca
- Hockey Hall of Fame, BCE Place, 30 Yonge St.; Hours vary by season. Open seven days a week; 416 360-7735, www.hhof.com
- Holocaust Education and Memorial

Centre, 4600 Bathurst St.; Open to the public by appointment only; 416 635-2883, www.utoronto.ca/museum/museums/museum/holocaust.html
- Textile Museum of Canada, 55 Centre Ave; Tues., Thurs., Fri. 11-5, Wed. 11-8, Sat. and Sun. 12-5; 416 599-5321, www.museumfortextiles.on.ca
- Scarborough Historical Museum, 1007 Brimley Rd.; Daily 10-5; 416 338-8807.
- Todmorden Mills Heritage Museum and Arts Centre, Pottery Rd. between Broadview Ave. and Bayview Ave.; Tues. to Fri. 10-5, Sat. and Sun. 12-5; 416 396-2819
- Toronto Police Museum, 40 College St.; Mon. to Fri. 8:30-4:30; 416 808-7020.
- R.C. Harris Filtration Plant. A shining example of Art Deco architecture. Tours Sat. 10, 11:30 and 1. 2701 Queen St. E. (In the Beaches); 416 392-3566.
- Redpath Sugar Museum, 95 Queens Quay E.; Mon. to Fri. 10-noon and 1-3; 416 366-3561. Group tours are by appointment; other visitors are also required to call in advance.
- Royal Ontario Museum, 100 Queen's Park; Mon. to Thurs. 10-6, Fri. 10-9:30, Sat. 10-6; Sun. 11-6; 416 586-5549 or 416 586-8000, www.rom.on.ca
- Zion Church Cultural Centre, 1650 Finch Ave. E.; 416 395-0321.
- Zion Schoolhouse, 1901 Finch Ave. E.; 416 395-7435.

GALLERIES

This list of public galleries is a select one. Consult the latest edition of *Slate*, available at most galleries, for listings of current shows.
- A Space, 401 Richmond St. W., #110; Tues. to Fri. 11-6, Sat. 12-5; 416 979-9633, Fax: 416 979-9683
- The Angell Gallery, 890 Queen St. W.; Thurs.-Sat. 12-6, 416 530-0444, www.angellgallery.com
- Art Gallery of Ontario, 317 Dundas St. W.; Tues.-Fri. 11-6, Wed. 11-8:30, Sat. and Sun. 10-5:30, closed all Mondays (including holidays); 416 979-6648, Fax: 416 979-6646, everyone@ago.net, www.ago.net
- Art Metropole, 788 King St. W.; Tues. to Fri. 11-6, Sat. 12-5; 416 703-4400, artmet@interlog.com, www.artmetropole.org
- Bau-Xi Gallery, 340 Dundas St. W.; Tues. to Sat. 10-5:30, 416 977-0600.
- Christopher Cutts Gallery, 21 Morrow Ave., #204; Tues. to Sat. 11-6; 416 532-5566, Fax: 416 532-7272, www.cuttsgallery.com
- Deleon White Gallery Art Culture Ecology, 223 Avenue Rd.; Tues. to Sat. 12-5, or by appt.; 416 964-7838, Fax: 416 964-9377, www.eco-art.com/deleon, White@eco-art.com
- The Drabinsky Gallery, 122 Scollard St.; Tues. to Sat. 11-5; 416 324-5766, www.drabinskygallery.com
- Gallery One, 121 Scollard St.; Tues. to Sat. 10:30-5:30; 416 929-3103, www.artgalleryone.com
- Gallery 44, Centre for Contemporary Photography, 401 Richmond St. W., #120; Tues. to Sat. 11-5; 416 979-3941, Fax: 416 340-8458
- Gallery Moos Ltd., 622 Richmond St. W.; Tues. to Sat. 11-6; 416 504-5445, Fax: 416 504-5446.
- Gallery TPW (Toronto Photographers' Workshop), 80 Spadina Ave. #310; Tues. to Sat. 12-5; 416 504-4242.
- Jane Corkin Gallery, 179 John St. #302; Tues. to Fri. 9:30-5:30, Sat. 10-5; 416 979-1980, www.janecorkin.com
- Kaspar Gallery, 86 Scollard St.; Tues. to Sat. 10-6; 416 968-2536.
- Katharine Mulherin, 1040, 1080 and 1086 Queen Street West; 416 537-8827.
- Leo Kamen Gallery, 80 Spadina Ave. #406; Tues. to Sat. 11-5; 416 504-9515.
- Lonsdale Gallery, 410 Spadina Rd.; Tues. to Sat. 11-6, Sun. 12-5; 416 487-8733, www.lonsdalegallery.com
- The McMichael Canadian Collection, 10365 Islington Ave., Kleinburg; 905 893-1121, www.mcmichael.on.ca
- Mira Godard Gallery, 22 Hazelton Ave.; Tues. to Sat. 10-5:30; 416 964-8197, www.godardgallery.com
- Olga Korper Gallery, 17 Morrow Ave.; Tues. to Sat. 10-6; 416 538-8220.

- Paul Petro Contemporary Art, 980 Queen Street West; 416 979-7874.
- Peak Gallery, 23 Morrow Ave.; 416 537-8108.
- The Power Plant, Harbourfront Centre, 231 Queens Quay W.; Tues. to Sun. 12-6, Wed. 12-8, Holiday Mondays 12-6; 416 973-4949.
- Propeller Centre for the Visual Arts, 96 Spadina Ave., #303; Tues. to Sat. 12-6; 416 504-7142.
- Sable-Castelli Gallery, 33 Hazelton Ave.; Tues. to Sat. 10-5; 416 961-0011.
- Sandra Ainsley Gallery, 55 Mill St., 416 214-9490.
- Susan Hobbs Gallery, 137 Tecumseth St.; Thurs. to Sat. 1-5, or by appt.; 416 504-3699, Fax: 416 504-8064.
- The Red Head Gallery, 401 Richmond St. W; Wed. to Fri. 12-5, Sat. 12-6; 416 504-5654.
- Toronto Imageworks, 80 Spadina Ave.; Mon. to Thurs. 8-10, Fri. 8-7, Sat. 10-6, Sun. 12-5; 416 703-1999, www.torontoimageworks.com
- Toronto Sculpture Garden, 115 King St. E.; 416 485-9658.
- Wynick/Tuck Gallery, 401 Richmond Street; 416 504-8716.
- Ydessa Hendeles Art Foundation, 778 King St. W.; Sat. 12-5 and by appt. (please fax or mail requests); 416 413-9400, Fax: 416 969-9889
- Zsa Zsa Gallery, 962 Queen St. W.

THEATRE AND DANCE

For tickets to most theatres, contact Ticketmaster, 1 Blue Jays Way; 416 870-8000. For same-day tickets, contact T.O. Tix, Toronto's Half-Price Ticket Centre, for a wide variety of theatre, dance and musical events. Half-price tickets are available only on the day of the performance and must be purchased in person at 220 Yonge Street. Call 416 536-6468 for recorded information.

LIVE THEATRE
- Artword Theatre, 75 Portland; 416 535-9998.
- Buddies in Bad Times, 12 Alexander St.; 416 975-8555.
- Canadian Stage Company, at Bluma Appel Theatre in the St. Lawrence Centre, 27 Front St. E.; 416 366-1656; and at the Berkeley Street Theatre, 26 Berkeley St.; 416 368-3110, www.canadianstage.com
- Canon Theatre, 244 Victoria St.; 416 364-4100.
- Elgin and Winter Garden Theatres, 189 Yonge St.; 416 314-2901.
- The Factory Theatre, 125 Bathurst St.; 416 504-9971.
- Famous People Players, 110 Sudbury St.; 416 532-1137.
- Ford Centre for the Performing Arts, 5040 Yonge St.; 416 733-9388.
- Harbourfront Centre, 235 Queens Quay W.; 416 973-3000.
- Hummingbird Centre for the Performing Arts. Home of the Canadian Opera Company and the National Ballet of Canada. One Front St. E.; 416 393-7474.
- Lorraine Kimsa Theatre for Young People (formerly Young People's Theatre), 165 Front St. E.; 416 862-2222.
- National Ballet of Canada, King's Landing, 470 Queens Quay W.; 416 345-9686.
- Premiere Dance Theatre, at Harbourfront Centre, 207 Queens Quay W.; 416 973-3000.
- Princess of Wales Theatre, 300 King St. W.; 872-1212 or 1-800-461-3333.
- Roy Thomson Hall, Home of the Toronto Symphony Orchestra. 60 Simcoe St.; 416 872-4255.
- Royal Alexandra Theatre, 260 King St. W.; 416 872-1212.
- Shaw Festival, Niagara-on-the-Lake; 1-800-511-7429, www.shawfest.com
- Solar Stage Children's Theatre, 4950 Yonge St.; 416 368-8031.
- Solar Stage Lunchtime Theatre, 40 King St.W.; 416 368-8031.
- St. Lawrence Centre for the Arts. Houses the Bluma Appel Theatre and the Jane Mallet Theatre. 27 Front St. E.; 416 366-7723, www.stlc.com
- Stratford Festival, Stratford; 416 363-4471 or 1-800-567-1600, Fax: 519 273-6173, orders@stratford-festival.on.ca, www.stratford-festival.on.ca
- Tarragon Theatre, 30 Bridgman Ave.; 416 531-1827.
- Theatre Passe Muraille, 16 Ryerson Ave.; 416 504-7529.
- Toronto Dance Theatre, 80 Winchester St.; 416 967-1365.

- Toronto Truck Theatre. Featuring The Mousetrap, 94 Belmont St.; 416 922-0084.

CINEMAS

For current movies, showtimes and venues, check the entertainment pages of the *Toronto Star*, *Now* magazine or *eye weekly*.

DINNER THEATRE

- The Laugh Resort. The city's newest stand-up comedy and variety artists. 370 King St. W.; 416 364-5233.
- Medieval Times Dinner and Tournament. Re-enactment of an eleventh-century medieval banquet with knights on horses competing in medieval games, sword fights and jousting. Exhibition Place, Lake Shore Blvd. W.; 416 260-1234 or 1-800-563-1190.
- Mysteriously Yours. A hilarious "whodunit." Join the fun at this interactive murder mystery! Dinner/Show or Show only. The Old Mill, 21 Old Mill Rd.; 416 486-7469 or 1-800-668-3323, www.mysteriouslyyours.com
- Second City. The well-known comedy troupe guarantees laughs. Second City Old Firehall Theatre, 56 Blue Jays Way; 416 343-0011.
- Yuk Yuk's Comedy Club. Canada's original home of stand-up comedy. 224 Richmond St. W.; 416 967-6425, www.yukyuks.com

SYMPHONY, CHAMBER MUSIC, OPERA

- Amadeus Choir, 75 The Donway W. #410.; 416 446-0188.
- Aradia Ensemble, Baroque Orchestra; 416 461-3471.
- Arraymusic. New music ensemble performs works by contemporary composers. 416 532-3019.
- Canadian Opera Company, Hummingbird Centre for the Performing Arts, One Front St. E.; 416 393-7469.
- Elmer Iseler Singers, chamber choir music, 1-800-884-0489, www.elmeriselersingers.com
- Esprit Orchestra, 174 Spadina Ave.; 416 815-7887,

www.espritorchestra.com
- Glenn Gould Studio, Canadian Broadcasting Centre, 250 Front St. W.; 416 205-5555, www.glenngouldstudio.cbc.ca
- The Music Gallery. Contemporary and experimental music and dance. 197 John St. 416 204-1080.
- Music Toronto, 8 King St. E., Suite 910; 416 214-1660.
- New Music Concerts, 20 St. Joseph St.; 416 961-9594.
- Off Centre Music Series, 968 Logan Ave.; 416 466-1870.
- Opera Atelier, 87 Avenue Rd.; 416 925-3767, Fax: 416 925-4895.
- Orpheus Choir, P.O. Box 662, Station F, Toronto; 416 530-4428.
- Toronto Symphony Orchestra, Roy Thomson Hall, 60 Simcoe St.; 416 872-4255.
- Tafelmusik, performing at Trinity-St. Paul's Church, 427 Bloor St. W.; 416 964-9562, Fax: 416 964-2782, info@tafelmusik.org
- Toronto Children's Chorus, 2180 Bayview Ave.; 416 932-8666.
- Toronto Consort, performing at Trinity-St. Paul's Church, 427 Bloor St. W.; 416 966-1045.
- Toronto Mendelssohn Choir, 60 Simcoe St.; 416 598-0422.

NIGHT LIFE

This list will help guide you through Toronto after dark. Refer to the Night Life section for more details and the map at the beginning of the book. Be sure to check local newspapers; there is something for everyone in Toronto. For up-to-date listings, try the most recent edition of *Now* magazine, or *eye weekly*, both available free of charge in bars and restaurants throughout Toronto.

LITTLE ITALY

- Bar Italia, 582 College St.; 416 535-3621. Attracts all types of people, including families. Billiards, football and live jazz upstairs.
- Ciao Edie, 489 College St.; 416 927 7774. A retro-kitsch home for scenesters.
- College Street Bar, 574 College St.; 416 533-2417. Attracts a large student crowd. Filling Italian food and microbrewery beers on tap.

- El Convento Rico, 750 College St.; 416 588-7800. Late-night dancing and Latin drag performers.
- El Rancho Night Club, 430 College St.; 416 921-2752. Dress code in effect.
- Kalendar, 546 College St.; 416 923-4138. Quiet and dignified. Wonderful imported beers.
- Lava Lounge, 507 College St.; 416 966 5282. Cool music entertains amidst groovy lava lamps and beaded curtains.
- The Midtown, 552 College St.; 416 920-4533. A modern cafe with the classic feel of a neighbourhood pub. Play pool at the back, or sit with creative types up front.
- Orbit Room, 580A College St.; 416 535-0613. Consistently filled to capacity. The resident band, the Dexters, plays classic R and B tunes loudly.
- Plaza Flamingo Restaurant Night Club, 423 College St.; 416 603-8884. Dress code in effect.
- Sottovoce, 595 College St.; 416 536-4564. A wine bar with a wrought-iron fenced patio. The most picturesque place to sit in Little Italy.
- Souz Dal, 636 College St.; 416 537-1883. Cozy and dark. Listen to the eclectic mix of music over a few martinis or margaritas (the best in town).

ENTERTAINMENT DISTRICT
- Horizons, 301 Front St. W.; 416 362-5411. Atop the CN Tower, with a spectacular view.
- The Apothecary, 340 Adelaide St.; 416 586 9858 An oasis of cocktails and cool in a loud land.
- The Beat Junkie, 306 Richmond St. W.; 416 599-7055. Hip-hop backbeat, gangsta-fashion and soul music.
- Cha Cha Cha, 11 Duncan St.; 416 598-3538. Come to mambo! A supper club with a tiny dance floor and a Latin menu.
- Fez Batik, 129 Peter St.; 416 204-9660.
- Fluid Lounge, 217 Richmond St. W.; 416 593-6116. Thursdays are the best night, with progressive house over the sound system.
- Joker, 318 Richmond St. W.; 416 598-1313. Explore all three floors to find your niche.

- Limelight, 250 Adelaide St.; 416 593-6126. Crowded and energetic.
- Orchid The Night Club, 117 Peter St.; 416 598-4990.
- Studio 69, 69 Bathurst St.; 416-703-6969.
- System Soundbar, 117 Peter St.; 416 408 3996. Star DJs spin for crowds on two dance floors.
- Vinnie's Midway and Social Club, 22 Duncan St.; 416 979-5565. A sports bar with a full games room.
- Joe, 250 Richmond St. W.; 416 971-6JOE. A landmark for the student crowd. Three floors take you from the plains to the forest to a Muskoka lake and from lounge to pop to club music.

QUEEN ST. WEST
- Big Bop, 651 Queen St. W.; 416-504-6699. Style code in effect.
- Cameron House, 408 Queen St. W.; 416 703-0811. Soul, R and B, alternative or acid-jazz.
- Element Bar, 553 Queen St W.; 416 359 1919. A party crowd comes for house, hip hop or techno on two floors.
- Gypsy Co-op, 817 Queen St. W.; 416 703-5069. An eclectic mix of vintage furniture and herbal teas attracts arty patrons.
- Horseshoe, 368 Queen St. W.; 416 598-4753. Features great local bands. A jeans-and-draught pub.
- Left Bank, 561 Queen St. W.; 416 504-1626. A must-be-seen, high-ceilinged temple with an overcrowded dance floor. Top 40 favourites from the DJ.
- NASA, 609 Queen St. W.; 416 504 8356. Hip hop to deep house to drum'n'bass.
- The Rivoli, 334 Queen St. W.; 416 596-1908. Dinner or drinks. The best place for live bands.
- Sanctuary, 732 Queen St. W.; 416 504-1917. Vampire-friendly establishment for initiates only.
- Savage Garden, 550 Queen St. W.; 416 504 2178. A gritty, dark, industrial, Goth dance bar.
- Velvet Underground, 508 Queen St. W.; 416 504-6688. Dark and unusual.

BLOOR-YORKVILLE
- Fritz, 140 Cumberland St.; 416 966-0111. Great espresso. Be prepared for the (loud) regulars.

- Ivory, 69 Yorkville Ave.; 416 927-9929. Cocktails in a sea of animal prints, gauzy fabrics and pillows.
- The Roof, Park Hyatt Hotel, 4 Avenue Rd.; 416 924-5471. Beautiful outdoor patio in summer.

GAY TORONTO
See page 249

DOWNTOWN
- Acqua, 10 Front St. W.; 416 368-7171. An uptown crowd gathers for an outstanding happy hour, weekdays from 5 p.m to 7 p.m.
- Betty's, 240 King St. E.; 416 368-1300. An informal, charming, comfortable bar.
- Bier Markt, 58 The Esplanade; 416 862-7575. A huge selection of beers from across the world.
- Canoe, 66 Wellington St. W.; 416 364-0054. A high-end lounge for pre-theatre or post-work cocktails. The view is fabulous from the 54th floor of the Toronto Dominion Bank Tower.
- Fionn McCool's, 70 The Esplanade; 416 362-2495. Irish is the theme in this comfortable pub.
- Phoenix Concert Theatre, 410 Sherbourne St.; 416 323-1251.
- Rockit Night Club, 120 Church St.; 416 947-9555.
- Rosewater Supper Club, 19 Toronto St.; 416 214-5888. A forties-style supper club with lavish details.
- Scotland Yard, 56 The Esplanade; 416 364-6572.

COMEDY
See Dinner Theatre, page 223

JAZZ
- Montreal Bistro and Jazz Club, 65 Sherbourne St.; 416 363-0179. Best local and visiting talent.
- The Rex, 194 Queen St.; 416 598-2475. Don't be fooled by the run-down appearance.
- Top o' the Senator, 249 Victoria St.; 416 364-7517. A cozy club that attracts any top names passing through town.

THE ANNEX
- Dance Cave, 529 Bloor St. W.; 416 532-1598.
- Lee's Palace, 529 Bloor St. W.; 416 532-1598.

- Ye Olde Brunswick House, 481 Bloor St. W.; 416 964-2242.

THE DANFORTH
- Dark City, 307 Danforth Ave.; 416 461-1606. A coffee bar up front and a fully stocked bar in the back.
- Myth, 417 Danforth Ave.; 416 461-8383. A mix of crowds and a mythic decor.

OTHER NEIGHBOURHOODS
- Academy of Spherical Arts, 38 Hanna Ave.; 416 532-2782. The ne-plus-ultra of pool halls.
- Atlantis Niteclub, Ontario Place, West Entrance, 955 Lakeshore Blvd. W.; 416 260-8000.
- Bambu by the Lake, 245 Queens Quay W.; 416 214-6000. Great Thai/Caribbean food at this live music spot. Features local bands like the Reggae Cowboys as well as artists from abroad.
- Berlin, 2335 Yonge St.; 416 489-7777. Tuesday is Latin night, with live music. Lessons are provided in the early evening.
- The Comfort Zone, 486 Spadina Ave.; 416 763-9139. Still raving late when other doors are shut.
- The Docks, 11 Polson St.; 416 461-3625. Patrons from all walks of life from bikers to yachters and college kids.
- Guvernment, 132 Queens Quay E.; 416 869-0045. A huge central dance space gives way to other unique rooms.
- Matador, 466 Dovercourt Rd.; 416 533-9311. Open from 1 a.m to 5 a.m., Friday and Saturday. Live bands.
- Mersini, 2120 Queen St. E.; 416 699-9444. The best espresso bar in the Beaches. Not licensed.
- Purple Pepper, 266 Queens Quay W.; 416 260-2095.
- Rebel House, 1068 Yonge St.; 416 927-0704. Try the cheese pennies and play Abalone, a terrific board game, in this pub.
- Silver Dollar Room, 484 Spadina Ave.; 416 975-0909. A Chicago-style house of blues. An easy-going, good-time place.
- Sneaky Dee's, 431 College St.; 416 603-3090. A sticky-floored beer hall. Ignore the feeling of being at a high school party and get caught up in the dancing.

- Tasting Rooms, First Canadian Place, 100 King St. W.; 416 362-2499. Three sections: a formal room, Wine Library and Smoke Lake Bar.

DINING

Toronto boasts some of the finest restaurants in North America. With a huge cultural diversity, there is something for everyone. The following is a select list of the restaurants available. Restaurants are listed alphabetically by category (e.g. Asian) and subcategory (e.g. Chinese). The sequence of the categories follows the sequence used in the dining chapter.

The map on page 9 shows the restaurants included in this selective listing which are located in central Toronto. The listings and brief descriptions which follow give you the numbers you can use to find central-city restaurants on the map.

Approximate prices are indicated, based on the average cost, at time of publication, of dinner for two including wine (where available), taxes and gratuity: $ = under $45; $$ = $45-$80; $$$ = $80-$120; $$$$ = $120-$180; $$$$$ = over $180. Meals served are indicated as: B = breakfast; L = lunch; D = dinner; Late = open past midnight; G = "grazing"; T-O = take-out. Credit cards accepted are also indicated: AX = American Express; V = Visa; MC = MasterCard.

CANADIAN
- 360, 301 Front St. W.; 416 362-5411. Atop the CN Tower, much better than expected meals for a revolving restaurant with a spectacular view. L/D, $$$$. **Map 67**
- Oyster Boy, 872 Queen St. W.; 416 534-3432.
- Patriot, 131 Bloor St. W.; 416 922-0025. Closed for weekend lunches. The best in modern Canadian cuisine and wine. L/D $$$.
- Rodney's, 469 King St. W.; 416 363-8105. Closed Sun. Go for the 2 dozen choices of raw oysters, opened while you watch. Intelligent, informed staff. L/D/Late/G/T-O, $$$, AX/V/MC. **Map 54**

ASIAN

Chinese
- Champion House, 480 Dundas St. W.; 416 977-8282. Wonderful Peking duck. Lots of vegetarian dishes. L/D/G, $$, AX/V/MC. **Map 37**
- Chung King, 428 Spadina Ave.; 416 593-0101
- Dragon Dynasty, 2301 Brimley Rd.; 416 321-9000. Peking duck with chive pancakes is worth the trek to suburbia. L/D/G/T-O, $$$, AX/V/MC.
- Eating Garden, 41 Baldwin St.; 416 595-5525
- Happy Seven Restaurant, 358 Spadina Ave.; 416 971-9820. Perfectly cooked fish at modest prices. Children welcome. L/D/G/Late/T-O, $$, V/MC. **Map 33**
- Kowloon, 5 Baldwin St.; 416 977-3773
- Lai Wah Heen, 108 Chestnut St.; 416 977-9899. Haute Cantonese and superlative Dim Sum. L/D, $$$, AX/V/MC. **Map 47**
- Lee Garden, 331 Spadina Ave.; 416 593-9524. Go early. Considered to be a notch above the rest. L/D/Late/T-O, $$$, AX/V/MC. **Map 32**
- Lucky Dragon, 418 Spadina Ave.; 416 598-7823. Excellent soups, noodle dishes, or anything with garlic; Jasmine tea, too. L/D/Late/G/T-O, $. **Map 28**
- Pearl Court, 633 Gerrard St. E.; 416 463-8778. Irreproachable seafood and interesting casseroles in a contemporary dining room. B/L/D/Late/G/T-O, $$$, V/MC.
- Peter's Chung King, 281 College St. W.; 416 928-2936
- Sai Woo, 130 Dundas St. W.; 416 977-4988
- Swatow, 309 Spadina Ave.; 416 977-0601
- Wah Sing, 47 Baldwin St.; 416 599-8822. Terrific two-for-one lobster specials. L/D/Late/G/T-O, $$, AX/V/MC. **Map 31**
- Xam Yu, 339 Spadina Ave.; 416 340-8603

Japanese

- Akane-ya, 2214 Queen St. E.; 416 699-0377
- Edo, 359 Eglinton Ave. W. Closed Mon; 416 481-1370. Dark and noisy. Fresh shrimp tempura in fragile batter and beef sashimi are magnificent. D/T-O, $$$, AX/V/MC.
- Ematei, 30 St. Patrick St.; 416 340-0472. Closed weekend lunch, Exquisite sushi and delicate soups. L/D/G/T-O, $$$, AX/V/MC. **Map 42**
- Hiro Sushi, 171 King St. E.; 416 304-0550. Hiro creates Toronto's most celebrated sushi. L/D, $$$$, AX/V/MC. **Map 61**
- Kaji, 860 The Queensway; 416 252-2166. Closed Monday. Impeccable sushi dinners at 3 price points. D, $$$$, V.
- Kobe, 9 Church St.; 416 365-1355. Closed Saturday lunch and Sunday. Sublime Kobe beef is featured in zenlike tatami rooms. **Map 53**
- Madoka, 252 Dupont St.; 416 924-3548. Closed Mon.; lunch Thurs. and Fri. only. Kindly sushi chefs are helpful to novices. Miso soup is particularly good. L/D/G/T-O, $$$, AX/V/MC.
- Rikishi, 833 Bloor St. W.; 416 538-0760. Closed weekend lunch/Mon. An enticing selection of small vegetarian dishes in humble surroundings. D/T-O, $$$, AX/V/MC.
- Tempo, 596 College St.; 416 531-2822. Closed Sunday. Tom Thai plates Toronto's most daring sushi and sashimi. D, $$$, AX/V/MC.

Korean

- Ho-Su Bistro, 254 Queen St. W.; 416 322-6860
- Korean Village Han Kuk Kwan, 628 Bloor St. W.; 416 536-0290. A dozen side dishes, including salads exploding with garlic and chillies accompany most dishes. Bring your appetite. L/D/T-O, $$, V/MC.

Thai/Laotian

- Ban Vanipha, 638 Dundas St. W.; 416 340-0491. Authentic, inexpensive Laotian food.. L/D, $$, AX/V/MC. **Map 39**
- Bangkok Garden, 18 Elm St.; 416 977-6748. Closed weekend lunch. Fabulous decor. Polished versions of traditional standards. L/D, $$$, AX/V/MC. **Map 35**
- Spice Thai Café, 250 Queen's Quay W.; 416 598-0600. Thai in an intimate setting. L/D, $$, AX/V/MC.
- Thai Magic, 1118 Yonge St.; 416 968-7366. Closed Sun. Other-worldly atmosphere. Food tastes even better presented on stunning dishes. D/T-O, $$, AX/V/MC.
- Vanipha Lanna, 863 St. Clair Ave. W.; 416 654-8068. Closed Sun. Admirable Laotian salads with vivid flavours: coriander, coconut, lemon grass. L/D/G/T-O, $$, V.
- Young Thailand, 165 John St.; 416 593-9291. Careful, balanced spicing and fresh ingredients. Pineapple-cashew salad is exceptional. L/D, $$$, AX/V/MC. **Map 50**

Tibetan

- Little Tibet, 712 Queen St. W.; 416 306-1896. Closed Sunday lunch/Monday. Nothing weird or scary. Terrific little dumplings; choose steamed or fried. Stir-fries, rice and noodle dishes. Admire the exotic wall murals. L/D/G/T-O, $$, AX/V/MC.

Vietnamese

- Indochine, 4 Collier St.; 416 922-5840. Closed Sun.; open for lunch and dinner Sat. Upper-class cuisine served without a trace of snobbery. L/D/G/T-O, $$, AX/V/MC. **Map 4**
- Pho Hung, 350 Spadina Ave.; 416 593-4274. The original. Same menu and quality fare in slightly humbler surroundings than 200 Bloor St. W. location. L/D/G/T-O, $$. **Map 11**
- Vien Dong, 359 Spadina Ave.; 416 593-6265. French influence adds refinements to classics. Exotic fruit milkshakes. L/D/G/Late/T-O, $$$, AX/MC. **Map 36**

Indian

- Babur, 273 Queen St. W.; 416 599-7720
- Bar-Be-Que Hut, 1455 Gerrard St. E.; 416 466-0411. Everything from the Tandoor oven tastes superb. Popular weekend brunch. L/D/Late/G/T-O, $$$, AX/V/MC.

- Blue Bay Café, 2443 Dundas St. W.; 416 533-8838. Closed Monday. Tropical Mauritian flavours: like Indian crossed with Thai. D, $$, AX/V/MC.
- Cuisine of India, 5222 Yonge St.; 416 229-0377. Discrete flavours with many vegetarian choices. L/D, $$$, AX/V/MC.
- The Host, 14 Prince Arthur Ave.; 416 962-4678. No lunch on Sun. Aristocratic cooking. Magical nut and cream sauces. L/D/G/T-O, $$$, AX/V/MC. **Map 10**
- Indian Rice Factory, 414 Dupont St.; 416 961-3472. No lunch on weekends. Owner-chef Amar Patel's attention to detail shows up in beguiling lamb and chicken curries. L/D/G/T-O, $$$, AX/V/MC.
- Madras Durbar, 1386 Gerrard St. E.; 416 465-2733. Inexpensive southern Indian vegetarian fare. L/D, $, AX/V/MC.
- Nataraj, 394 Bloor St. W.; 416 928-2925. Northern cuisine includes marvellous breads, tandoori chicken and expertly prepared seafood. L/D/G/T-O, $$, AX/V/MC.

CONTINENTAL

Greek
- Christina's, 492 Danforth Ave.; 416 463-4418. Straightforward Mediterranean cooking in the convivial din. B/L/D/Late/G/T-O, $$, AX/V/MC.
- Myth, 417 Danforth Ave.; 416 461-8383. No lunch Sun.-Wed. Weird and wonderful. Anything in phyllo pastry's a winner. L/D/Late/G/T-O, $$$, AX/V/MC.
- Ouzeri, 500-A Danforth Ave.; 416 778-0500. Ordinary braises and filo pies shine with cinnamon, mint and anise flavours. L/D/Late/G/T-O, $$, AX/V/MC.
- Pan, 516 Danforth Ave.; 416 466-8158. Lamb with figs and refined sweets in a hip atmosphere. D/Late/G, $$$, AX/V/MC.
- Pappas Grill, 440 Danforth Ave.; 416 469-9595. Straightforward comfort food. Children are welcome. L/D/Late/G/T-O, $$$, AX/V/MC.

French/Belgian/Bistro
- Arlequin, 134 Avenue Rd.; 416 928-9521. Closed Sun. Grilled sardines, chicken couscous with lemons, calamari with olives, baguettes and salads. D/G/T-O, $$$, AX/V/MC. **Map 1**
- Bier Markt, 58 The Esplanade; 416 862-7575. A huge selection of beers from across the world complements brasserie food. L/D $$ **Map 63**
- Brownes Bistro, 4 Woodlawn Ave. E.; 416 924-8132. No lunch on weekends, closed Mondays in summer. Robust pastas and wines by the glass are the big sellers. L/D/G/T-O, $$$$, AX/V/MC.
- Café Brussel, 124 Danforth Ave.; 416 465-7363. Mussels a dozen ways and more in magic art deco room. Great brunches. L/D, $$$, AX/V/MC.
- Cities, 859 Queen St. W.; 416 504-3762
- Epicure Cafe, 512 Queen St. W.; 416 504-8942
- Gamelle, 468 College St.; 416 923-6254.Closed Monday, no lunch Tuesday. Asian influenced bistro with ambitious wine list. L/D, $$$, AX/V/MC.
- Jacques' Bistro du Parc, 126A Cumberland St.; 416 961-1893. Closed Sunday lunch. Classic bistro cooking, great omelettes. L/D, $$$, AX/V/MC. **Map 5**
- La Maquette, 111 King St. E.; 416 416 366-8191. Closed Saturday lunch and Sunday. French and Italian fare served in garden-side setting. L/D $$$
- Le Matignon, 51 St. Nicholas St.; 416 921-9226
- Le Nouveau Parigo, 1675 Bloor Street W.; 416 531-8850. Bistro classics, including beautiful salads. D, $$$, V.
- Le Papillon, 16 Church St.; 416 363-0838. Closed Mon. Crepes are the point here but the onion soup is a hit with Saturday crowds. L/D/Late, $$, AX/V/MC. **Map 57**
- Le Paradis, 166 Bedford Rd.; 416 921-0995. Bistro with a turn towards Morocco. L/D, $$$, AX/V/MC.
- Le Sélect, 328 Queen St. W.; 416 596-6405
- Pastis, 1158 Yonge St. ; 416 928-2212. Bistro and high-end French fare. L/D, $$$$, AX/V/MC.

- Provence, 12 Amelia St.; 416 924-9901. A great wine list complements southern french cuisine. L/D, $$$$, AX/V/MC.
- Quartier, 2112 Yonge St.; 416 545-0505. Beautifully executed bistro. L/D, $$$$, AX/V/MC.
- Quigley's, 2232 Queen St. E.; 416 699-9998
- Richard's, 2006 Queen St. E.; 416 698-2066
- Torch Bistro, 249 Victoria St.; 416 364-7517. Closed Mon. Solid upscale cooking with extensive wine list. Close to theatres. L/D/G, $$$$, AX/V/MC. **Map 40**
- Zola, 162 Cumberland St.; 416 515-1222. Upscale food and wine with a patio smack dab in the Yorkville shopping district. L/D, $$$$, V/MC.

Italian
- Bar Italia, 582 College St.; 416 535-3621. Fabulous sandwiches of cured meats, greens and fine olive oil on crusty buns. L/D/G/Late, $$, AX/V/MC.
- Bar One, 924 Queen St. W.; 416 535-1655
- Barolo, 193 Carlton St.; 416 961-4747. No lunch Sat.-Sun. High-roller Italian wines, bold pasta sauces and primo grilled meats. L/D/Late/G, $$$, AX/V/MC.
- Biagio, 155 King St. E.; 416 366-4040. Closed Saturday lunch and Sunday. Traditional northern Italian fare pared with great Italian wines. L/D $$$ **Map 55**
- Bravi, 40 Wellington St. E..; 416 368-9030. Closed Sunday and Saturday lunch. Comfort food accented with invention. L/D, $$$, AX/V/MC.
- Ci Vediamo, 1970 Queen St. E.; 416 694-5966
- College St. Bar, 574 College St.; 416 533-2417. Energetic young staff. Pasta with fresh pesto sauce. Shows what a tiny kitchen can do. D/G/T-O, $$, AX/V/MC.
- Coppi, 3363 Yonge St.; 416 484-4464. Sublime seafood plus great Italian wines. L/D, $$$, AX/V/MC.
- Focaccia, 17 Hayden St.; 416 323-0719. International starters with comfy Italian mains. L/D, $$$$, AX/V/MC. **Map 22**
- Galileo, 193 King St. E.; 416 363-

6888. Closed Sun. Unique variations on traditional preparations. Smoked quail and salmon taste splendid. L/D/G, $$$$, AX/V/MC.
- Giancarlo Trattoria, 41 Clinton St.; 416 533-9619. Closed Sun. Romantic little room with neighbourhood-style terrace. Remarkable seafood and wine list. D, $$$, AX/V/MC.
- Grano, 2035 Yonge St.; 416 440-1986. Closed Sun. A stylish room features several metres of fresh antipasti under glass. L/D/Late/G/T-O, $$$, AX/V/MC.
- Grappa Restaurant, 797 College St.; 416 535-3337. Closed Mon. Baked sea bass stands out. D/Late, $$$, V/MC.
- Il Fornello, 2901 Bayview Ave.; 1968 Queen St. E.; 214 King St. W. **Map 60**; 55 Eglinton Ave. E.; 1560 Yonge St.; 35 Elm St.; 576 Danforth Ave.; 416 920-9410. Consistently high-caliber pizzas from wood-fired ovens. Families welcomed. L/D/Late/G/T-O, $$, AX/V/MC.
- La Fenice, 319 King St. W.; 416 585-2377. Closed Sun.; dinner only Sat. Outstanding shrimp grilled with olive oil. Pasta with fresh truffles in season. L/D/G/, $$$, AX/V/MC. **Map 62**
- Masquerade Caffe, 42 Yonge St.; 416 363-8971 Closed Sunday. Expert ravioli in colourful surroundings. L/D $$
- Mezza Luna, 999 Eglinton Ave. W.; 416 787-8787. Beguiling antipasti table in stylish surrounding. D/G/T-O, $$$, AX/V/MC.
- Noce, 783 Queen St. W.; 416 504-3463
- O Sole Mio, 3186 Yonge St.; 416 482-6000. No lunch July-Oct. Homemade gnocchi, grilled fish are favourites. Children welcome. L/D, $$$, AX/V/MC.
- Prego della Piazza, 150 Bloor St. W.; 416 920-9900. Closed Sun. Spot the celebrities over veal chops and a bottle of Barolo. L/D/G, $$$$, AX/V/MC. **Map 9**
- Sazio, 3185 Yonge St.; 416 484-0745. Closed Sun.; lunch Mon.-Fri.; dinner Mon.-Sat. Warm olives, seafood soup and contemporary ingredients all work. L/D/G/T-O, $$$, AX/V/MC.

- Sotto Sotto, 116A Avenue Rd.; 416 962-0011. Romantic, subterranean setting. Irresistible grilled dishes, especially the radicchio. D, $$$$, AX/V/MC. **Map 2**
- Terroni, 106 Victoria St.; 416 955-0258, 720 Queen St. W.; 416-504-0320. Closed Sunday. Upmarket pastas and thin crispy pizzas in a relaxed setting. L/D $$ **Map 29**
- Zizi Trattoria, 456 Bloor St. W.; 416 533-5117. Friendly, nostalgic atmosphere. Checkered tablecloths, memorable home-made desserts. D/T-O, $$$, AX/V/MC. **Map 14**
- Zucca, 2150 Yonge St.; 416 488-5774. Rustic, traditional food from the heel of Italy's boot. L/D, $$$, AX/V/MC.

OTHER EUROPEAN
- Amadeu's, 184 Augusta St.; 416 591-1245
- Country Style Hungarian Restaurant, 450 Bloor St. W.; 416 537-1745. Waitresses whisk hefty schnitzels and smoked pork with beans to tables at record speed. L/D/T-O, $. **Map 12**
- Millie's Bistro,1980 Avenue Rd.; 416 481-1247. Mediterranean spices inspire a changing menu. L/D, $$$, AX/V/MC.
- Segovia, 5 St. Nicholas St.; 416 960-1010. Dinner Mon.-Sat., lunch Mon.-Fri.; closed Sun. Authentic Spanish flavours in paella; garlicky chicken. Flamenco dancers upstairs. L/D, $$$, AX/V/MC. **Map 24**
- The Boat, 158 Augusta St.; 416 593-9218
- Vienna Home Bakery, 626 Queen St. W.; 416 703-7278

ETHNIC
- Boulevard Café, 161 Harbord St.; 416 961-7676. Solid, home-style South American fare. Shaded patio is the most popular in the neighbourhood. L/D/G/T-O, $$$$, AX/V/MC.
- Byzantium, 499 Church St.; 416 922-3859. Moroccan and Middle Eastern specialties in two design-award-winning rooms. D/G/, $$$$, AX/V/MC. **Map 25**
- Ethiopian House, 4 Irwin St.; 416 923-5438. Earthy stews served in traditional covered platters.

L/D/Late/G/T-O, $$, AX/V/MC. **Map 23**
- Jerusalem, 955 Eglinton Ave. W.; 416 783-6494. Reliable, Middle Eastern cooking. Eggplant is special. L/D/G/T-O, $$, AX/V/MC.
- Kensington Kitchen, 122-24 Harbord St.; 416 961-3404. Lovely rooms and a leafy roof patio in summer. Distinguished Lebanese dishes predominate. L/D/G/T-O, $$$, AX/V/MC. **Map 16**
- Southern Accent, 595 Markham; 416 536-3211. Blackened chicken livers a must. Festive patio music. D, $$$, AX/V/MC. **Map 15**

À LA MODE
- Axcess, 3185 Yonge St.; 416 482-8485. Closed for lunch Sat, all day Sunday. Colourful, inventive fusion food. L/D, $$$$, AX/V/MC.
- Cafe La Gaffe, 24 Baldwin St.; 416 596-2397. Pizza menu only 4-6 pm. Brunch on weekends. Romantic bohemian environment. Valiant portions of home-style cooking. Don't miss dessert. L/D/G, $$$, V/MC. **Map 30**
- Citron, 813 Queen St. W.; 416 504-2647. No lunch Monday to Friday in winter. Funky fusion foods throughout the day. L/D, $$, AX/V/MC.
- Goldfish, 372 Bloor St. W.; 416 513-0077. Fusion with a Canadian flare. L/D, $$$, AX/V/MC. **Map 6**
- Gypsy Co-op, 817 Queen St. W.; 416 703-5069
- Jump, 16 Wellington St. W.; 416 363-3400. Closed Saturday lunch and Sunday. A Cal-Ital bistro at the city's financial heart. L/D, $$$, AX/V/MC.
- Left Bank, 567 Queen St. W.; 416 504-1626
- Lemon Meringue,2390 Bloor St. W.; 416 769-5757. Closed Sunday and Monday. Signature pie preceded by beguiling mains. D, $$$, AX/V/MC.
- Marché, 42 Yonge St.; 416 366-8986. Eclectic bistro food, cafeteria style, in fun, bustling atmosphere. Late. L/D $$ **Map 66**
- Messis, 97 Harbord St.; 416 920-2186. Tweedy profs from nearby U of T enjoy warm salads, stylish pizza and well-priced wines. D, $$$, AX/V/MC. **Map 17**

- Mildred Pierce, 99 Sudbury St.; 416 588-5695. Lunch Mon.-Fri.; brunch Sun.; Cal-Ital flavours from talented kitchen. L/D, $$$, AX/V/MC.
- Opus, 37 Prince Arthur Ave.; 416 921-3015. Enjoy Toronto's best lamb and an awe-inspiring wine list. D, $$$$, AX/V/MC.
- Pony, 488 College St.; 416 923-7665. Closed Sunday. Nifty appetizers can be ordered as mains for $5 more. D, $$$, AX/V/MC.
- Red Tea Box, 696 Queen St. W.; 416 203-8882
- Superior, 253 Yonge St.; 416 214-0416. Closed Sunday. Pre-show fine dining for nearby Canon, Elgin, Winter Garden theatre crowds. L/D $$$
- Swan, 892 Queen St. W.; 416 532-0452
- Terra, 8199 Yonge St.; 905 731-6161. Closed Monday. Ironically for a place named "Earth," fresh seafood is the standout. D, $$$$, AX/V/MC.
- YYZ, 345 Adelaide St. W.; 416 599-3399. Asian inspired dishes and modernist room are equally gorgeous. D, $$$$, AX/V/MC.

FOUR-STAR DINING

- Accolade, 225 Front St. W.; 416 597-8142. Closed Sunday & Saturday lunch. Chef Michael Potters serves star tasting menus. L/D, $$$$, AX/V/MC. **Map 65**
- Avalon, 270 Adelaide St. W.; 416 979-9918. Closed Sunday. Lunch only Thursday. Discover chef Christopher McDonald's sublime Italian-influenced cooking. L/D, $$$$, AX/V/MC. **Map 52**
- Black and Blue, 150 Bloor St. W.; 416 920-9900. Closed Sun. The city's hottest steakhouse. Big ticket wines and pampering service. D/Late, $$$$, AX/V/MC. **Map 8**
- Boba, 90 Avenue Rd.; 416 961-2622. Closed Sun. Splendid fusion cooking by top chefs Barbara Gordon and Bob Berman. D, $$$$, AX/V/MC. **Map 3**
- Canoe, Toronto Dominion Tower, 66 Wellington St. W.; 416 364-0054. Closed weekends. Finest local ingredients cooked with Japanese refinement. L/D, $$$$, AX/V/MC. **Map 59**

- Centro, 2472 Yonge St.; 416 483-2211. Closed Sun. High-end Italian food with contemporary twists. Awe-inspiring wine cellar. D/Late, $$$$, AX/V/MC.
- Chiado, 864 College St.; 416 538-1910. Light, elegant Portuguese cooking in graceful surroundings. D/G/T-O, $$$$, AX/V/MC.
- The Fifth, 225 Richmond St. W.; 416 979-3005. Luxury ingredients, a gifted chef, on the fifth floor of a warehouse. Go figure. D/Late, $$$$$, AX/V/MC.
- J.K. ROM, 100 Queen's Park Cres.; 416 586-5578. Right inside the Royal Ontario Museum. Chef Jamie Kennedy's stellar dishes available at lunchtime. L/G, $$, AX/V/MC. **Map 20**
- Oro, 45 Elm St.; 416 597-0155. Closed Sunday and Saturday lunch. Thorough pampering in a lovely dining room. L/D, $$$$, AX/V/MC. **Map 34**
- Pangaea, 1221 Bay St.; 416 920-2323. Closed Sun. Inventive culinary notions backed by technical expertise. Afternoon tea. L/D, $$$$, AX/V/MC. **Map 21**
- Rain, 19 Mercer St.; 416 599-7246. Closed Sunday and Monday. Superb fusion food in the one of the continent's most beautiful rooms. D, $$$$, AX/V/MC. **Map 38**
- Scaramouche Pasta Bar/Restaurant, 1 Benvenuto Place; 416 961-8011. Closed Sun. A gifted chef, top-drawer service and lavish dining room. D/G, $$$$$, AX/V/MC.
- Sen5es, 318 Wellington St. W.; 416 935-0400. Fusion perfection in cool modern elegance. L/D, $$$$, AX/V/MC.
- Splendido, 88 Harbord St.; 416 929-7788. Closed Sun. Meaty green olives to fruit garnishes are chosen and prepared with care. D, $$$$, AX/V/MC. **Map 18**
- Susur, 601 King St. W.; 416 603-2205. Closed Sunday. Star chef Susur Lee is the king of Fusion. D, $$$$, AX/V/MC.
- Truffles, 2nd floor, Four Seasons Hotel, 21 Avenue Rd.; 416 928-7331. Closed Sun. Canadian Heart Association's stamp of approval on haute cuisine selections. Deluxe ingredients. D, $$$$$, AX/V/MC.

Map 7

- Zoom, 18 King St. E.; 416 861-9872. Both food and the room itself compete for the best design. Awesome desserts. L/D/Late, $$$$, AX/V/MC.

ART SCENE

- Peter Pan, 373 Queen St. W.; 416 593-0917. Sunday brunch. Burgers, warm salads and Thai noodles. No gaffes. L/D/Late/G, $$$, AX/V/MC. **Map 49**
- Queen Mother Cafe, 208 Queen St. W.; 416 598-4719. Lots of arty atmosphere. Choice of excellent small dishes. L/D/Late/G/T-O, $$, AX/V/MC. **Map 43**
- Rivoli, 332 Queen St. W.; 416 596-1908. Elegant fare borrows flavours from the Orient. Quirky decor and staff. L/D/Late/G, $$$, AX/V/MC. **Map 48**
- Tiger Lily's Noodle House, 257 Queen St. W.; 416 977-5499. Healthy East-Asian soups and noodle dishes with flair. L/D/G/T-O, $$, AX/V/MC. **Map 44**

NEIGHBOURHOOD SPOTS

- Allen's, 143 Danforth Ave.; 416 463-3086. Wide selection of imported beers. Backyard patio. Burgers carefully grilled to order. L/D/Late/G/T-O, $$$, AX/V/MC.
- Barberian's, 7 Elm St.; 416 597-0335
- C'est What?, 67 Front St. E.; 416 867-9499. Plenty of suds from outstanding local microbreweries. Live jazz. L/D/Late/G/T-O, $$, AX/V/MC. **Map 56**
- Carman's Club Steak House and Seafood, 26 Alexander St.; 416 924-8697. Glorious beef. Olives and dill pickles pass as vegetables. Hundreds of celebrity photos. New steak house section. D/, $$$$, AX/V/MC. **Map 26**
- Cultures Fresh Food Restaurant, Eaton Centre, **Map 41**. 208 Bloor St. W.; 43 Eglinton Ave. E.; 120 Adelaide St. W.; 200 King St. W. (Sunlife Centre); Royal Bank Plaza (200 Bay St.). 416 368-1440. Closed Sun. Cafeteria-style. Fresh soups, salads, sandwiches and quiche. B/L/D/G/T-O, $.
- Express Café, 254 Queen St. W., 416 596-0205. Hip and happening. Choose fresh salads and sandwich makings from glass display cases.

B/L/D/G/T-O, $$, V. **Map 46**
- Free Times Café, 320 College St.; 416 967-1078. Live folk music, wholesome light meals and kindly staff. L/D/Late/G/T-O, $, AX/V/MC. **Map 27**
- Montana, 145 John St.; 416 595-5949. Superb wood oven-baked pizzas, everything from the grill's in top form. A perennial favourite with singles. L/D/Late/G/T-O, $$$, AX/V/MC. **Map 51**
- The Paddock, 178 Bathurst St.; 416 504-9997. Lunch Tues.-Fri. Reopened deco beverage room features live jazz and lots of pizzazz. L/D/Late/G, $$, AX/V/MC. **Map 45**
- Pauper's, 539 Bloor St. W., 416 530-1331. Well-executed pub food with happy hour bargains and rooftop patio. L/D/G/T-O, $$, AX/V/MC. **Map 13**
- Room 338 Diner, 338 Huron St.; 416 979-2486. Cheerful staff dish out hearty student fare. Right on U of T campus. B/L/D/G/T-O, $. **Map 19**
- Rosetta, 924 Kingston Rd.; 416 690-6081
- Shopsy's Delicatessen, 1535 Yonge St., 416 967-5252; 33 Yonge St.; 416 365-3333; 284 King St. W.; 416 599-5464. A stone's throw from the Hummingbird Theatre. All-beef hot dogs are a hit. B/L/D/G/T-O, $$, AX/V/MC. **Map 58**
- Tulip, 1610 Queen St. E.; 416 469-5797
- Wheat Sheaf, 667 King St. W., 416 504-9912. Toronto's oldest pub. Unpretentious and decent fare. L/D/Late/G/T-O, $, AX/V/MC. **Map 64**

SHOPPING

ANTIQUES AND COLLECTIBLES

Toronto's antique dealers are diverse and far-flung. It's easiest if you pick a neighbourhood and start by visiting all the shops in the vicinity. After some individual locations of general interest, key shops in areas rich with antiques are listed below.

General
- Bayview Village Shopping Centre: Antique Market. Bayview and Sheppard, 416 226-0404. Runs one Sunday each month and spans the

entire mall from 10 a.m. to 5 p.m.
- Harbourfront Antique Market, 390 Queens Quay W., 416 260-2626. Permanent antique market with more than 100 exhibitors. High-quality jewellery, ceramics, glass, silver, carpets and other items. Open Tues.-Sun. 10 a.m.-6 p.m.
- Old China Patterns Ltd. 1560 Brimley (at Ellesmere). Scarborough, 416 299-8880, Fax: 416 299-4721. Off the beaten track, but the best place to call to replace that broken dish from Grandma's china set. Extensive selection of discontinued patterns.
- The Sunday Market, St. Lawrence North Market, Front and Jarvis Streets, 416 410-1310. Popular antique and collectibles market every Sunday.

North Yonge St., Mount Pleasant Blvd., and Bayview
- Acanthus Antiques, 612 Mount Pleasant Blvd., 416 483-8510. 18th century desks and other fine furnishings.
- Antiquers, 561 Mount Pleasant Blvd., 416 481-4474. Jewellery, sterling silver, china, glass and furniture.
- Art of Design, 207 Queen's Quay W., 416 214-5809 and other locations.

Queen St. West
- Arcadia Antiques, 1702 Queen St. W. (at Roncesvalles), 416 534-0348. Large selection of furniture and collectibles; part of an enclave of antique stores east of Roncesvalles.
- Quasi-Modo Modern Furniture, 789 Queen St. W. 416 703-8300. Vintage furniture and collectibles.
- Red Indian Art Deco, 536 Queen St. W., 416 504-7706. Very cool vintage furniture and collectibles: Deco lamps, cocktail shakers, chrome items.

Queen St. East
- Antique Aid, 187A Queen St. E., 416 368-9565. Estate and antique jewellery, fine china, ceramics, glass and silver as well as other interesting items; repair silver, glass and china; the place to go if your antiques need restoring.
- Clutters Art Deco Gallery Antiques, 692 Queen St. E., 416 461-3776. Specializing in art deco furniture, accessories and antique lighting of

the period.
- Zig Zag, 1107 Queen St. E., 416 778-6495

Markham Village
- Journey's End Antiques Ltd., 612 Markham St., 416 536-2226. Estate silver, crystal, glass and china.
- Plantation Antiques, 608 Markham St., 416 533-6466. Small, quaint, cluttered shop packed with antique jewellery, silver, cloissone, Victorian glass and porcelain. Lots of treasures.

Yorkville and Avenue Road
- David Gillies Antiques, 21 Avenue Rd., 416 967-9753. Fine furnishings and decorative items.
- The Paisley Shop Ltd., 77 Yorkville, 416 923-5830. Specializing in 18th and 19th century furniture, porcelain and decorative accessories.
- R.A. O'Neil Antiques, 100 Avenue Road, 416 968-2806. Country furniture, primitive ceramics and other decorative accessories.
- Stanley Wagman and Sons Antiques Ltd., 224 Davenport Rd., 416 964-1047.

Yonge St. at Rosedale and Summerhill
- Absolutely Inc., 1132 Yonge St., 416 324-8351. Vintage desk lamps, club chairs, 19th century paisley shawls.
- L'Atelier, 1224 Yonge St., 416 966-0200. European fine furniture, hand-blown antique light fixtures, ottomans and architectural prints.
- Prince of Serendip, 1073 Yonge St., 416 925-3760. Antique furniture, chandeliers, decorative accessories.
- Perkins Antiques, 1198 Yonge St., 416 925-0973. Fine Canadian pine furniture and primitive ceramics.

BEAUTY AND HEALTH
- Aveda Environmental Lifestyle Store, 95 Bloor St. W. 416 413-1333. Full line of Aveda products, including shampoo, hair care products, and cosmetics.
- Beauty Queen, 249 Queen St. W., 416 977-4277. A full service salon with a wide range of products for your hair.
- The Body Shop, 100 Bloor St. W., 416 928-1180; most major malls and assorted other locations. Toronto Eaton Centre, 220 Yonge

St., 977-7364; 71 Wellesley at Church, 416 323-1878. Environmentally-friendly skin care products, cosmetics and toiletries.
- Crabtree and Evelyn, Hazelton Lanes, 416 929-0109; Toronto Eaton Centre, 416 340-1488 and most upscale malls. A line of soaps and body lotions from the U.K.; also cotton dressing gowns, pajamas and nightgowns.
- Hooper's Pharmacy, 2124 Queen St. E. in the Beaches, 416 928-3366. A full-range pharmacy which also carries homeopathic supplies.
- Lush, 312 Queen St. W., 416 599-5874; 116 Cumberland St., 416 960-5874 277 Yonge St., 416 703-5874; 633 Yonge St., 416 924-5874. A blitz of bath bombs from London, England, along with other bubbly concoctions.
- M.A.C., 89 Bloor St. W., 416 929-7555; Hudson's Bay Centre (at Bloor and Yonge), 416 972-3363; The Bay at Queen and Yonge, 416 861-4508 as well as 12 other locations. A makeup store that contributes to AIDS charities through a wide range of cruelty-free products.
- Mirella Parfums and Cosmetics, Manulife Centre, 55 Bloor St. W., 416 923-9302. French and Italian fragrances, cosmetics for men and women, and hair accessories and costume jewellery.
- Thompson's Homeopathic Supplies Ltd., 844 Yonge St., 416 922-2300. One of Toronto's main homeopathic suppliers.
- Thuna Herbals and Wholistic Centre (Since 1888), 298 Danforth Ave., 416 465-3366. A 19th century apothecary atmosphere pervades this long-established shop.

BOOKS
New
- Another Man's Poison, 29 McCaul St., 416 593-6451. A design bookstore with hefty volumes on architecture, packaging, tin soldiers and even Bakelite; not for the weak of wallet, but a great browse.
- Another Story, 164 Danforth Ave., 416 462-1104. Great selection of books on politics, women's studies and labour, with a multicultural bent; excellent children's selection; knowledgeable staff.

- BAKKA Science Fiction Bookstore, 598 Yonge St. (north of Wellesley), 416 963-9993. Knowledgeable staff always have something new to suggest; this is the place to whet your inter-galactic whistle.
- Ballenford Books on Architecture, 600 Markham St., 416 588-0800. A gallery-like atmosphere for books on all things built, located in Mirvish Village.
- Books for Business, 120 Adelaide St. W., 416 362-7822, www.booksforbusiness.com. Well-stocked store in the heart of the Financial District.
- Book City, 348 Danforth Ave., 416 469-9997, 180 Bloor St. W., 416 922-3557; 1430 Yonge St. 416 961-1228; 1950 Queen St. E., 416 698-1444. The best stop for remaindered titles in the city, but they also stock everything else.
- Chapters, 110 Bloor St. W. 416 920-9299. The first of its kind in Toronto with much to recommend it: Selection, location and the obligatory big comfy couches and lattes. A new location has opened as part of the Paramount at Richmond and John.
- The Constant Reader Books for Children. 111 Harbord St., 416 972-0661.
- The Cookbook Store, 850 Yonge St., 416 920-2665. Not far from Chapters; a great specializer.
- Librairie Champlain, 468 Queen St. E., 416 364-4345. Bilingual staff make this large, French bookstore, housed in an old brewery, a welcome haven for anyone.
- Glad Day Bookshop, 598A Yonge St., 416 961-4161. Eclectic mix serves the Gay and Lesbian community.
- IndigoBooks, Music and Café, 2300 Yonge St. 416 544-0049; Manulife Centre, 55 Bloor St. W., 416 925-3536 and several other locations; A huge selection of books, thematically arranged, plus CDs and great coffee in two locations.
- Maison de la Presse Internationale, 124 Yorkville Ave., 416 928-2328. A wide selection of international newspapers and magazines.
- Nicholas Hoare, 45 Front St. E., 416 777-2665. A publisher's dream

and cornucopia of colour: Almost all the books face out, framed by fine wood display stands and walls.

- David Mirvish Books and Books on Art, 596 Markham St., 416 531-9975. Best selection of art books in Toronto in the heart of Mirvish Village.
- Mabel's Fables Children's Book Stores, 662 Mount Pleasant, 416 322-0438.
- The Omega Centre Bookstore, 29 Yorkville Ave., 416 975-9086. New Age titles and related paraphernalia.
- Open Air Books & Maps, 25 Toronto St., 416 363-0719. If you're coming or going, this is the place to find out how to get there. It's below street level, so look for the sign leading down.
- Pages Books and Magazines, 256 Queen St. W., 416 598-1447. Queen West's most popular newsstand and bookroom.
- Parentbooks, 201 Harbord St., 416 537-8334. Books on all things adult, from pregnancy or adoption to divorce and bereavement.
- Sleuth of Baker St., 1600 Bayview Ave., 416 483-3111. Toronto's mystery bookstore.
- Smithbooks, Toronto Eaton Centre, 220 Yonge St., 416 979-9376; Fairview Mall, 416 499-0581; 2187 Queen St. E., 416 698-9536. Some of the many locations of this stalwart chain are listed above; you'll also find them at Terminals 1 and 2 of the Toronto International Airport.
- Spoken Word Audiobooks, 350 Bay St., 416 368-1027. A great find in the Financial District for books on tape and CDs.
- Theatrebooks, 11 St. Thomas St., 416 922-7175. If this is how Toronto runs specialist bookrooms, it can never have enough: An excellent store for all things dramatic in a fine redbrick building.
- This Ain't The Rosedale Library, 483 Church St., 416 929-9912. A great store for fiction in the heart of the Church Street community.
- Toronto Women's Book Store, 73 Harbord St., 416 922-8744. Well-positioned to serve the gender studies crowd at the University of Toronto, and a fine bookstore in its

own right.
- University of Toronto Bookstore, 214 College St., 416 978-7900. Housed in the Koffler Centre, the old U of T library. Since Robarts reared its beak, it's up to bookstores to look like libraries; this one does a fine job and has a huge academic selection.
- World's Biggest Bookstore, 20 Edward St., 416 977-7009. Before Chapters and Indigo, there was this two-floor giant. It's still a contender.

Used
- Abelard Books, 519 Queen St. W., 416 504-2665. Always a good feel to this well laid-out bookroom, not to mention good bookmarks to go with your purchases.
- Atticus, 84 Harbord St., 416 922-6045. The best second-hand scholarly bookstore in Toronto, one of a row of used and specialized bookstores just west of the U of T campus.
- Balfour Books, 601 College St., 416 531-9911. A book lover's surprise in the heart of Little Italy; the green awning takes you back to the storefront shopping era.
- Hugh Anson-Cartwright, 229 College St. W., Rm. 107, 416 979-2441. A trusted and experienced antiquarian and academic dealer, just south of the U of T campus.
- David Mason Books, 342 Queen St. W., 416 598-1015. A long-time survivor on what is now a trendy section of Queen; walk up a flight and lose yourself among ancient spines.
- McBurnie and Cutler, 698 Queen St. W., 416 504-8873. The gem of Queen St. west of Bathurst; there are always new arrivals and old favorites in this fine shop.
- Steven Temple Books, 489 Queen St. W., 2nd Fl., 416 703-9908. Another Queen Street survivor, with a fine selection of Canadian antiquarian books.

CANADIANA
- Arctic Nunavut, Queens Quay Terminal, 207 Queens Quay W., 416 203-7889. Inuit carvings and other arctic arts and crafts; also located at Pearson International Airport, Terminal 2.
- Canadiana Shoppe, Toronto Eaton

Centre, 416 977-6547. All things Canadian, from traditional to contemporary.

- Canadian Naturalist, 207 Queen's Quay W., 416 203-0365, Eaton Centre, 416 581-0044
- Hudson Bay Company Gallery, 401 Bay St., 9th Floor, 416 861-4626.
- Native Canadian Centre of Toronto: Gift Store, 16 Spadina Rd., 416 964-9087. Moccasins, beadwork, cards, and other Native-made items.
- Oh Yes! Toronto, Queens Quay Terminal, 416 203-0607, two locations in Eaton Centre, 416 593-6749 and 416 596-0443. Clothing for all ages to take home as souvenirs from Toronto.
- Toronto Dominion Gallery of Inuit Art, 66 Wellington St. W., 416 982-8473. Open Monday to Friday 8 am to 6 pm, Saturday and Sunday 10 am to 4 pm.

CHINA AND CRYSTAL
- William Ashley, 55 Bloor St. W., 416 964-2900. Toronto's largest selection of fine china, crystal, silver and gifts.
- Du Verre, 280 Queen St. W., 416 593-0182. Hand-blown glassware and hand-crafted iron furnishings.
- Amarynth, 131 Bloor St. W., 416 515-9191, 1-800-551-9190. This is the only Lalique boutique in Canada and features the exquisite crystal work of René Lalique, the most successful glassmaker of the twentieth century.
- Lincraft, 276 Danforth Ave., 416 406-6996. Canadian-made gifts vie for your attention among Royal Copenhagen, Royal Doulton, Wedgwood and others.
- Muti and Company, 88 Yorkville Ave. 416 969-0253. An ample selection of imported Italian majolica ceramics.

CLOTHING: CANADIAN DESIGNERS
- Blue Angel, 2237 Bloor St. W., 416 763-2098
- Comrags, 654 Queen St. W., 416 360-7249. Canadian duo Joyce Gunhouse and Judy Cornish offer feminine clothing such as ethereal floral rayon dresses and tight-fitting cotton-Lycra knits.
- Eriettas, 320 Danforth Ave., 416 778-8363.
- Fashion Crimes, 395 Queen St. W., 416 592-9001. Velvet wear for the goth crowd, Edwardian morning coats, Empire-waisted bodice gowns and glamourous accessories.
- Finishing Touches, 3281 Yonge St., 416 482-9034. Offers the best in Canadian women's fashion.
- Hoax Couture, 114 Cumberland St., 416 929-4629. Men's and women's wear cut with panache and invention by designers Jim Searle and Chris Tyrell.
- Lida Baday Studio, 70 Claremont St., 416 603-7661. Simple, elegant, high-end women's fashion, using excellent fabrics and knits.
- Linda Lundstrom, 136 Cumberland St., 416 927-9009; Bayview Village (Bayview and Sheppard), 416 225-7227. Women's outerwear including the four-coats-in-one La-Parka.
- Lowon Pope Design, 779 Queen St. W., 416 504-8150
- Marilyn Brooks, 132 Cumberland St., 416 961-5050. A well-known line of fine, sensible women's clothing.
- Motion Clothing Co., 106 Cumberland St., 416 968-0090.
- Ms. Emma Designs, 1721 Bayview Ave., 416 322-1849; 87 Harbord St., 416 323-8800; 1230 Yonge St., 416 924-6304. Here's a happy marriage of handmade clothing in exotic, imported natural fabrics; alterations included in the price.
- Price Roman, 267 Queen St. W., 416 979-7363. Elegant women's suits and dresses, with simple lines and subtle detailing.
- Psyche, 352 Queen St. W., 416 599-4882

CLOTHING: CHILDREN'S
- Athenian Originals, 523 Danforth Ave. 416 461-1086. A thorough selection of kids' clothing.
- Bon Lieu, 890 Yonge St., 416 963-4322. A fine selection of European and Canadian children's clothing and accessories.
- Cotton Basics, 16 Baldwin St., 416 977-1959. Carries its own line of children's clothing exclusively.
- Gap Kids, Toronto Eaton Centre, 218 Yonge St., 416 348-8800; 80 Bloor St. W., 515-0668; 2574 Yonge St., 416 440-0187. Well-

made clothing for babies and children in natural fabrics; a bit on the preppy side.

- Jacadi, Hazelton Lanes, 87 Avenue Rd., 416 923-1717; 2901 Bayview Ave., 416 733-1717. Jacadi's line of clothing, nursery furnishings and shoes for newborns to 14-year-olds.
- Kid's Wardrobe, 12 Wineva Ave., 416 778-6153.
- Little Ones Fashions, 372 Eglinton Ave. W., 416 483-5989. Designerwear from Canada and abroad for newborns to pre-teens; extensive selection.
- Misdemeanours, 322 1/2 Queen St. W., 416 351-8758. This wonderful shop makes you step through the looking-glass: storybook dresses for girls, accented with Victorian frills.
- Roots, 100 Bloor St. W., 416 323-3289; Toronto Eaton Centre, 416 593-9640, 12 other stores, plus 3 factory outlets; www.roots.com. Look for the Baby Roots line at each of these locations.
- Snug, 348 Danforth Ave. 416 463-6133. A good selection of children's clothing.

CLOTHING: MEN'S

- Banana Republic, 80 Bloor St. W., 416 515-0018; Toronto Eaton Centre, 416 595-6336. Trendy chain featuring casual and office wear for young professionals; also carries accessories and shoes.
- Boomer, 309 Queen St. W., 416 598-0013. A variety of mid-range to upscale men's clothing.
- Eddie Bauer, 50 Bloor St. W., 416 961-2525; Toronto Eaton Centre, 416 586-0662. Outdoor gear, hiking boots, down vests, flannel shirts and other icons of the comfortable male.
- The Gap, 60 Bloor St. W., 416 921-2711; First Canadian Place, 416 777-1332; 375 Queen St. W., 416 591-3517; Toronto Eaton Centre, 416 599-8802. Casual wear for some, workwear for others, and dancewear if you watch too much television.
- Harry Rosen, 82 Bloor St. W., 416 972-0556; Toronto Eaton Centre, 416 598-8885; Yorkdale Shopping Centre, 416 787-4231. Upscale men's business and casual wear, including Giorgio Armani, Hugo

Boss, Canali, Brioni and Versace, and the V2 collection; also shoes and accessories.

- Holt Renfrew, 50 Bloor St. W., 416 922-2333; Yorkdale Shopping Centre, 416 789-5377. Fine fashions for men; Giorgio Armani, Calvin Klein and Holt Renfrew's own label.
- Salvati Men's Wear, 138 Cumberland St., 416 961-3309; Fine Italian suits and casual wear, with excellent service.
- Moores: The Suit People, 100 Yonge St., 416 363-5442. The Canadian Tire of menswear: reasonable, dependable, and, every now and then, surprising; all sizes available and attentive service.
- Walter Beauchamp Tailors Inc., 145 Wellington St. W., 416 595-5454. Custom and ready-to-wear business and casual clothing since 1908; includes military wear and tails.

CLOTHING: SECOND-HAND

- Cabaret Nostalgia, 672 Queen St. W., 416 504-7126
- Circa Forty, 456 Queen St. W, 416 504-0880
- Courage My Love, 14 Kensington Ave., 416 979-1992. Standby funky vintage clothing with all the trappings (beads, chains, charms); reasonably priced.
- Dancing Days, 17 Kensington Ave., 416 599-9827.
- Divine Decadence, 136 Cumberland St.., 416 324-9759. Vintage designer clothing, mostly upscale, evening and bridal wear; pricey but wonderful.
- Ex-Toggery, 115 Merton St., 416 488-5393. Worth searching through for rare gems.
- Goodwill, 234 Adelaide St. E., 416 362-4711. It can be dispiriting to see so much homeless stuff, but everything's here, from furniture to clothing to books; always worth a visit.
- Preloved, 613 Queen St. W., 416 504-8704. Features clothes from the l970s.
- Previously Loved Designer Kids Clothing, 986 Bathurst St., 416 516-3613. High-quality used kids designer clothing.
- Pineapple Room, 2 Kensington Ave., 416 340-7859. Great for good vintage clothing; reasonably priced

but not a steal.
- Salvation Army Thrift Store, 1447 Queen St. W., 416 536-3361. The cousin to Goodwill for furniture and clothing, along with a wide range of castoffs.
- Value Village, 924 Queen St. E., 416 778-4818; A mecca for youth in search of cool party wear and low prices.
- Zinc, 471 Richmond St. W., 416 504-6013.

CLOTHING: WOMEN'S
High-end
- Andrew's, Hazelton Lanes, 416 969-9991. Women's department store with upscale eveningwear, sportswear, coats, lingerie, and cosmetics and fragrances.
- Bra Bar, 118 Yorkville Ave., 416 921-4567. Great selection of undergarments and swimwear; post-mastectomy prosthetics.
- The Cashmere Shop, 24 Bellair St., 416 925-0831. Sweaters, scarves, throws and blankets; you can have them customized, too.
- Chanel Boutique, 131 Bloor St. W., 416 925-2577. Fragrances, shoes, clothes and leather bags.
- French Accents, 126 Yorkville Ave. 416 964-1171. Imports fashion by French designers; exclusive, friendly service; tailored to the individual.
- Holt Renfrew Centre, 50 Bloor St. W., 416 922-2333. Flagship store carries fine fashions for men and women, as well as accessories, cosmetics and fragrances; also has a tea room.
- Irish Shop, 150 Bloor St. W., 416 922-9400. Women and men's clothing by Irish designers, fabulous Edwardian suits, dresses, Irish woolen sweaters, hats and scarves; also carries books, music and giftware.
- Lacoste, 131 Bloor St. W., 416 513-1212. Casual, athletic, club and weekend wear displayed in clusters to encourage mixing and matching.
- Narnia, 3236 Yonge St, 416 487-7287. Good quality dressy and casual clothes stocked by an independent buyer.
- Plaza Escada 110 Bloor St. W., 416 964-2265. Escada designer lines, including Couture, Elements, Laurèl and Escada Sport.

- The St. Regis Room, The Bay (Yonge and Queen), 416 861-9111. Exclusive women's boutique, including Armani, Lida Baday, The Room's own label, Dejac and other European designers.
- Sophia's Lingerie, 527 Danforth Ave. 416 461-6113. A great selection of exclusive women's lingerie.

Medium Range and Casual Wear
- Club Monaco, 157 Bloor St. W., 416 591-8837; 403 Queen St. W., 979-5633; Toronto Eaton Centre, 416 593-7299. Canadian company with trendy, fashionable clothing including suits, dresses, club and athletic wear.
- Banana Republic, 80 Bloor St. W., 416 515-0018; Toronto Eaton Centre, 416 595-6336. Another trendy chain featuring casual and office wear for young professionals; also carries accessories and shoes.
- Eddie Bauer, 50 Bloor St. W., 416-961-2525. This flagship store offers jackets and corduroy pants, as well as classic career wear.
- Fairweather, Toronto Eaton Centre, 416 586-7700; First Canadian Place, 416 586-7718; Yorkdale Shopping Centre, 416 781-9105. Reasonably-priced work wear for young women who want to preserve a touch of funk; a good source for sweaters and t-shirts.
- The Gap, 60 Bloor St. W., 416 921-2711; First Canadian Place, 416 777-1332; 375 Queen St. W., 416 591-3517; Toronto Eaton Centre, 416 599-8802. Trendy, well-made clothing in the younger line; t-shirts, khakis and cotton.
- Talbots, 2 Bloor St. W., 416-927-7194. Conservative women's clothing, reasonably priced.
Large
- Marina Rinaldi, 131 Bloor St. W., 416 969-9677. Very elegant line of Italian women's clothing in large sizes; high-end, beautiful stuff.
- Tall Girl, Atrium on Bay, 416 977-4023. A complete line of women's fashions in sizes 8-20 tall.
Petite
- Laura Petites, Toronto Eaton Centre, 416 585-2367; Scarborough Town Centre; 416 296-7388; Yorkdale Shopping Centre, 416 781-1462. Petite proportioned

contemporary fashions for women 5'4" and under in sizes 2-16.

CRAFTS AND HOBBIES

- Arton Beads and Crafts Inc. 523 Queen St. W., 416 504-1168. Beads and findings, buttons, and jewellery-making materials.
- Curry's Art Store, 490 Yonge St., 416 967-6666; 344 Queen St. W., 416 260-2633. Signmaking, drafting and graphic supplies; airbrushes and compressors; in business since 1911.
- George's Trains, 510 Mount Pleasant Rd., 416 489-9783. Best train shop in the city; knowledgeable staff.
- The Needlepoint Shoppe, 108A Cumberland St., 416 920-9006. Lovely collection of needlepoint supplies, including gorgeous knits from England.
- Romni Wools Ltd., 658 Queen St. W., 416 703-0202. Dedicated knitters will go wild in here. Great selection of wool and knitting patterns.
- Timbuktu, 39 Front St. E., 416 366-3169
- Woolfitt's Art Enterprises, 1153 Queen St. W., 416 536-7878; Brushes, paints, canvas and the best selection of paper in the city.

FLOWERS

- Black-eyed Susan's, First Canadian Place, 416 361-3500. Downtown florist with a unique and unusual selection of flowers.
- Demarco-Perpich, 1116 Yonge St., 416 967-0893. Upscale, artistic floral arrangements for all occasions.
- Posies, 590 Markham St., 416 588-9061; Owner Karina Lemke makes this lovely shop the best reason to visit Mirvish Village; imaginative arrangements.

HATS AND ACCESSORIES

- Accessories by Eva, 402 Eglinton Ave. W., 416 481-0892. Family-owned business fitting gloves since 1958; also handbags, hats and scarves.
- Accessity, 136 Cumberland St., 416 972-1855. Interesting assortment of hats, belts, leg coverings, jewellery and hair ornaments by Canadian accessory designers.
- Lilliput Hats, 462 College St.., 416 536-5933. Wonderful assortment of hand-made hats; fairly pricey, but worth it.
- Pleasant Pheasant, 35 Lisgar St., 416 599-5408. The source for their own, well distributed line of accessories.

HEALTH FOOD STORES

- Baldwin Natural Foods (since 1975), 20 1/2 Baldwin St., 416 979-1777. Natural food, organic produce and macrobiotic foods.
- The Big Carrot, 348 Danforth Ave., 416 466-2129. Natural food market, organic produce, groceries and bulk foods; holistic dispensary.

HOME FURNISHINGS

- Art Shoppe, 2131 Yonge St., 416 487-3211. Upscale home furnishings in a wide range of styles.
- Barrymore Furniture Co., 1137 King St. W., 416 532-2891. Venerable Canadian manufacturer of fine-quality upholstered furniture, with a good selection of conservative fabrics and styles; discounted models are also for sale.
- Constantine Interiors, 1110 Yonge St., 416 929-1177. Beautiful furnishings, mostly antique, as well as an eclectic assortment of home accessories; great Venetian overhead lamps, some fabrics; friendly service.
- Eye Spy, 1100 Queen St. E., 416 461-4061
- Homefront, 371 Eglinton Ave. W., 416 488-3189.
- Ikea, 15 Provost Dr., 416 222-4532. Sturdy, inventive, diverse and at the extreme end of the subway line.
- Morba, 665 Queen St. W., 416 364-5144
- The Original Brass Bed, 119 Yorkville Ave., 416 968-6932. Brothers Josh and Ivor Parker have a large selection of imported and domestic ornamental iron and brass furniture and accessories; the sole Canadian distributor of Lipparini of Italy.
- Pack-Rat, 1062 Yonge St., 416 924-5613. Custom lampshades, upholstery and furnishings; an eclectic mix of neat stuff for your home.
- Pavilion, 739 Queen St. W., 416

504-9859.
- Pottery Barn, 100 Bloor St. W., 416 962-2276, Toronto Eaton Centre, 416 597-0880, Yorkdale Shopping Centre, 416 785-1233
- Proud Canadian Design, Queens Quay Terminal, 207 Queens Quay W., 416 603-7413. Canadian lines such as Umbra and Atelier Oda.
- Residential Lighting Studio, 489 Dupont St., 416 537-3138. New and antique lighting fixtures.
- Ridpath's, 906 Yonge St., 416 920-4441. Another long-established Toronto quality furniture shop.
- En Provence Nord Sud, 20 Hazelton Ave., 416 975-9400. French furnishings and home accessories, including fabrics, lampshades, and ceramics.
- Table of Contents, Queens Quay Terminal, 207 Queens Quay W., 416 203-1182. International kitchenware, houseware, dinnerware, textiles and glassware; custom orders and shipping worldwide.
- Up Country, 214 King St. E., 416 777-1700. Comfortable couches, lamps, and wooden furniture in a trendy industrial setting; personal items also.
- Urban Mode, 389 Queen St. W., 416 591-8834. Hip modern furnishings.
- Wonderful and Whites, 83 Front St. E., 416 363-7606. Victorian bath, bedding and gift shop.
- Williams-Sonoma, Toronto Eaton Centre, 416 260-1255, Yorkdale Shopping Centre, 416 781-3770, 100 Bloor St. W., 416 962-8248

JEWELLERY AND WATCHES
- Birks, 55 Bloor St. W., 416 922-2266; Toronto Eaton Centre, 416 979-9311 and six other locations. Extensive, conservative collection of jewellery, silverware, crystal, watches and china.
- Cartier Boutique, 130 Bloor St. W., 416 413-4929. Fine watches, earrings, brooches, rings and necklaces from France.
- European Jewellery, Toronto Eaton Centre, 416 599-5440.
- Fabrice, 55 Avenue Rd., 416 967-6590.
- First Toronto Jewellery Exchange, 215 Yonge St., 416 216-7062. A showcase for more than 30 independent jewellers, selling diamonds, gold, silver and watches.
- Magi Jewels, Queens Quay Terminal, 207 Queens Quay W., 416 203-0594. Intriguing designer jewellery and a hand-picked selection of leather bags.
- Metamorphosis Jewellery Gallery, 29 Bellair St., 416 944-0134. Looking for a unique and romantic gift? Check out the custom silver and amber jewellery.
- Peter Cullman Inc., 99 Yorkville Ave., 416 964-2196. Goldsmith; finely crafted custom jewellery.
- Sassy Bead Company, 2076 Yonge St., 416 488-7400. Create your own stone and bead jewellery, or choose from items already crafted. A welcome relief from silver and gold.
- Tiffany and Co., 85 Bloor St. W., 416-921-3900. The jewellery here includes collections by Elsa Peretti, Paloma Picasso and Jean Schlumberger; also diamonds, pearls, gold, silver, and platinum. Watches, flatware, sterling silver, china, fragrances, and even stationery.

LEATHER
- Bart Leather Fashions, 144 Yorkville Ave., 416 960-3096. Great leather clothing, sheepskin coats and jackets, hats and gloves.
- Betty Hemmings Leathergoods, 131 Bloor St. W., 416 921-4321. High quality leathergoods, including purses, briefcases, wallets; German and Italian imports.
- Danier Leather, Toronto Eaton Centre, 416 598-1159; Yorkdale Shopping Centre, 416 783-8304. In-house designs at reasonable prices from this Canadian chain.
- De Catarina, Manulife Centre, lower level, 55 Bloor St. W., 416 966-0562. A large assortment of good-quality briefcases, purses and other items.
- Doc's Leathers, 726 Queen St. W., 416 504-8888. Park your Harley Davidson outside and get your new or old jackets, patches, pants and vests here, as well as unusual custom stuff.
- Lanzi of Italy, 123 Yorkville Ave., 416 964-2582. An executive's leather dreamhouse, with desk sets,

appointment books, briefcases, wallets, and more.

- Louis Vuitton, 110 Bloor St. W., 416 968-3993. Canada's flagship store for the famous 144-year-old French company, manufacturers of fine leather and canvas goods.
- Northbound Leather, 586 Yonge St., 416 924-5018. Hip clothing and fetish wear in leather, PVC and rubber; classic jeans and skirts, too.
- Perfect Leather Goods, 555 King St. W., 416 205-9775. A great place for leather, located in Toronto's old garment district.
- Roger Edwards, 339 Queen St. E., 416 366-2501.
- Roots, 100 Bloor Street W., 416 323-3289; 195 Avenue Road, 416 927 8585; Toronto Eaton Centre, 977-0041 and five other locations. In addition to the trademark clothing and shoes, this Canadian company also produces jackets, handbags and luggage, plus a new line of leather furniture.
- Taschen! 162 Cumberland St., Renaissance Court, 416 961-3185. An intimate shop with designer purses, leather bags and smaller items.

MALLS

- Bayview Village Shopping Centre, 2901 Bayview Ave. at Sheppard, 416 226-2003. Almost 100 shops, restaurants and services, including Talbots, Havana Tobacconist, La Vie En Rose, Capezio Shoes and Rodier.
- Commerce Court, 199 Bay St. at King, 416 364-4994. Get your hair cut at Tony's, and then wander among the court's 50 shops and restaurants in the heart of Toronto.
- Hazelton Lanes, 55 Avenue Road, 416 968-8600. Over 80 unique boutiques and a few chain stores, with mid- to high-end shops for fashion and the home. Toronto's serious shopping zone.
- Toronto Eaton Centre, 220 Yonge St., 416 598-8700. The place visitors to Toronto visit first and most often, with over 320 shops, restaurants and services, under the protective wings of Michael Snow's geese.
- Holt Renfrew Centre, 50 Bloor St. W., 416 922-2333. Over 25 shops, including HMV, Eddie Bauer,

Sunglass Hut and Science City, as well as unusual boutiques.
- Manulife Centre, 55 Bloor St. W., 416 923-9525. 50 upscale shops, including Indigo!, William Ashley, Mephisto, and an LCBO; a Thomas Cook Foreign Exchange is upstairs.
- Queens Quay Terminal, 207 Queens Quay W., 416 203-0510. A magnificent Deco terminal building on the waterfront, renovated to house specialty shops with a Canadian focus. Also features restaurants and special events.
- Royal Bank Plaza Merchants Mall, 416 974-5570. Over 60 shops, restaurants and various services; underground accessibility from Union Station makes this mall one of the most-travelled in the city.
- Sherway Gardens, 25 The West Mall, Etobicoke 416 621-1070. Over 50 shops, including Holt Renfrew and Co., Eddie Bauer, Harry Rosen, Japan Camera and SmithBooks.
- Yorkdale Shopping Centre, Hwy 401 and Allen Rd., 416 789-3261. Over 200 shops and services, including Benetton, Club Monaco, Harry Rosen, Holt Renfrew, Marks and Spencer, Nine West, Roots and Tall Girl, La Senza Lingerie and P.J.'s Pet Centre.

MUSEUM SHOPS

- Bata Shoe Museum, 327 Bloor St. W., 416 979-7799. Everything in this unique shop, from jewellery, scarves and umbrellas to books, has a shoe focus.
- Fort York, 1 Garrison Rd. (off Fleet St.) 416 392-6827. A small shop dedicated to military books and reproductions from fifes to buttons, plus a selection of prints. You can visit the shop separately from the site, if you wish (but you probably won't: Fort York is an urban gem).
- Gallery Shop, Art Gallery of Ontario, 317 Dundas St. W., 416 979-6610. A great shop with an extensive collection of Canadian and international art prints, plus cards, books, toys for children and grownups, and jewellery.
- George R. Gardiner Museum of Ceramic Art, 111 Queen's Park, 416 586-5699. A fine selection of contemporary Canadian ceramic art highlights this museum shop.

- Royal Ontario Museum, 100 Queen's Park Cres., 416 586-5551. Three shops, each with its own emphasis. The ROM Shop carries jewellery, objets d'art, distinctive cards and books; the ROM Reproduction Shop offers sculpture and jewellery inspired by the museum's collections; and the Museum Toy Shop, underground, contains a wide variety of inventive and educative toys.
- Swipe Books on Advertising and Design, The Design Exchange, 234 Bay St., 416 363-1332. Much more than books; cool setting, and the old Deco Exchange building is always worth a visit, not least for the reliefs outside.

MUSIC

- L'Atelier Grigorian, 70 Yorkville Ave, 416 922-6477. Classical and jazz music shop. Knowledgeable, helpful staff. Great selection without being overwhelming.
- Bay Bloor Radio, Manulife Centre, 55 Bloor St. W., 416 967-1122. One of the best hi-fi shops in the world. A huge selection of audio and video equipment, in a family business that's been at Bay and Bloor for over half a century.
- HMV, 333 Yonge St., 416 596-0333; 50 Bloor St. W., 416 324-9979. The flagship store on Yonge St. is the challenger to Sam's; 4 floors of music, videos, and magazines.
- Long and McQuade Musical Instruments, 925 Bloor St. W., 416 588-7886. Instrument sales and rentals; sheet music.
- Remenyi House of Music, 210 Bloor St. W., 416 961-3111, 1-800-667-7625. A very good selection of classical and popular music and books on music.
- Rotate This, 620 Queen St. W., 416 504-8447. New and used CDs and vinyl.
- Sam the Record Man, 347 Yonge St., 416 977-4650; Bayview Village, 2252 Bloor St. W., 416 767-9964; 1500 Yonge St., 416 324-8624. Canada's home-grown music superstore.
- Song and Script, 1200 Bay St., 416 923-3044. A good selection of popular sheet music and recordings.

OUTFITTERS AND SPORTS

- The Dock Shoppe, 162 Queens Quay West, 416 362-3625. A good selection of high-quality marine clothing, equipment and supplies.
- Europe Bound, 47 Front St. E., 416 601-1990. A worthy challenger to Mountain Equipment Co-op when both were on Front St.
- Genco Marine Ltd., 544 King St. W., 416 504-2891. A great selection of boating equipment and supplies, including clothing; everything imaginable and knowledgeable service.
- Mountain Equipment Co-op, 400 King St. W., 416 340-2667. A new, custom-built location for Toronto's best outfitter, carrying practical clothing and other gear for hiking, skiing, climbing, biking and everyday living.
- Nike Toronto, 110 Bloor St. W., 416 921-6453. Canada's first Nike-only store offers a full range of shoes, apparel, and accessories for basketball, hiking, tennis, golf, and running, as well as skates. The store is divided into pavillions for each sport.
- The Sign of the Skier, 2794 Yonge St., 416 488-2118. The place to go to get your skis and boots properly fitted; great service from a family business.
- Spirit of Hockey, BCE Place, lower level, 416 360-7765. The Hockey Hall of Fame's retail store: jackets, heritage sweaters, hockey cards, and books.
- Sporting Life, 2665 Yonge St., 416 485-1611; Sherway Mall, 416 620-7750; and Sporting Life Bikes and Boards, 2454 Yonge St., 416 485-4440. An excellent all-round sports shop, but especially good if you cycle; also a great shoe selection.
- Sport Swap, 2063 Yonge St., 416 481-0249. Inexpensive, used ski equipment, snowboards and bikes.
- Tam Dive Ltd., 246 King St. E., 416 861-1664. The place to go for diving gear and equipment.
- Tilley Endurables, Queens Quay Terminal, 207 Queens Quay W., 416 203-0463 and 900 Don Mills Rd., 416 441-6141. Signature outdoor clothing including the virtually indestructible hat.

- Wilson's Sporting Tradition, 61 Front St. E., 416 869-3474. Gone fishin'? Make sure you go to this place first. Rods, reels, weights, threads and outerwear.

OUTLETS

- Benetton, 4700 Keele St. (south of Steeles Ave. on the York University campus), 416 736-1659. Up to 70 per cent off on casual Italian wear for women and men.
- B. Silverstein and Son (Chocky's), 327 Spadina Ave., 416 977-1831. Wholesale dry goods importers, men's and women's underwear, and some camping wear.
- Dacks Outlet, 595 Trethewey Dr., 416 241-5170. Classy men's shoes with minor flaws or discontinued lines can be had at 50 per cent off.
- Danier Leather Factory Outlet, 365 Weston Rd., 416 762-6631. Quality leather and suede clothing for men and women; discounts of up to 70 per cent.
- Dixie Outlet Mall, Dixie Rd. and the QEW, 905 278-7492. Over 120 factory outlets make this mall the mother of all discount outlets; wear your best walking shoes.
- Honest Ed's, 581 Bloor St. W., 416 537-1574. Legendary, loud and labyrinthine. What's better, it really is cheap, and quite well organized. Look to find something of everything.
- Irwin Toy Factory Outlet, 13 Hanna Ave., 416 533-3521. Especially good for the holidays; over 25,000 items mix discontinued and current lines of toys.
- Roots Canada Factory Store, 1168 Caledonia Rd., 416 781-8729. Great bargains year round from Canada's retailing wunderstore.
- Tom's Place, 190 Baldwin St. (Kensington Market), 416 596-0297. Racks and racks of high quality business and casual clothing for men and women; don't forget to haggle.
- Winners, 57 Spadina Ave., 416 585-2052. Not as cheap as it used to be, but still worth a try for almost anything, including toys.

SHOES

- Aldo Shoes, Toronto Eaton Centre, 416 979-2477 and various other locations.
- B2, 399 Queen St. W., 416 595-9281.
- Birkenstock, 8 Alcorn Ave., 416 921-0779. A thorough selection of comfortable Birkenstock sandals.
- Browns, at Holt Renfrew Centre, 50 Bloor St. W., 416 960-4925; Sherway Gardens, 416 620-1910. Three in-house lines complement a good selection of fine footwear for men and women.
- Capezio, 70 Bloor St. W., 416 920-1006 and 218 Yonge St., 416 597-6662. Trendy, cutting-edge women's shoes by Guess, Steve Madden, Nine West, Unisa and others; also stocks belts, handbags and leathergoods.
- Cole-Haan, 101 Bloor St. W., 416 926-7575. The only branch in Canada of this American manufacturer of fine shoes and leather goods for men and women.
- Corbo Boutique, 131 Bloor St. W., 416 928-0954.
- Davids, 66 Bloor St. W., 416 920-1000. Top designer shoes and accessories for men and women, including David's own line. Large selection of fashionable boots.
- Get Out Side, 437 Queen St. W., 416 593-5598
- Harry Rosen, 82 Bloor St. W., 416 972-0556. The upscale men's clothier also has a shoe salon upstairs.
- Harry Young Shoes, 1421 Yonge St., 416 924-4431; 67 Front St. E., 416 363-2015. Quality shoes for women and men, including Amalfi, Neos and Sioux; top-of-the-line narrow and wide fittings; an old Toronto business that pays special attention to its customers.
- John Fluevog, 242 Queen St. W., 416 581-0132. Wild platform shoes, go-go boots and more. Not for the tame or weak of sole.
- Mephisto, Holt Renfrew Centre, 50 Bloor St. W., 416 963-3668. 1177 Yonge St., 416 968-7026. Mephisto walking shoes: the best there are and good for your feet.
- Nine West, Toronto Eaton Centre, 220 Yonge St., 416 977-8126; First Canadian Place, King west of Bay, 416 368-0611; 99 Bloor St. W., 416 920-3519.
- Pegabo, Toronto Eaton Centre, 416 977-6185, 91 Bloor St. W., 416 323-3722, 778 Yonge St., 416 928-

1213, 349 Queen St. W., 416 977-3401.

- Peter Fox, 24 Bellair, 416 960-5572. High-end shoes designed by Peter Fox; leather and satin shoes and wedding boots for brides.
- Petit Pied, 890 Yonge St., 416 963-5925; 2651 Yonge St., 416 322-6067; Bayview Village, 1534 Bayview Ave., 416 225-3038. European children's footwear by Elefanten, Minibel, Buckle My Shoe and others, as well as athletic shoes.
- Susanne Shoe Salon, 2506 Yonge St., 416 489-3290. A pleasing assortment of quality women's shoes; a small shop with good service.
- Tallcrest, Atrium on Bay, 595 Bay St., 416 598-5532; Yorkdale Shopping Centre, 416 781-1275, Square One 905 276-9067. Larger-sized shoes (sizes 10 to 14) for women in elegant styles: casual, dress, and athletic.
- Taylor's Shoes, 2934 Dundas St. W., 416 769-2045. Men's and women's shoes, specializing in hard-to-fit sizes, narrow and wide widths, in classic and contemporary styles including Stonefly, Rockport, Clarks and Mephisto. Widths from AAAA to EEEEE.
- Town Shoes, 131 Bloor St. W., 416 928-5062; Toronto Eaton Centre, 220 Yonge St., 416 979-9914; Toronto-Dominion Centre, 416 362-1921; St. Clair Centre, 416 967-4131.

TOYS

- Barbie on Bay, the Bay at Richmond and Yonge, 416 861-9111. Barbie's world entire: dolls, houses, cars, clothes and stickers; also Barbie collectibles.
- Dollina, Queens Quay Terminal, 207 Queens Quay W., 416 203-0576. Dolls and dollhouses for both collectors and kids.
- Kidding Awound, 91 Cumberland St., 416 926-8996. Funky selection of new and vintage wind-up toys, paper-dolls, puppets, fridge magnets and Gumby!
- Kidstuff Toy Store Inc., 738 Bathurst St., 416 535 2212. Baby developmental toys, Lego, Brio, puzzles books and lots more.
- Science City, 50 Bloor St. W., 416

968-2627. Educational toys, science kits, lab wear, puzzles and games.
- The Toy Shop, 62 Cumberland St., 416 961-4870. Wonderful selection of children's toys, dolls, books, arts and crafts supplies, as well as other items. Great place to visit; lots of fun.
- Treasure Island Toys, 581 Danforth Ave., 416 778-4913. The place parents would like their children to spend their allowance: a great selection of toys with an educational bent.

WEIRD AND WONDERFUL

- Curved Space, 2030 Yonge St., 416 484-0850. Great bean-bag furnishings in a store from the era of peace, love and no back support.
- The Door Store, 43 Britain St., 416 863-1590. A portal fantasy of antique and ornate doors of every description located on an old industrial street downtown.
- F/X, 515 Queen St., 416 504-0888. A favourite with the kids.
- Hollywood Canteen, 1516 Danforth Ave., 416 461-1704. There's no business like this business: Films, books, stills, memorabilia, with helpful, knowledgeable owners.
- Ice, 163 Cumberland St., 416 964-6751. Imaginative gift items for grown-ups and kids, including artist-designed clothing and accessories, cosmetics and Beanie Babies.
- Mokuba, 577 Queen St. W., 416 504-5358. Racks and racks of ribbons: Every width, lace pattern, colour and texture imaginable.
- Menagerie Pet Shop, 549 Parliament St., 416 921-4966. If you can't make it to the Toronto Zoo, visit the shop with the giant iguana wrapped around the door, and exotic pets including turtles, lizards, birds, small mammals, fish, and a wide range of pet supplies inside.
- Ontario Specialty Company, 133 Church St., 416 366-9327. Keeps an almost vanished word in the world of retail alive, along with all its trappings: crass, crazy and incredible novelties.
- Sugar Mountain, 320 Richmond St. W., 416 204-9544; 1920 Queen St. E., 416 690-7998; 571 Queen St.

W., 416 861-1405; 2299 Yonge St., 416 486-9321. The decor alone makes these colourful cavities worth a visit; you'll see an entire wall of Pez dispensers.

- Tap Phong Trading Company, 360 Spadina Ave., 416 977-6364. One of the great Chinese Canadian trading companies; a kind of Zeller's of the East.

SPORTS

PRO SPORTS

- Toronto Maple Leafs Hockey. Toronto's National Hockey League team. Air Canada Ctr., 40 Lower Bay St.; Individual tickets: 416 872-5000, www.mapleleafs.com
- Toronto Argonauts Football. See the CFL at its best. SkyDome, 1 Blue Jays Way; Individual tickets: 416 872-5000, www.argonauts.on.ca
- Toronto Raptors Basketball. See the Toronto Raptors hit the court. Air Canada Ctr., 40 Lower Bay St.; Individual tickets: 416 872-5000, www.nba.com/raptors/
- Toronto Blue Jays Baseball. Another season of exciting American League baseball. SkyDome, 1 Blue Jays Way; Individual tickets: 416 872-5000, www.bluejays.com
- Toronto Rock Lacrosse Club. Maple Leaf Gardens, 60 Carlton St.; Individual tickets: 416 872-5000, www.ontariolacrosse.com/rockinfo.htm
- Molson Indy. 175 Bloor St. E., North Tower, Ste. 1500. Features the superstars of Indy Car racing. Exhibition Place, Lake Shore Blvd.; Tickets: 416 872-4639, www.molsonindy.ca

HALLS OF FAME

- Canada's Sports Hall of Fame, Exhibition Place; 416 260-6789.
- Hockey Hall of Fame. The ultimate tribute to the fastest game on earth. Open year-round. 30 Yonge St., BCE Place; 416 360-7735.
- Canadian Motorsport Hall of Fame, Exhibition Place; 416 263-3223.

FISHING

- Canadian Trophy Fishing. Fishing and sightseeing charters for groups up to twelve. Lake Simcoe ice-fishing in winter; 905 472-8000.
- Klancy's Fishing Charters. Try Klancy's for fishing or a lazy afternoon cruise. May to Oct. 1001 Bay St., Ste. 718; 416 866-8489.
- Albion Hills Conservation Area, Municipal #1655, Hwy. 50, Palgrave; 905 880-4855.

GOLF

- Canadian Golf Registry Ltd. Canada's golf information network. 1895 Commerce Park Dr.; 705 431-GOLF
- Don Valley Golf Course, 4200 Yonge St., south of Hwy. 401. 416 392-2465.
- Glen Abbey Golf Club. Home of the PGA Tour's Bell Canadian Open and the Canadian Golf Hall of Fame. 1333 Dorval Dr., Oakville, ON L6J 4Z3; 905 844-1811.
- Scarlett Woods Golf Course, 1000 Jane St., 416 392-2484.
- Humber Valley Golf Course, 40 Beattie Ave., 416 392-2488.

RECREATION

- Playdium. Canada's first physical and interactive entertainment centre. Open daily. Twenty minutes west of downtown, in Mississauga. Highway 403 or 401 to Highway 10 (Hurontario St.) and south to 99 Rathburn Road West; 905-273-9000.
- ProKart Indoor Raceway. Kart racing machines! Let loose on this challenging indoor track. Special group rates available for Grand Prix style races and corporate meetings with catering. Must have a valid driver's licence. 120 North Queen St.; 416 236-5278.

FESTIVALS AND EVENTS

All winter
- Harbourfront Centre's Skating Rink. Outdoor skating, skate rentals, change rooms, rental lockers and skate-sharpening. Open daily, 10 am to 10 pm. The Rink at Harbourfront, York Quay Centre, 235 Queens Quay W.; 416 973-3000.

November
- Santa Claus Parade. This crowd-pleasing parade takes place the third Sunday in November each year; 416 249-7833.
- Royal Agricultural Winter Fair. Featuring the Agricultural Show, the Royal Horse Show, and the Winter Garden Show among other attractions. National Trade Centre, Exhibition Place; 416 263-3400, www.royalfair.org
- The Hobby Show. The International Centre, 6900 Airport Rd.; www.thehobbyshow.com

All of December
- The Nutcracker. National Ballet of Canada at the Hummingbird Centre for the Performing Arts; 416 345-9595, www.national.ballet.ca
- Tafelmusik's Sing Along Messiah. 416 964-6337.
- Allan Gardens Victorian Christmas Flower Show. A display of seasonal Christmas plants. Allan Gardens Conservatory, 19 Horticultural Ave.; 416 392-7288.

Mid-December
- The Christmas Story. Mimed story of the nativity with narration, organ music and carols. Church of the Holy Trinity, Trinity Square, behind Toronto Eaton Centre; 416 589-8979.

Christmas Eve
- Cavalcade of Lights Christmas Carol Concert. Features Toronto's finest choirs, including the Toronto Mendelssohn Choir. Rotunda, Toronto City Hall, Queen and Bay Sts.; Events Hotline 416 395-0490.

New Year's Eve
- Cavalcade of Lights New Year's Eve Celebration. Toronto's alcohol-free New Year's party. Nathan Phillips Square, Toronto City Hall, Queen and Bay Sts.; Events Hotline 416 395-0490.
- First Night. An alcohol-free New Year's Eve celebration for all ages with theatre, dance, musical and visual-arts performances, People's Parade and Imagination Market. Multiple locations along Front St., between John St. and Jarvis St.; 416 395-0490.

Mid-January
- Toronto International Boat Show. National Trade Centre, Exhibition Place; 416 203-3934.
- Speedorama Custom Car and Bike Show. Automotive Bldg., Exhibition Place; 1-877-250-4550; 905 634-7736.

Early February
- Canadian International Auto Show. Canada's premier automotive showcase. Metro Toronto Convention Centre, 255 Front St. W.; 905 940-2800.
- Cavalcade of Lights Canadian Flag Day. A salute to our nation's flag. Nathan Phillips Square, Toronto City Hall, Queen and Bay Sts.; Events Hotline 416 395-0490.
- Computer Fest/Mac Fest. More than 130 exhibitors; shows in February and September. Automotive Bldg., Exhibition Place; 416 925-1070.
- Cottage Show. West Annex Bldgs., Exhibition Place; 416 393-6000.
- Psychics, Mystics and Seers' Fair. Queen Elizabeth Bldg., Exhibition Place; 416 461-5306.

Third week of February
- Toronto Festival of Storytelling. Storytelling, workshops, evening concerts and free afternoon storytelling; over 70 storytellers from Canada and beyond. York Quay Centre, Harbourfront Centre; 416 656-2445.

Mid-March
- Toronto International Bicycle Show. National Trade Centre, Exhibition Place; 416 369-0515.
- Spring Fling. Midway rides, kiddieland ride area, games of skill and live entertainment. SkyDome, 1 Blue Jays Way; 416 341-3663.
- Toronto Sportsmen's Show. Coliseum, Exhibition Place; 416 695-0311.
- Canada Blooms. Metro Toronto Convention Centre; 416 585-8000.
- International Home and Garden Show. The International Centre, 6900 Airport Rd.; 416 512-1305, www.home-show.net

Late March
- Molson Export Ice Canoe Race and Barrel Jumping Contest.

Harbourfront; 416 973-3000.
- National Motorcycle Swap Meet and Bike Show. A retail motorcycle and custom bike show. Queen Elizabeth Bldg., Exhibition Place; 705 778-2275.
- One of a Kind Spring Canadian Craft Show and Sale. Automotive Bldg., Exhibition Place; 416 960-3680.

Early April
- Canadian Craft Supply Show. International Centre, 6900 Airport Rd.; 416 674-4636.
- Home Office Show/Business Show. Metro Toronto Convention Centre, 255 Front St. W., 416 585-8000.
- National Home Show/National Kitchen and Bath Showcase. Exhibition Place; 416 263-3000.

Mid-April
- Creative Sewing and Needlework Festival. National Trade Centre, Exhibition Place; 905 709-0100.
- International Spring Bike Show. International Centre, 6900 Airport Rd.; 416 674-4636.
- Postage Stamp Show. Queen Elizabeth Exhibit Hall, Exhibition Place; 416 393-6000.
- Spring Classic Car Auction. International Centre, 6900 Airport Rd.; 416 674-4636.
- Spring Family Show. International Centre, 6900 Airport Rd.; 416 674-4636.
- Toronto Toy Show. International Centre, 6900 Airport Rd.; 416 674-4636.

Late April
- Hobby Ceramic Show. International Centre, 6900 Airport Rd.; 416 674-4636.
- Old Clothing Show and Sale. Automotive Bldg., Exhibition Place, Lake Shore Blvd. W.; 416 393-6000.
- Travel and Leisure Show. International Centre, 6900 Airport Rd.; 416 674-4636.

May
- Victoria Day Fireworks. Celebrate Victoria Day while witnessing an exciting fireworks presentation. Paramount Canada's Wonderland, 9580 Jane St.; 905 832-7000.
- Victoria Day Musical fireworks. Celebrate the Queen's birthday and

witness an exciting fireworks extravaganza put to music. Ontario Place, 955 Lakeshore Blvd. W.; 416 314-9990.

Early May
- Hot Docs Canadian International Documentary Festival. Showcasing the best in documentary film and television; 416 203-2155.
- Cabbagetown's Forsythia Festival in Riverdale Park W.; 416 921-0857.
- The Good Food Festival. Automotive Bldg, Exhibition Place, Lakeshore Blvd. W.; 416 393-6000.

Early June
- Toronto Aviation and Aircraft Show. Canadian Airline Hangar, Pearson International Airport; 1-800-776-5976, www.canadianaviationexpo.com.

All of June
- Milk International Children's Festival. North America's largest performing arts festival for the whole family. Performers from around the world, as well as right here in Canada. For seven days visitors can see the very best the world has to offer in theatre, dance, music, visual arts, storytelling, physical comedy and puppetry for young audiences. Harbourfront Centre, 973-3000.
- Northern Encounters. This month-long festival showcases the traditional music, arts and culture of Canada and seven other members of the Arctic Council, including Greenland, Iceland, Alaska, Siberia and five Scandinavian nations. Various venues; 416 979-1282.

Mid- to late June
- Toronto Worldwide Short Film Festival; 416 445-1446, ext. 815, www.worldwideshortfilmfest.com..
- Bloom in the Beaches. A literary festival. Various venues; 416 365-7877.
- Pride Week-Toronto. The largest Lesbian and Gay Pride event in North America. Church and Wellesley neighbourhood. 65 Wellesley St. E, Suite 501; 416 927-7433, www.pridetoronto.com
- Du Maurier Downtown Jazz.

Featuring high-profile international and Canadian jazz favourites. Various venues; 416 928-2033, Tickets: 416 870-8000, www.torontojazz.com

- Toronto International Caravan. Visit fifty pavilions located throughout Toronto representing the world's greatest cities. 263 Adelaide St. W., 416 977-0466.
- North by Northeast. Enjoy up-and-coming rock bands over a three-day festival. June 5 to 7, 2003. Various venues; 416 863-6963, www.nxne.com
- Queen's Plate. The running of this internationally renowned race. June 3-8, 2003. Woodbine Racetrack, 555 Rexdale Blvd; 416 675-7223 or 675-6110.
- Toronto International Dragon Boat Race Festival. Dragon boat racing and multicultural performances on the Toronto Islands; 416 595-1735, www.torontodragonboat.com

July
- Toronto Outdoor Art Exhibition. This free outdoor exhibit showcases the original paintings, ceramics, jewellery, sculpture and mixed-media creations of talented Canadian and international artists. July 11-13, 2003. Nathan Phillips Square, 100 Queen St. W.; 416 408-2754, www.torontooutdoorart.org
- Molson Indy. 175 Bloor St. E., North Tower, Ste. 1500. Features the superstars of Indy Car racing. Exhibition Place, Lake Shore Blvd.; Tickets: 416 870-8000, www.molsonindy.com/toronto

Late July
- Beaches International Jazz Festival. This popular jazz streetfest features over forty bands performing everything from calypso, to Latin, fusion and steel drum nightly on selected street corners, balconies and parks. Queen St. E., between Woodbine Ave. and Victoria Park Ave.; 416 410-8809.
- Fireworks, Ontario Place, 955 Lake Shore Blvd. W.; June 21, 28, July 2, 2003. 416 314-9900, Tickets: 416 870-8000, www.ontarioplace.com
- CHIN Picnic, Exhibition Place; 416 531-9991, www.chinradio.com

- Toronto Fringe Theatre Festival. June 28-July 1, 2003. Ten days of theatre in the Annex area (near Bloor and Spadina Sts.); 416 966-1062, www.fringetoronto.com

August
- Caribana. A two-week celebration attracting more than one million people, capped with a parade. Various venues; July 18 to Aug. 4, 2003. www.caribana.com
- Circle Ball Fair. A ten-day fair with busker competitions; 416 929-5566.
- Fringe Festival of Independent Dance Artists. Various indoor and outdoor sites. August 5 to 17, 2003. www.ffida.org
- SummerWorks. Ten days of theatre. Various venues; 416 410-1048.
- Rogers AT&T Cup. New box seating and upper stand seating available, National Tennis Centre, York University Aug. 9-17, 2003. Ticket info: 1-800-398-8761, www.tenniscanada.com

Mid-August to Labour Day
- Canadian National Exhibition. The world's largest and longest annual exhibition in Canada. Featuring midway rides, display buildings, top-name concert performers, roving entertainers, live music and much more. Exhibition Place, Lake Shore Blvd. W.; 416 393-6000, www.theex.com

Fall
- Word on the Street. Open-air book and magazine festival celebrating literacy and the printed word. Queen St. W. between Spadina Ave. and Simcoe St.; 416 504-7241.
- Artsweek. Various venues; 416 977-2787.
- Made in Canada Festival of Canadian Music. 416 593-7769 ext. 335.
- Bell Canadian Open. Hamilton Golf & Country Club, Ancaster, Ontario. 1-800-571-6736.
- International Festival of Authors. The world's largest literary festival. Harbourfront Centre, 235 Queens Quay W.; 416 973-4760.
- Toronto International Film Festival. Sept. 4 to 13, 2003. 416 968-3456, www.bell.ca/filmfest/

DAY TRIPS

- Butterfly Conservatory at the Niagara Parks Botanical Gardens; www.niagaraparks.com.
- Bruce Trail Association; 905 529-6821 or 1-800-665-4453, www.brucetrail.org
- Crawford Lake Conservation Area. May through October. At Steeles Ave. and Guelph Line; 905 854-0234, www.conservationhalton.on.ca/Crawford.html
- Elora Festival. July/August. P.O. Box 370, Elora ON N0B 1S0; 519 846-0331, Fax: 519 846-5947, info@elorafestival.com, www.elora.org
- Fort George, Niagara-on-the-Lake. A recreated British garrison. Open April 1 to Oct. 31; 905 468-4257, www.niagara.com/~parkscan/
- Kortright Centre for Conservation, 9550 Pine Valley Dr., Woodbridge; 10 am to 4 pm every day; 905 832-2289.
- Maid of the Mist, Niagara Falls; 905 358-5781, www.maidofthemist.com
- Marineland Theme Park, open May 7 to Oct. 12, 2003, 7657 Portage Rd., Niagara Falls; 905 356-9565, www.marinelandcanada.com
- The McMichael Canadian Collection, 10365 Islington Ave., Kleinburg; 1-888-213-1121, 905 893-1121, www.mcmichael.on.ca
- Niagara Grape and Wine Festival. A ten-day celebration of the grape harvest, featuring winery tours, concerts, and parades. 905 688-0212, www.grapeandwine.com
- Niagara Parks Botanical Gardens and School of Horticulture, on the Niagara Parkway 9 km north of Niagara Falls. 905 356-2241 (Niagara Parks) or 1-877-642-7275.
- Presqu'ile Provincial Park. Off the 401, 155 km east of Toronto; 613 475-4324, www.ontarioparks.com
- St. Jacobs Farmers' Market and Flea Market. In the heart of Mennonite country. St. Jacobs; tourist@stjacobs.com, www.stjacobs.com
- Shaw Festival, Niagara-on-the-Lake; April 3 to Nov. 30, 2003, 1-800-511-7429, www.shawfest.com
- South Simcoe Railway, Tottenham; www.steamtrain.com/
- Stratford Festival, Stratford; 416 363-4471 or 1-800-567-1600, Fax: 519 273-6173, orders@stratford-festival.on.ca, www.stratford-festival.on.ca

GAY TORONTO

Festivals and Theatres
- Pride Committee of Toronto, Pride Week of Toronto, the largest Lesbian and Gay Pride event in North America. Church and Wellesley neighbourhood. 65 Wellesley St. E; 416-927-7433. webmaster@pridetoronto.com.
- Inside Out Lesbian and Gay Film and Video Festival. End of May. Multiple venues. 416 977-6847.

Bars and Restaurants
- Bar 501, 501 Church St.; 416 944-3272.
- Babylon, 553 Church St.; 416 923-2626.
- The Barn/Stables, 418 Church St.; 416 977-4702.
- Black Eagle, 457 Church St.; 416 413-1219.
- Bootscomplex, 592 Sherbourne St. (Selby Hotel); 416 921-0665.
- Byzantium, 499 Church St.; 416 922-3859.
- The Devon, 556 Church St.; 416 921-4121.
- El Convento Rico, 750 College St,; 416 588-7800.
- Living Well Cafe, 692 Yonge St.; 416 922-6770.
- Sneakers, 502 Yonge St.; 416 961-5808.
- The Rivoli, 332 Queen St. W; 416 596-1908.
- The Toolbox, 508 Eastern Ave,; 416 466-8616.
- Trattoria Al Forno, 459 Church St,; 416 944-8852.
- Trax V, 529 Yonge St,; 416 963-5196.
- Village Rainbow Restaurant, 477 Church St.; 416 961-0616.
- Wilde Oscar's, 518 Church St.; 416 921-8142.
- Woody's/Sailor, 465-67 Church St.; 416 972-0887.

Lesbian Bars
- Pope Joan, 547 Parliament St.; 416 928-6662.
- Tango, 508 Church St. 416 972-1662.

INDEX

PHOTO CREDITS

Legend: Top – T; Centre – C; Bottom – B

Photography by Vincenzo Pietropaolo except for those listed below:
A Space: 59B; Graig Abel: 88T, 118B; Art Gallery of Ontario: 48T&B, 49T&B, 50T&B, 51T&B, 52T&B, 114B; Bata Shoe Museum: 54B; BDS Studios: 69T&B; Black Creek Pioneer Village: 56T&B, 112T; Blue Jays: 22B, 89C; Canada Blooms: 120T; CanStage: 62C; CN Tower: 3T, 110B; Comrags: 85B, 86T; Dwayne Coon: 126T; David Cooper: 126B, 127C; Danny Grossman Dance Company: 63C
Gera Dillon: 106T, 107B; Don Hunstein/Sony Classical: 68T; Steven Evans: 128B; Gallery One: 57B, 59T; Mary Gerry: 130T; Heritage Toronto: 16B, 35B, 36T&B, 55B, 112B; Hike Ontario: 132T; Textile Museum of Canada (Raoul): 41B; Michael Mahoulic: 75T; Joan Marcus: 10, 60T & 159T; Barbara McCracken: 131; Molson Indy: 92T; National Ballet: 115, 116, 119B; National Trade Centre: 29T; Niagara National Historic Sites: 126C; Ontario Place: 27B, 111B; Ontario Science Centre: 30T, 31T, 31C, 111C; Opera Atelier: 66B; Power Plant: 57T; Premiere Dance Theatre: 63B; Royal Ontario Museum: 42T&B, 43T,C&B, 44T,C&B, 45T,C&B, 46T,C&B, 47T&B 110T, 111T; Roy Thomson Hall: 64B, 67T, 67C; Sable-Castelli Gallery: 58T; Sandra Ainsley Gallery: 58B; Textile Museum of Canada (Rachel Ashe): 41T, 55C; Textile Museum of Canada (Simon Glass): 55T; Shaw Festival: 61T&B, 62B, 126B; South Simcoe Railway: 134T; Stratford Festival: 60, 128; Tafelmusik: 64T; Ted Rhodes: 25T; Toronto Mendelssohn Choir: 66T; Toronto Raptors: 90T; Toronto Rock: 91B; Toronto Symphony Orchestra: 66T; Toronto Zoo: 2B, 31B, 32T,C&B, 109B, 113B; Toronto Transit Commission: 7; William Van Veen: 130C; William Ashley: 2B, 81T; Scott Wishart: 128T&B; Willy Waterton: 132C; Woody's: 135T; Word on the Street: 124T&B

National Library of Canada Cataloguing in Publication
Coopersmith, Penina
    Toronto colourguide / Penina Coopersmith ; photography by Vincenzo Pietropaolo. — 4th ed.
(Colourguide series)
Includes index.
Title of previous edition: Toronto : a colourguide.
ISBN 0-88780-584-1

    1. Toronto (Ont.)—Guidebooks.   I. Pietropaolo, Vincenzo II. Title. III. Series.
FC3097.18.C66 2003   917.13'541044   C2003-900467-8
F1059.5.T683C66 2003